Strategies for Healthcare Information Systems

Robert A. Stegwee

Ton A.M. Spil

University of Twente, The Netherlands

ST. PHILIP'S COLLEGE LIBRARY

IDEA GROUP PUBLISHING
Hershey • London • Melbourne • Singapore

RA
971.23
.S74
2001

Aquisitions Editor:	Mehdi Khosrowpour
Managing Editor:	Jan Travers
Development Editor:	Michele Rossi
Copy Editor:	Maria Boyer
Typesetter:	Tamara Gillis
Cover Design:	Deb Andree
Printed at:	Sheridan Books

Published in the United States of America by
 Idea Group Publishing
 1331 E. Chocolate Avenue
 Hershey PA 17033-1117
 Tel: 717-533-8845
 Fax: 717-533-8661
 E-mail: cust@idea-group.com
 Web site: http://www.idea-group.com

and in the United Kingdom by
 Idea Group Publishing
 3 Henrietta Street
 Covent Garden
 London WC2E 8LU
 Tel: 44 20 7240 0856
 Fax: 44 20 7379 3313
 Web site: http://www.eurospan.co.uk

Copyright © 2001 by Idea Group Publishing. All rights reserved. No part of this book may be reproduced in any form or by any means, electronic or mechanical, including photocopying, without written permission from the publisher.

Library of Congress Cataloging-in-Publication Data
Stegwee, Robert A., 1962-
 Strategies for healthcare information systems / Robert A. Stegwee, Ton A.M. Spil.
     p. cm.
 Includes bibliographical references and index.
 ISBN 1-878289-89-6 (paper)
  1. Health services administration--Computer networks. 2. Medical care--Computer networks.
 3. Medicine--Computer networks. 4. World Wide Web. I. Spil, Ton A.M. II. Title.
 RA971.23 .S74 2001
 362.1'068'4--dc21   2001013192

British Cataloguing in Publication Data
A Cataloguing in Publication record for this book is available from the British Library.

NEW from Idea Group Publishing

- ❏ **Developing Quality Complex Database Systems: Practices, Techniques and Technologies/** Shirley Becker, Florida Institute of Technology/ 1-878289-88-8
- ❏ **Human Computer Interaction: Issues and Challenges/**Qiyang Chen, Montclair State University/ 1-878289-91-8
- ❏ **Our Virtual World: The Transformation of Work, Play and Life via Technology/**Laku Chidambaram, University of Oklahoma and Ilze Zigurs/1-878289-92-6
- ❏ **Text Databases and Document Management: Theory and Practice/**Amita Goyal Chin, Virginia Commonwealth University/1-878289-93-4
- ❏ **Computer-Aided Method Engineering: Designing CASE Repositories for the 21st Century/**Ajantha Dahanayake, Delft University/ 1-878289-94-2
- ❏ **Managing Internet and Intranet Technologies in Organizations: Challenges and Opportunities/**Subhasish Dasgupta, George Washington University/1-878289-95-0
- ❏ **Information Security Management: Global Challenges in the New Millennium/**Gurpreet Dhillon, University of Nevada Las Vegas/1-878289-78-0
- ❏ **Telecommuting and Virtual Offices: Issues & Opportunities/**Nancy J. Johnson, Capella University/1-878289-79-9
- ❏ **Managing Telecommunications and Networking Technologies in the 21st Century: Issues and Trends/**Gerald Grant, Carleton University/-878289-96-9
- ❏ **Pitfalls and Triumphs of Information Technology Management/**Mehdi Khosrowpour/1-878289-61-6
- ❏ **Data Mining and Business Intelligence: A Guide to Productivity/**Stephan Kudyba and Richard Hoptroff/1-930708-03-3
- ❏ **Internet Marketing Research: Theory and Practice/**Ook Lee, University of Nevada, las Vegas/1-878289-97-7
- ❏ **Knowledge Management & Business Model Innovation/**Yogesh Malhotra/1-878289-98-5
- ❏ **Strategic Information Technology: Opportunities for Competitive Advantage/**Raymond Papp, Central Connecticut State University/1-878289-87-X
- ❏ **Design and Management of Multimedia Information Systems: Opportunities and Challenges/** Syed Mahbubur Rahman, Minnesota State University/1-930708-00-9
- ❏ **Internet Commerce and Software Agents: Cases, Technologies and Opportunities/**Syed Mahbubur Rahman, Minnesota State University,& Robert J. Bignall, Monash University/ 1-930708-01-7
- ❏ **Environmental Information Systems in Industry and Public Administration/** Claus Rautenstrauch and Susanne Patig, Otto-von-Guericke University Magdeburg/ 1-930708-02-5
- ❏ **Strategies for Managing Computer Software Upgrades/**Neal G. Shaw, University of Texas Arlington/1-930708-04-1
- ❏ **Unified Modeling Language: Systems Analysis, Design and Development Issues/** Keng Siau, University of Nebraska-Lincoln and Terry Halpin, Microsoft Corporation/ 1-930708-05-X
- ❏ **Information Modeling in the New Millennium/**Keng Siau, University of Nebraska-Lincoln and Matti Rossi, Erasmus University Rotterdam/ 1-878289-77-2
- ❏ **Strategies for Healthcare Information Systems/**Robert Stegwee and Ton Spil, University of Twente/ 1-878289-89-6
- ❏ **Qualitative Research in IS: Issues and Trends/** Eileen M. Trauth, Northeastern University/ 1-930708-06-8
- ❏ **Information Technology Evaluation Methods and Management/**Wim Van Grembergen, University of Antwerp/1-878289-90-X
- ❏ **Managing Information Technology in a Global Economy** (2001 Proceedings)/Mehdi Khosrowpour/1-930708-07-6

Excellent additions to your library!

Receive the Idea Group Publishing catalog with descriptions of these books by calling, toll free 1/800-345-4332
or visit the IGP Web site at: http://www.idea-group.com!

Strategies for Healthcare Information Systems

Table of Contents

Preface i

Section 1. Introduction

1. Strategies for Healthcare Information Systems 1
   Ton A.M. Spil & Robert A. Stegwee
   University of Twente, The Netherlands

2. Experiences in Strategic Information Systems
   Implementation in UK Healthcare 11
   Stuart J. Barnes, University of Bath, UK

3. Streamlining Operations in Healthcare with ICT 31
   Reima Suomi, Turku School of Economics and
   Business Administration, Finland

Section 2. Standardization in Healthcare IS

4. Standardization Strategies in Practice—
   Examples from Healthcare 46
   Nina Lundberg, Gothenburg University, Sweden
   Ole Hanseth, University of Oslo, Norway

5. Healthcare Information and
   Communication Standards Framework 66
   Peter J.B. Lagendijk & Robert A. Stegwee
   University of Twente, the Netherlands

6. The Electronic Patient Record as an Organizational Artifact 78
   Pieter Toussaint, Leiden University Medical Centre, The Netherlands
   Marc Berg, Erasmus University Rotterdam, The Netherlands

Section 3. Transformation In Healthcare Chains

7. The Introduction of EDI Systems in Healthcare
   Supply Chains: A Framework for Business Transformation 91
   Stefan Klein, University of Muenster, Germany
   Heike Schad, CapGemini Ernst & Young

8. Telecommunications as a Medicine for General Practitioners 114
   Peter J.B.Lagendijk, Roel W. Schuring and Ton A.M. Spil
   University of Twente, The Netherlands

9. Reengineering the Healthcare Supply Chain in Australia:
   The PeCC Initiative 126
   Elizabeth More & G. Mike McGrath
   Macquarie University, Australia

Section 4. Network Organizations in Healthcare

10. Understanding Health Information Networks in Canada 143
    Yolande E. Chan & David J. Ramsden
    Queen's University, Canada

11. Exploring ICT Enabled Networking in Hospital Organizations ... 164
    Ronald Spanjers, Ryan Peterson & Martin Smits
    Tilberg University, The Netherlands

    Willi Hasselbring
    University of Oldenburg, Germany

Section 5. Knowledge Management Healthcare Information Systems

12. Distributed Knowledge Management
    in Healthcare Administration 182
    Michael Holm Larsen & Mogens Kühn Pedersen
    Copenhagen Business School, Denmark

13. IS/IT: Enabling Medical Group Practices
    in a Managed Care Environment 198
    Nilimini Wickramasinghe, University of Melbourne, Australia
    J.B. Silvers, Case Western Reserve University, USA

About the Authors 214

Index 220

Preface

Many conferences and publications have focused on the requirements and possibilities of Electronic Patient Record systems as the ultimate goal of Healthcare Information Systems. This book takes a radically different approach and views the Electronic Patient Record system as a possible outcome of several initiatives for innovative use of information systems, not as a system to design and implement. This book gives an overview of the research of the e-health group at the University of Twente:
- Information Strategies in Healthcare Organizations;
- Global Standardization Frameworks:
- Transformation of the Healthcare Chain and Process Management in Healthcare;
- Networks of Healthcare Organizations;
- Knowledge as an Innovation Enabler in Healthcare.

Strategies for Healthcare Information Systems covers the strategic and organizational issues that arise in the application of information and communication technology in the healthcare industry. It takes a broad perspective, discussing both the strategic challenges facing healthcare and the strategic opportunities provided by modern information and communication technology. They blend together in a framework for the strategic deployment of information and communication technology in the healthcare industry. Process innovation surfaces as a key area for success in healthcare information systems, as is described in studies from different continents. The process approach is analyzed in more detail, by describing the necessary interactions between healthcare providers and other parties involved. A description of full-scale implementation of such information systems uncovers the tremendous complexity when working in healthcare on a national scale. Stakeholder analysis and various other tools for organizational change management are described as a means to carry out effective process management in healthcare information systems implementation.

By looking beyond the individual organizations in the healthcare

Chapter I

Strategies for Healthcare Information Systems

Ton A.M. Spil and Robert A. Stegwee
University of Twente, The Netherlands

It is widely recognized that the healthcare industry does not use information technology to its full potential. This book uncovers many of the reasons why large-scale implementation of healthcare information systems has not come to fruition yet. The authors provide a broad coverage of the field, ranging from strategic analysis to real-life project implementation. Moreover the book provides strategies to avoid pitfalls and direct your healthcare organization to strategic use of healthcare information systems. This section of the book will introduce the five main themes of the book and will show that the healthcare organizations are realistic laboratories for the information and communication technology scientists to do research. The five main themes are: Strategy, Network Healthcare Chain, Process Management, Knowledge Management, Standardization.

INTRODUCTION

The environment of the professional healthcare organizations handled in this chapter is changing. Where it should be complex and stable, according to reference models (Mintzberg, 1983;, Heijnsdijk, 1990), the environment is becoming more and more unstable. The size of most healthcare organizations in the Netherlands is growing by mergers and natural growth. This means that these professional organizations have to use strategic variables that they have never used before with a new technical system. There is need for structural changes to strengthen middle management but even more need for cultural changes to balance the autonomous and heteronomous powers in the organization (Scott, 1982). This book argues that information management can contribute in these changes for the good and the bad.

Figure 1. Strategies of Healthcare Information Systems Themes

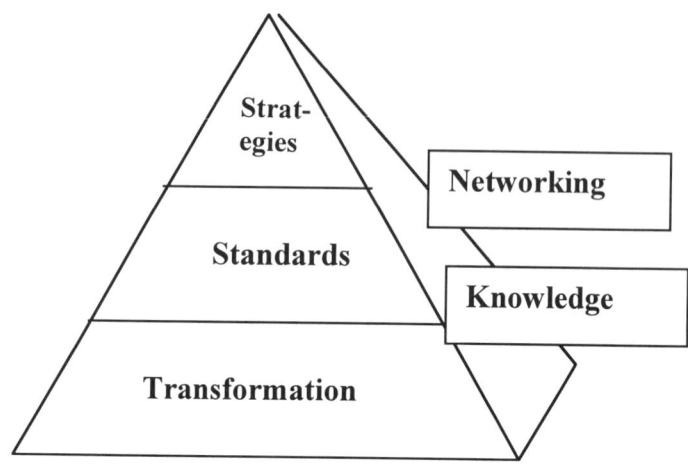

Information Strategy in healthcare organizations is an ad hoc static planning process (Spil, 1998) which does not fit the dynamic environment the healthcare organizations are facing. In this research, a more dynamic approach is developed to adapt to the specific organization and the specific environment. The environment (government, suppliers, patients, professional groups) determines for a great deal which planning possibilities are available. That is why in four cycles--agreeing, aligning, analyzing and authorizing--a yearly planning approach is built in which the information projects can be chosen and monitored and changed when necessary (Spil & Salmela, 1999). An action study plan is built to put this approach into healthcare practice in both Finland and the Netherlands.

Information Structure is well developed in healthcare organizations where we regard information structure as heterogeneous socio-technical networks (Hanseth & Lundberg, 1999), in which both social and technical actors take part. Agreements and standards, like healthlevel seven, can support a wide range of applications and create a common language both internal and external. Still, healthcare organizations are struggling with all kinds of new developments on a structural level. The developments focus on management information, Internet, intranet and archiving. Management information is implemented in various ways as networks (Lines, 1999), as clinical management systems (Spil, 1998) and as information warehouses (Zviran & Armoni, 1999). Our e-health group wants to make a comparative study on management information systems and wants to study standardization and specifically HL7 in depth.

Many Internet possibilities in healthcare organizations are not implemented because of privacy problems concerned with opening up the internal network. In cooperation with the National Insurance Netherlands, our healthcare research group wants to support new implementations, especially between hospital physicians, home physicians and pharmacies. This study has started with a thorough description of a hospital information system with system components (Sikkel et al., 1999) that both fit the HIS and the structure of the hospital. The second phase is to investigate the workflow and relate this workflow to the (electronic) information flows. The functional integration of all system components (in a hospital admission, outpatients agenda, medical services communication) is an objective that might be utopia, but HIS and EMR combined with the strong communication facilities create many possibilities to put a step into the right direction.

Communication is a strong weapon for the strategic use of information systems. E-health will open possibilities that were only for imagination three years ago. We think healthcare information systems can be the enablers of transformation in the healthcare chain, and to become an enabler there is need for strategies for healthcare information systems. The next five sections introduce the five sections of this chapter.

STRATEGIES

The editors of this book have assisted in many information strategy studies in healthcare organizations and have never seen such an external view on information systems like it is today. The subjects of the book support this external thinking by showing that you should not look at one organization but have to look at healthcare organizations as a chain. The interactions between the actors in this chain are the main subjects of research in our research group.

Strategy is the definition of the overall end goals and the means of action to meet these goals. To measure these strategies we look at seven dimensions (Burton & Obel, 1995):
- Product and process innovation,
- Product and market breadth,
- Concern for quality,
- Price level,
- Control level,
- Technology and
- Capital requirement.

In this introduction we will not handle every dimension but some highlights will introduce other sections in this book.

In the third section *process innovation* is preferred above *product innovation* because we expect a longer lasting effect. This does not mean that ICT is not apparent in product innovation, because the medical technology is highly dependent on ICT. The implementation of healthcare information systems can be seen as a process innovation . Stuart Barnes argues in the next chapter that without a framework for strategic IS implementation, many healthcare information systems are doomed for failure.

The cooperation of many healthcare organizations shows the changes that are taking place on the dimension *product and market breadth*. Healthcare organizations have to rethink their strategy and start strategic alliances. In the fourth chapter the role of ICT in forming these networks is described.

Concerns of quality is always a dimension that is seen as important in healthcare organization. It is not a coincidence that the first three dimensions mentioned are the main objectives of a hospital in one of our case studies (Spil, 1996). Three changes are taken from the corporate strategy-plan. The hospital wants to:
- grow to be a top hospital with many educational facilities and with clinical and technical research of high quality;
- derive economy of scale reached by the merger of several smaller institutions;
- deliver high quality healthcare to the patients.

These three objectives do not always go together because economic factors, like the *price level*, often collide with quality factors. In our recent research we explicitly study the cost reduction of medicine prescription as described in the third chapter. One of the conclusions of that section is that time seems to be far more important to the professional than price levels.

The *control level* is a completely different issue. Management of healthcare organizations complain that they do not have enough management information to control the organization. Although many systems exist to deliver this information, the problem seems to have a more organizational nature. On one hand the professionals do not want to be controlled, on the other hand management does not have much variety of alternatives. New information and communication technology like datawarehouses and intranet solutions explore a new kind of control systems. This book does not specifically address these problems, but in literature there are some examples that look promising but are not yet established (Berndt, 2000; Zviran & Armoni, 1999).

Technology requirements therefore are high both on product and process of the healthcare organizations. Reima Suomi and his research group try to find explanations why ICT adoption in healthcare seems to be gaining momentum as described further on in this section.

Finally, when discussing strategy, the budget determines what can be implemented. The dimension *capital requirements* is often questioned in the following way: "How much money should we invest in ICT?" In general terms the ICT budgets vary from 1% to 15% of the revenue when the role of ICT is respectively support and strategic. In most healthcare organizations ICT is seen as the latter . Experience learns that although the budget is rather high, there is not that much strategic variety because many ICT projects are determined by contingency. One big example of the last year is the millennium bug which absorbed a huge pie of the ICT budget in healthcare, but also the government and the suppliers determine ICT actions.

STANDARDIZATION

In the previous paragraph we described the strategic wish of healthcare organizations to gain more control on the operational core. Professionals will see monitoring systems as a reduction of their autonomy. The scale of hospitals urges managers to implement management information systems but up till now these systems are mainly used financially. Managers try to standardize medical processes and the control is mainly on the procedures. The professionals are responsible for the quality of the products and processes.

In light of external collaboration, we want to broaden the scope of the use of standards. Lundberg and Hanseth show the difference between local standards and global standards, and we like to grasp which global standards have to be developed at this moment and in the future. To this end Stegwee and Lagendijk have developed a framework which helps in specifing the need for standardized information exchange by specific applications. Using this framework to categorize available standards enables us to select appropriate standards for our application and to assess possible blind spots and overlaps when using a combination of standards. This assessment can also guide the future development of standards.

The need for standards becomes more clear when looking at the Electronic Patient Record in terms of a constellation of independent yet integrated information systems. Toussaint and Berg elaborate the topic of the Electronic Patient Record and show us new ways to look at it, both from a technical and from an organizational point of view. In the long run many EPR systems will consist of specialized modules, tailored to the needs of specific user groups, and standardized to communicate efficiently and effectively with other such components in a global network.

TRANSFORMATION

The professionals who work in the operating core want to be free to do what they think is best. They will not allow managers to decide on professional matters. An occupational group that regulates the access to the profession establishes the power of the professionals. There are healthcare organizations that are very autonomous, meaning that the professional or his representatives determine the strategy, structure and operational activities of the organization. Other healthcare organizations are heteronomies by nature in which the management regulates the activities and also feels responsible for the content of the primary process.

Business transformation is now the central management challenge and the primary, if not the sole, task of business leaders (Gouillart & Kelly, 1995). According to these authors the business management should change from a mechanical to a biological model. This transformation should go in four stages:
- Reframe (mind)
- Restructure (body within)
- Revitalize (body and environment)
- Renew (spirit)

The institutional mind of healthcare organizations should change from intramural to extramural. In chapter four these thoughts are put to paper, but before the healthcare organizations can change their vision to the environment, they have to restructure internally. Process management can help with the restructuring.

Process management tries to identify the most important processes of the organization and integrate them by means of information interaction. Instead of suboptimalization of functions in the organization, there is a chance of optimizing the overall process. The process management literature has grown from the business process reengineering thoughts but also stems from process-oriented development methods. The first group described radical change of the processes of organization, but this is nowadays seen more evolutionary. The second group thoroughly described the processes of the organization but only made small changes. Process management can be the best of both worlds and can be used to transform the healthcare chain.

We think the internet will be the medium to link the institutional healthcare bodies to the environment. In five chapters in this book, the Internet technologies take an enabling role to revitalize the healthcare community. To reach this revitalization it is necessary that on a standardization level, global agreements have to be made to accelerate the developments.

Last but not least we are back in this chapter where the spirit of healthcare organizations has to be renewed by building strategies for healthcare information systems. Renewal deals with the people side of transformation and therefore information systems should be seen as sociological interactive systems in stead of computer systems. With the renewal we also arrive at the last section of the book, knowledge management, because it involves the rapid dissemination of knowledge inside the firm.

An important new development is that process management is not only internally oriented any more but focuses on the processes and information flows in between organizations. The two chapters, network organizations and process management, therefore are rather strongly connected to each other. Especially the chapter of Klein and Schadt combines both worlds. Another clear connection is to the standardization chapter (chapter 4) because there is no interorganizational process management possible if there are no standards to communicate between the different stakeholders.

This book shows that the transformation can take place on different levels and in different places in the healthcare organizations. Klein and Schadt focus on the transformation of the hospital–supplier relation. Lagendijk, Schuring and Spil evaluate the first processes in the healthcare chain, and More and McGrath look at the same problem from a macro perspective for the whole of Australia--again global and local initiatives that have to get together in the future.

NETWORK ORGANIZATIONS

Healthcare organizations have to rethink their borders and have to make strategic alliances to be able to cope with the changes in the environment. This does not only mean a changing relation with the supplier, as described in the process management chapter by Klein and Schadt, but also a changing relationship with other kinds of healthcare organizations. Spanjers, Hasselbring, Peterson and Smits suggest an evolution from intradepartmental to interdepartmental to interorganizational healthcare chains. In their case a relation is sought with specialistic healthcare organizations but alliances can take form in many different constellations. Chan and Ramsden studied the electronic networks in Canada where the client is directly involved in the external interaction from and to the healthcare organizations. Many changes will occur in this area in the near future, and therefore more research in this direction is needed.

A network of organizations can be defined as a decentralized organism without steady borders and without a specific center. There is no top or bottom, just relationships (Kelly, 1996). Healthcare organizations have made their first step into this insecure, relative virtual world as we can see in the cases in Germany, The Netherlands, Australia, the United States and Canada.

KNOWLEDGE MANAGEMENT

The main focus of information management in organizations went through an evolution from costs via functionality and integration towards knowledge as described in Table 1 (Spil, 1996).

Many healthcare organizations are still concerned with integration but start to recognize the possibilities of knowledge management in healthcare. Professionals learn by doing and therefore can make use of knowledge systems, expert systems and decision support systems. The last group can have a large influence on the specialist's job (Boonstra, 1994) but is not yet common in the operational kernel.

Davenport et al., (1998) identify four broad types of objectives for knowledge management:
- Create knowledge repositories
- Improve knowledge access

Table 1. The information system evolution (Spil, 1996)

Period	Performance	Market	IS
1950-1975	Efficiency	Price	Costs
1975-1985	Quality	Quality	Functionality
1985-1995	Flexibility	Choice	Integration
1995-200?	Innovation	Uniqueness	Knowledge

- Enhance knowledge environment
- Manage knowledge as an asset

If we look at these objectives, we must observe that healthcare organizations still have some work to do to start reaching them.

Professionals have a high educational level and can pick up new developments in communication relatively easy if they are supported in the right way. A distinction can be made in external and internal communication. External possibilities for scientists are evident. External access to Internet, electronic mail, electronic journal (Boonstra, 1994), but also video conferencing for consultancy of colleagues and other links with outside professionals (Jordan, 1994), are essential for the professional of the future. Yet there are not that many movements in healthcare organizations. They are still focused on the patient flow and the internal databases and basic hospital information systems.

The last two chapters in this book explore this future direction, one in the administrative function with a thorough knowledge management base (Larsen & Pedersen) and one trying to enable medical working groups (Wickramasinghe & Silvers). We think part of the medical future lies in the knowledge area, but we have to notice that the promise of decision support and expert systems in healthcare has not shown many results in the past decade. It might be that the Internet possibilities speed up these developments because knowledge gets more and more available, as is happening in the world of the academic library.

CONCLUSIONS

Although it is impossible to show all developments that take place around the world on healthcare information systems, we think this book shows the main streams in which these information systems are moving on strategic level:
- Standardization and integration of the healthcare chain;
- Transformation of the healthcare processes (from push to demand);
- Externalization of healthcare organizations.

Global standards and clear local definitions must pave the way to integrated care pathways in the future. In an optimal situation all healthcare information interactions will have an international standard with enough freedom to apply local systems for specific situations.

The changing environment forces the healthcare organization to transform their processes from a client push to a client demand situation. The patient will change in the near future from a will-less victim to a knowing client.

There is a need for innovation in the healthcare organizations, and the main way of bringing innovation is using knowledge as a driver. An important support for knowledge in the organization will be the information and communication technology.

REFERENCES

Arrow, K.J. (1974). *The Limits of Organizations*, New York:Norton.

Berndt, D., Hevner, A. R. & Studnicki, J. (2000). Community Health Assessments: A datawarehousing approach, *Proceedings of the European Conference on IS*, Vienna.

Boonstra, A. (1994). Strategieen voor informatiemanagement bij professionele organisaties, *Informatie*, 36(5), 333-342.

Broadbent, M., Weill, P. & O'Brien, T. (1996). Firm context and patterns of IT infrastructure capability, *ICIS 96*, Cleveland.

Brown, A D (1995). *Organizational Culture*, Pitman, London.

Burton, R. & Obel, B. (1995). *Strategic Oorganizational Diagnosis and Design, Developing Theory for Application*, Kluwer Academic Publishers, Boston.

Cash, J. I., Mc Farlan F. W., Mc Kenney, J. L. & Applegate, L. M. (1992). *Corporate I S Management* Irwin, Boston.

Chandler, A. D. (1962). *Strategy and Structure: Chapters in the History of the Industrial Enterprise*, MIT press, Cambridge.

Child, J. (1973). Predicting and understanding organization structure, *Administrative Science Quarterly*, 18, 168-185.

Daft, R. L. (1997). *Organization Theory and Design*, South-Western College Publishing, Cincinnati, Ohio.

Davenport, T. H., De Long, D. W. & Beers, M. C. (1998). Successful knowledge management projects, *Sloan Management Review*, Winter 1998, 43-57.

Duncan, R B.(1979),What is the right organization structure, *Organizational Dynamics*, winter, 59-79.

Earl, M. J. (1989). *Management Strategies for Information Technology*. Prentice Hall, London.

Gouillart, F. J. & Kelly, J. N. (1995). *Transforming the Organization*, Mc Graw Hill, New York.

Handy, C. (1978). *Gods of Management*, Penguin, London.

Handy, C. (1996). Find meaning in uncertainty In: Gibson, R, *Rethinking the Future*, Nicholas Brealey publishing Ltd, London.

Hanseth, O. & Monteiro, E. (1998). Changing irreversible networks: Institutionalisation and infrastructures, *Proceedings of the Sixth ECIS*, June, Aix en Provence, France.

Harrison, R. (1972). Understanding your organization's character, *Harvard Business Review*, 50(2), 119-128.

Heijnsdijk, J. (1990). *Vitale Organisaties (in Dutch)*, Wolters Noordhof, Groningen.

Jans, E. J. (1996). *Grondslagen Administratieve Organisatie(in Dutch)*, Samson, Alphen a/d Rijn.

Jordan, E. (1994). Information strategy and organization structure, *Information Systems Journal*, 4, 253-270.

Kelly, K. (1996). The company as a living organism, In: Gibson, R, *Rethinking the Future*, Nicholas Brealey publishing Ltd, London.

Lederer, A. & Sethi, V. (1988). The implementation of Strategic IS Planning methodologies *MIS Quarterly* 12,3, September.

Leifer, R. (1988). Matching computer-based IS with organizational structures, *MIS Quarterly*, 12, March, 63-73.

Lines, K. (1999). MIS in local government health care organizations, *Proceedings of the 22th IRIS Conference*, August, Keuruu, Finland, volume 2, 337-348.

Mantz, E. A. & Kleijne, D. & Zijden, F. A. P van der (1991). Planning en realisatie informatie-voorziening nog ver uit elkaar (in Dutch), *Informatie* 33,12, pp. 847-856.

Markus, L. (1984). *Systems in Organizations,* Pitman, London.

McDonald, P. & Gandz, J. (1992). "Getting value from shared values," *Organizational Dynamics,* Winter, 64-77.

Miller, D. (1987). Strategy making and structure: analysis and implications for performance, *Academy of Management Journal,* 30(1), 7-32.

Mintzberg, H. (1979). *The Structuring of Organizations,* Prentice Hall, Englewood Cliffs.

Mintzberg, H (1983).*Structures in fives:Designing effective organizations,* Prentice Hall, Englewood Cliffs, New York.

Nicholson, N., Rees, A. & Brooks-Rooney, A. (1990). "Strategy, innovation and performance," *Journal of Management Studies,* 27(5), 511-534.

Perrow, C (1967). A framework for the comparative analysis of an organization, *American Sociological Review*, 32(2).

Porter, M & Millar, V (1985). How information gives you competitive advantage. *Harvard Business Review*, July/August, 149-160.

Quinn, R G & McGrath, M R (1985). The transformation of organizational cultures: a competing values perspective, in Frost, Moore, Louis, Lundberg & Martin (eds),*Organizational Culture,* Newbury Park, California Sage, 315-334.

Raelin, J A (1991). *The clash of cultures; Managers managing professionals*, Harvard Business School Press, Boston.

Robbins, S P (1990). *Organization Theory:Structure, Design and Application*,Prentice Hall,Englewood cliffs

Sääksjarvi, M (1988) . Information Systems Planning: What makes it uccessful? *Australian Computer Conference proceedings*, 523-542.

Scott, W R (1982)'Managing professional work: Three models of control for health organizations. Healthservices *research,*17(3), 213-240.

Scott Morton, M S (1991). *The Corporation of the 1990s: Information Technology and Organizational Transformation,* Oxford Press, New York.

Sikkel, K, Spil, T A M, Weg, R L W van de (1999). A real world case in information technology for undergraduate students, *Journal of systems and software,* 49, 2-3, 30 December.

Spil, T A M (1996). *The effectiveness of strategic information systems planning in professional organizations*, PhD thesis University of Twente, Enschede, ISBN 90 90009588-8.

Spil, T A M (1998). From professional healthcare to where? A healthcare information management reference model. *Proceedings 1998 IRMA conference,* Boston, USA, 285-294.

Stolz, C (1987). Corporate culture and strategy – the problem of strategic fit. *Long Range Planning*, 20(4), 78-87.

Wassenaar, D A (1995). *Informatieplanning in transactioneel perspectief (in Dutch),* PhD Thesis, Free University, A'damWeggeman, M, Wijne, G & Kor, R (1994)*Ondernemen binnen de onderneming:* essenties van organisaties (in Dutch), Deventer, 1994, ISBN 90 267 1660 5.

Woodward, J (1965). *Industrial Organization Theory and Practice,*Oxford University Press, Oxford.

Zuurbier, J J (1993). *Financial control in hospitals,*PhD thesis University of Twente.

Zviran, M & Armoni, A (1999). Integrating hospital information systems, *International journal of Healthcare Technology and Management*,1(1), 168-179.

Chapter II

Experiences in SIS Implementation in UK Healthcare

Stuart J. Barnes
University of Bath, UK

Implementing large strategic IS in the UK health sector has recently become the subject of much debate, as hospitals have undergone wide-reaching government-led institutional reforms involving the introduction of IT. Many of the developments have followed the patterns in the U.S. One such example is that of Case Mix, introduced strategically as part of the Resource Management Initiative and aimed at the facilitation of both clinical and financial audit. Moreover, Case Mix was implemented alongside significant changes in hospital structure and culture, requiring clinicians to get involved in management tasks and decision making within the structure of the hospital, supported by a new information infrastructure.
Case Mix was implemented blanket-fashion throughout many UK hospitals, and the success of such systems has varied significantly. A number of lessons can be learned from the way that the implementation was approached. This chapter stems from a research project focusing longitudinally on the implementation of Case Mix in four UK hospitals. It draws a number of findings from the cases, and importantly, explicates a framework for strategic IS implementation, as generated from the cases and supported by the extant literature. Such a framework has implications for both theory and practice, and assists in the understanding of what is often a dynamic and poorly understood situation.

INTRODUCTION

The implementation of information systems (IS) is an important theme in the literature (Cooper and Zmud, 1990; Keen, 1981; McFarlan, 1981; Swanson, 1988). Much of it appears to suggest a gloomy outlook, with many systems doomed to failure. Indeed, there are many case examples to support this (e.g., Computing, 1993; Beynon-Davies, 1995a; Oz, 1994; Tate, Hunter, McPartlin and Duffy, 1993), and numerous statistics of IS failure (e.g. Lyytinen and Hirschheim, 1987; Willcocks and Lester, 1993). Hockstrasser and Griffiths (1991), for example, suggest that around two-thirds of all large IS implementations are not successful.

The overwhelming focus for most studies of IS has, until recently, been the private sector. However, in the last decade, the public sector in the UK has been the subject of wide-ranging reforms involving the introduction of competitive practices, and significantly, the introduction of IS and information technology (IT) to aid in this task (Brown, 1992; 1995; Beynon-Davies, 1995a). Among these has been the health care sector, which previously had very little in the way of IT infrastructure. Included within this new area of IS implementation, we find systems associated with the National Health Service (NHS) Resource Management Initiative (RMI). The Initiative revolves around cultural and structural change, and the provision of relevant information for clinical and management audit. At the heart of the Initiative are Case Mix systems, which are patient-centered databases for all aspects of hospital operations.

Although it is a large-scale and expensive development and the UK NHS is the largest employer in Europe, Case Mix has received very little attention in the IS literature. The study presented here investigates the organizational changes that influence the successful implementation of Case Mix. It presents some of the results from the study, and in particular, draws a number of important lessons for those attempting to implement IS in healthcare. To this end, it provides a framework for considering IS implementation at a strategic level.

BACKGROUND TO THE RESEARCH

Despite the notable increasing sophistication of information technologies, systems continue to fail either during development, or at the points of implementation and use (Holmes & Poulymenakou, 1995). In the words of Lyytinen (1987):

The information systems community faces a paradox: despite impressive advances in technology, problems are more abundant than solutions; organizations experience rising costs instead of cost reductions, and information systems misuse and rejection are more frequent than acceptance and use.

Until very recently in the UK, these problems have largely focused upon organizations in the private sector. However, during the last decade, the public sector has been the subject of wide-ranging reforms involving the introduction of IS and IT. A major objective of such change has been to push public sector units into becoming more competitive. The external pressures, in the form of legislation and direct Government control, have sought to elicit changes in organizational culture, often in the face of significant resistance. Change has been sought in the ways that services are managed and delivered, the evaluation of the quality of aforesaid services, and in accountability and costing. One of the most predominant of such changes has been the introduction of competition for services, the motivation of which has been to invite efficiency, effectiveness and related benefits ensuing from the accrual of economies. These reforms, pursued over the last 15 years or so, have been introduced by a series of mechanisms. For example, in the NHS, competition has been catalyzed by the imposition of an internal market; while in local authorities, a major component of reforms has involved the extension of compulsory competitive tendering for their services (Hackney and McBride, 1993).

Pivotal to such change has been an explosion in the introduction of a variety of information systems to meet such challenges. Focusing on healthcare, a large part of the work of the NHS involves collecting and handling information, from lists of people in the population to medical records (including images such as X-ray pictures), to prescriptions, letters, staffing rosters and huge numbers of administrative forms. Yet until recently, the health service has been woefully backward in its use of the technology to handle information by the standards of private industry.

This has been quickly changing in recent years, and the UK public sector now typically spends an estimated £2 billion per annum on IT, equating to around 1% of the public purse (Holmes & Poulymenakou, 1995), while the NHS spends around £220 million annually on IT in hospitals (Audit Commission, 1995). This investment is still small by the standards of the private sector, at less than 1% of operating costs compared to around 2-15% for a forward-looking business (dependent on industry sector). However, it is all the more significant when we consider that healthcare is an industry which has been slow to adopt IT, and one which presents some of the biggest IT opportunities (Cross, 1992).

Subsequently, and increasingly as a result of this investment, the public sector is beginning to experience problems with the implementation of IT. In fact, estimates suggest that problems with projects in the public sector in the last 12 years have cost over £5 billion (Collins, 1994). Associated with the technological change, there are an increasing number of examples of IS failure in the NHS, including that of Wessex Regional Health Authority's Regional Information Systems Plan (RISP; at a cost £63 million) (Health Economics Research Group, 1991), the London Ambulance Service's Computer Aided Dispatch (LASCAD) system (£1.1 to £1.5 million) (Beynon-Davies, 1995a), and more recently various Resource Management Initiative (RMI) Case Mix failures (£1 to £3 million) (Brown, 1995).

The Resource Management Initiative was a driving force in the move towards information systems and cultural change in the NHS (DHSS, 1986). First announced in 1986, the functions of RMI were twofold: (1) to provide clinicians and other hospital managers with the information they required to use the resources they controlled to maximum effect, generally by the introduction of new IT; and, (2) to encourage clinicians to take more interest and involvement in the management of the hospital and community units in which they worked, by making them responsible for the operational and strategic decisions taken in their place of work.

Put bluntly, the RMI was going to help clinicians and other hospital managers to make better-informed judgments surrounding how the resources they control can be used most effectively. The Initiative was not only aimed at persuading clinicians to own the management process, but to provide them with accurate, up-to-date and relevant information which could be used to cost medical activities and improve patient care. The response to this need for improved information services available to hospital units was the development and implementation of a sophisticated and extensive package of IT referred to as the 'Case Mix' information system (CMIS) with the purpose of clinical and management audit (Black and Moore, 1994; Kramer and Ellertson, 1993; Rea, 1994; Richards, 1986).

Prior to RMI, the introduction of IT in the NHS was patchy and limited (Cross, 1992; Hackney and McBride, 1993). Where systems existed, the technology was very varied, incompatible, archaic, and dependent upon Regional computer departments to deliver necessary operational systems. The development of Case Mix, with its dependence on data fed from other systems such as the Patient Administration System (PAS), radiology, pathology, theatre and nursing systems, provided a catalyst for the adoption of operational systems throughout the hospital (Naude, Proudlove and Bellingham, 1994).

Case Mix takes a central position in the hospitals' IT infrastructure, as shown in Figure 1 (an illustrative example, specifications may vary depending upon the hospital), providing a tool for collecting and analysing data from all areas of hospital operations. As we can see from Figure 1, there are two main types of data feed: financial and medical. The financial feed consists of pulling data from the general

Figure 1. The role of case ix in NHS hospitals (after Brown, 1995)

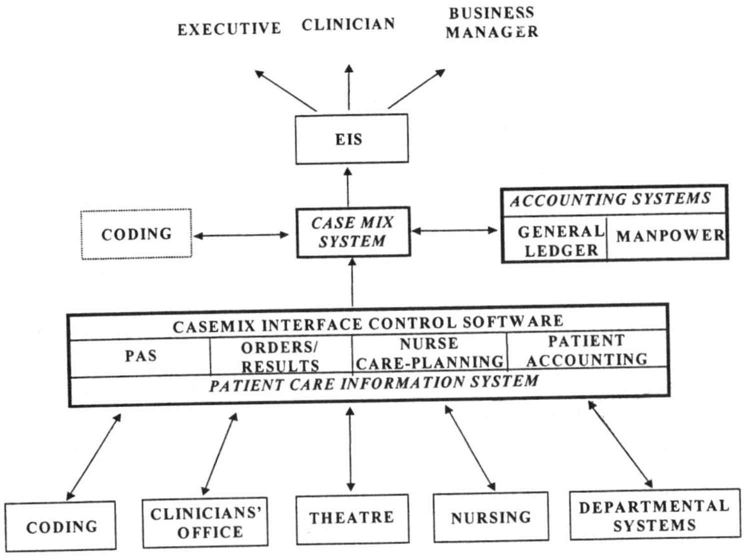

ledger and manpower systems, particularly standard costs and budgets. This contrasts with the other main feed to Case Mix, that of the 'patient care information system' which is a label given to the array of feeder sub-systems providing information on all aspects of patient treatment and care (Brown, 1995).

Each of the feeder systems is interfaced with Case Mix, so as to provide appropriate data in an acceptable format. Such data is accumulated by Case Mix within the care profile sub-system: this stores the actual tests, treatments, costs, number of cases and so on to be compared with expected 'ideal' profiles or projected activity levels as drawn from the financial data, enabling financial audit.

Regarding clinical audit, Case Mix provides the tool for assessment of the professional clinical practices of each clinician. The kinds of general information that is routinely provided in Case Mix includes lengths of stay (LOS), deaths, re-admissions and so on, whilst more specific information such as drugs administered and operative procedures performed is available via the appropriate feeder systems. The data allows aspects of Case Mix, clinical management, diagnostic accuracy and patient outcomes to be compared. For these purposes, at the apex of the architecture is an executive information system (EIS). This system takes summary data from the Case Mix (and therefore its feeders) and enables, for example, graphical and tabular analysis of the aggregated data by clinicians, executives and business managers.

On reflection, the Case Mix experiment may have turned sour. Evidence suggests that success has been difficult to achieve, and that hospitals have found it difficult to achieve any tangible benefits (e.g., see Brown, 1992, 1995; Cross, 1992; Hackney and McBride, 1993; Health Economics Research Group, 1991; Jones and Worsdale, 1993; Rea, 1994; Robinson, 1992). Evaluating investments is made all the more difficult by the fact that published evidence is scarce. Lock (1996a, 1996b) found that only 5% (by value) of all investments were the subject of published assessment, which may be an indicator of the poor value of such investments. Even published studies are far from conclusive: the 'official' Resource Management evaluation conducted by Brunel University found "no measurable patient benefits" in its review of the six pilot sites, while costs were more than double those expected (Health Economics Research Group, 1991). Thus, the situation can be characterised as one of uncertainty.

The research examined here was part of a larger study aimed at giving a detailed insight into the context, process and outcomes of the CMIS development. It is one of very few IS-oriented academic studies into this recent area of IS implementation. The purpose was to find determinants of the outcomes (success or otherwise) of such developments to assist in understanding the phenomena. Moreover, it sought to develop explanatory and normative frameworks to meet such ends. The following section briefly examines the methodology used for the research.

METHODOLOGY

The research design involves intensive grounded theory research (Strauss and Corbin, 1990). The units of data within this methodology are four quasi-longitudinal case studies of CMIS introduction in NHS hospitals, and as a consequence, aspects of the case study method (Eisenhardt, 1989; Yin, 1984, 1994) and some of those of longitudinal research (Pettigrew, 1990, 1992) are integrated in a complementary manner. The longitudinal case research provides an in-depth and time-integrated view, enabling the identification of causal processes between events over a period of time. In this study, data was collected in three key phases of IS introduction: planning and evaluation, mid-implementation and post-implementation.

Most of the study data was gathered by means of semi-structured interview schedule using a cross-section of stakeholder groups: senior management, IT staff, users and heads of user departments. In total, 96 interviews were conducted on 32 respondents in each of three time periods. The main focus for the discussion were 'anchor' themes/concepts drawn from preliminary interview sessions, supported by a synthesis of themes in the literature (e.g., King and Grover, 1991; Roberts and Barrar, 1992; Schultz, Slevin and Pinto, 1987). In each case, the respondents were asked about each theme/concept, its causes or antecedents and its effects or outcomes as they see them. Further emerging concepts were similarly treated.

THE DEVELOPMENT OF AN IMPLEMENTATION FRAMEWORK

While all the hospitals studied implemented Case Mix as part of RMI, their experiences differ significantly. Comparative analysis implied that differences can be attributed to disparity in the process of change, the contextual environment within which the implementation is situated, plus the behaviour of key agents around the implementation of Case Mix.

A very brief summary of the cases, as structured around the core conceptual grounded theory categories, is given in Table 1. Moreover, it is possible to attempt to generalise the patterns distinguished. By approaching the possible association of the grounded theory with elements of present formal theory, a more general substantive theory can be produced (Glaser and Strauss, 1967, p. 34). Eisenhardt (1989, p. 545) also advocates this method, suggesting:

Overall, tying the emergent theory to existing literature enhances the internal validity, generalizability and theoretical level of theory building from case study research.

In approaching this issue, it is important to be selective. There are a great many frameworks that could be used to tell us about the studies. Here we attempt to confine ourselves to one major framework stemming from the literature, drawing some comparisons and making some developments to fit the frame of the results.

Sauer's Framework

A useful framework for analysing organizational interactions surrounding IS implementation and its resultant outcomes is that deriving from Sauer's case analysis of IS failure (Sauer, 1993). He refers to the complex intertwining of relationships in the context of IS as a *web model* of explanation (see Figure 2), pointing out that web explanations are necessarily complex and do not offer simple linear explanations of phenomena.

Sauer's focus for the model he develops is on exchange relations. He suggests that there are three components which play a part in IS development (ISD), which he portrays as an innovation process: the project's organization, the IS itself and the supporters of the IS. These elements are linked together in a triangle of dependencies, as given in Figure 2. The information system depends on the project organization, requiring the efforts and expertise of the project organization to sustain it. The project organization in turn depends on its supporters, support coming in the form of material resources to help cope with contingencies. Finally, the supporters depend on the information system. Thus, we have a cyclical pattern of dependencies.

Figure 2. The dependencies model of IS failure (after Sauer, 1993)

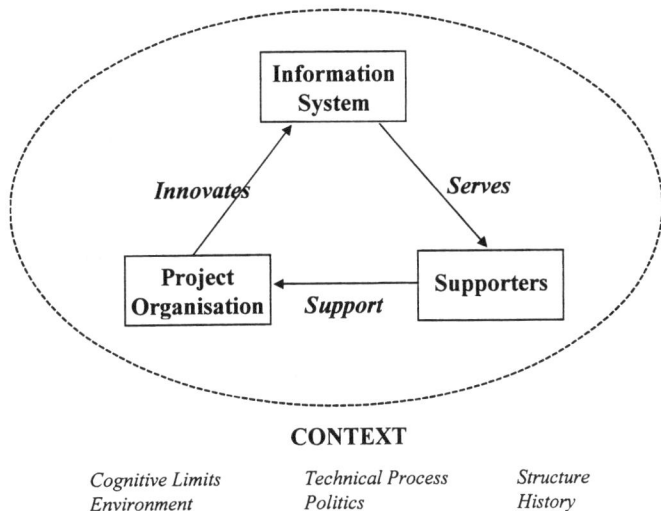

However, this is by no means a closed system. Contextual factors can control the ways in which each of the dependencies are instigated. Sauer suggests that context is made up of six dimensions:
- cognitive limits, such as the limits of communication;
- technical process constraints, arising from the nature of the IS (e.g., developing and fixing an abstract specification for organizational processes), or the development process (e.g., the constraints of the ISD methodology);

Table 1. Case summaries

GROUNDED THEORY CATEGORY	CASE 1: ALPHA	CASE 2: BETA	CASE 3: GAMMA	CASE 4: DELTA
EXTERNAL CONTEXT	Central directives exercised locally by Region, including RM. Regional data requirements and project milestones. News of NHS IS failure prevalent in the media. Competitive pressures from purchaser/provider split. Immature systems and stretched resources of vendors.	IS failure in the Media. Internal competition. Local Political agenda as 'flagship.' Pressure and requirements from Region, and tenuous relations. Kept local not Regional IS focus. Procurement effort to find mature system and resourced company. Unclear coding signals, kept to central ICD.	Regional and Government policies. Unclear central messages regarding clinical coding. Regional control, funding, and criticism of coding and third party information, fading after Trust status. Hospital cynical of poorly developed and supported systems from well-known companies.	Regional and Government influences of policy, and control of the RMI. Issues regarding the choice of vendor and Regional influence, falling away after Trust status. Failure of CMIS in the media forced the hospital to look beyond standard solution towards underdeveloped OC/CMIS market.
ORGANIZATIONAL CONTEXT	Non-RM initiatives including contracting. Centralised, fragmented structure and cultures, difficult to devolve. Traditional NHS culture, inert, alien to IT. Autonomous clinical culture. Clinicians into management. Isolated status of RM. Politics over clinical coding. Top management had some changes, resistance to devolvement, and lacked understanding of IT.	Central to devolved organization. Progressive, fragmented subcultures, two sites. Improved management-clinician relations. Issues of IT vs. patient care, clinical vs. financial use, data confidentiality. Lacked IT awareness/skills, culturally inert. Integrated project via clinical RMI manager. Top mgt. support new structure and IT. Other NHS initiatives and priorities.	Devolved, fragmented structure on two sites. Political friction between subcultures, e.g. RM/CS, coding clerks/medical secretaries, and clinicians/managers. Lacked awareness of IT value: traditional culture, inert and devoid of IT. Positive, enlightened management appreciated IT in new structure. Issue of clinical priority of CMIS via clinicians.	Other changes, inc. quality initiatives, directorates, and DHA split into two Trusts. New senior management, opposed to devolvement, forced RM re-evaluation. Traditional cultural and structural divisions, inertia, and general lack of IT awareness. RM in difficult political situation between supportive clinicians and unsupportive top management.
RMI & IS CONTEXT	Limited existing IT. PAS data mistrusted. Formal RM structure, some individuals from outside NHS, inexperienced in IT. First manager had finance role, left/replaced. No IS/IT strategy. Funds tight - required extra resources for completion.	Few areas of IT. No IS/IT strategy. Structured project. Respected RMI manager, a clinician, facilitator and communicator. Technically able team which 'gelled'. Delays diminished resources.	Little IT and strategy. Project structured, headed by a respected nurse, organizational rather than IT oriented. Experienced, able team, worked together. Resources restrained by delay, and required extension for completion.	Limited existing IT. Defined structure with strong, ambitious but insensitive manager and cohesive, competent RM team. Clear path and IT strategy mapped during re-evaluation. Uncertainty about long-term funds.
CONDITIONS FOR IMPLE-	Central evaluation and objectives. Benefits realisation. Direction affected by contracting. Procure-	Central justification. Localised objectives and procurement, user sensitive. Affected by introduction of	Evaluation of CMIS centrally. Tailored objectives to meet needs, e.g. clinicians, contracting. Leng-	Re-evaluation for a locally-specific solution. Resultant objectives were heavily clinically-oriented.

MENTING CASE MIX (cont.)	ment inexperience, poor OR/MOS, limited user involvement. Underdeveloped CMIS market. Vendors oversold systems.	contracting. Strong documentation and negotiation. Vendors professional, aimed for mutual benefit.	thy procurement, tightly controlled and documented, influenced by political relationships.	Procurement influenced by existing vendor relationships and appeared to be cost-effective, although system not fully developed.
IMPLEMENTING CASE MIX	Good initial hospital communication, later limited to within project structure. No user groups. System not user-friendly, underdeveloped, problems with feeders. Limited user involvement. Inadequate training resource. Informal project management/control. Weak vendor management, poor vendor support. Debate - ICD vs. Read.	Organization-wide communication. Discussion with other hospitals. Tight contract. Slow to develop clinical card, feeder interfacing difficult. Selective user involvement. Limited training and priority. Formal project management, firm vendor mgt. Vendor supportive. Single ICD coding and HRGs.	Communication limited to key stakeholders. Project management "loose". Binding contract. Network, interfacing and software issues. User involvement conservative. Sufficient quality of training, and much still outstanding. Problematic vendor support and flexibility. Coding problems - political and practical.	Limited communication outside of RM. Poor contract: difficult to control supplier, slow to develop CMIS and give support. High clinical involvement and training for pilot clinicians in OC. Poor senior management control. Difficult to formalise project management. Clinical coding remained central in ICD.
ACTIONS AND REACTIONS TO IMPLEMENTATION AND USE	Positive, committed, motivated team, some friction. Morale fell with progress. Dual role for RMI manager in finance, not accountable, high commitment/motivation fell with delays. Manager left/replaced. top mgt. apathetic, no ownership. Clinical users sceptical, inert, apathetic. Business users more supportive. Difficulties with medical secretaries' clinical coding. 'Cut and run' vendor.	Positive, committed team and manager with common goals. Morale fell with poor progress. Ownership and accountability from RMI manager to clinical RM manager. Top management interest, commitment, support. Vendor aimed for mutual benefit.	Team committed and enthusiastic. Manager motivated, influential, technically limited. Clinical user ownership, support, diminishing with poor progress. Other users less supportive. Secretaries' difficulties with Read. Top management interested, supportive. Vendors GHI committed and supportive, but not JKL.	RM team and manager motivated and committed, strong leadership. Morale affected by politics and uncertainty about project. Clinicians supportive and committed to 'their' system. Other users felt distanced or sceptical. Top management unsupportive. Vendors slow, lacked commitment and resources.
OUTCOMES	Exceeded budget and time-scale, required extra funds. Objectives not fulfilled. Incomplete system and information. Financial benefits. Lack of clinical benefits. Introduced IT infrastructure, strategy, facilitated cultural/structural change, IT awareness.	Ran over time and budget. Long-term funds required. Financial and planning benefits. No clinical card/audit. IT infrastructure, feeders interfaced. Catalyst for change, IT awareness. Experience to help other hospitals.	IT awareness and infrastructure. Project delays. Require funds to complete. System/information incomplete, but some clinical pilot use. Few benefits and objectives met, but some potential.	Delayed. Required resources for completion. System incomplete. Operational OC benefit. Infrastructural and cultural benefits. Overall, both clinical and financial benefits, & the main objectives, were not met.

Notes/Key: Region = Regional Health Authority (RHA), one of 14 regional administrative zones; DHA = District Health Authority, a subdivision of each RHA; Trust = semiautonomous hospitals which manage their own budgets; OR = operational requirements; MOS = memorandum of specifications; CS = computer services department; Read = an alternative coding standard to the International classification of diseases (ICD); HRG = health-related grouping, a clustering of ICD codes.

- environment, referring to the constraints and contingencies instigated by customers, suppliers, competitors and so on;
- politics, the exercise of power in the organization;
- structure, particularly internal project structure; and
- history, that is antecedents in the form of prior constraints and contingencies (e.g., those set up by previous information systems projects).

Sauer suggests that IS is the product of a process which is, by nature, open to flaws. By a flaw, we mean that stakeholders perceive that they are confronted with undesired situations, posing problems to be solved. In fact, every IS is likely to be flawed in some way. However, flaws do not necessitate failure: flaws may be corrected within an innovation process at a cost, or accepted at a cost. Examples of such flaws are organizational changes, and technical issues about hardware and software.

The idea of a flawed IS is one of the key ways that Sauer distinguishes his conception of termination failure to that of Lyytinen and Hirschheim's expectation failure (Lyytinen & Hirschheim, 1987). Expectation failure is defined as the inability of an IS to meet a specific stakeholder group's expectations: there is a gap between some existing and desired situation for members of such a group. Stakeholders are defined as any group of people who hold a set of values that define what desired IS features are, and how one should go about implementing them. Termination failure occurs only when development or operation of an IS actually ceases, leaving a vacuum where stakeholders are dissatisfied with the extent to which the system has served their interests. In this latter definition then, a system cannot therefore be considered a failure until all interest in progressing an IS project has ceased.

Beynon-Davies (1995b), building upon the work of Land (1976), makes some changes to Sauer's framework. Beynon-Davies points out the ambiguous and misleading nature of the term supporter as used in Sauer's framework, suggesting that not all interest groups with a stake in an IS may necessarily support it. Indeed, Beynon-Davies points out examples where stakeholder groups may have a negative interest in the success of a project. Thus, the term supporter is substituted by the term stakeholder.

The Implementation Cube

Sauer's model has some parallels to the grounded theory drawn from the case studies. In particular, the cases emulate the importance and interrelationships of the IS, the project and stakeholders, all within a specific context.

However, in order to provide a more useful framework by which to generalise and provide explanation of CMIS implementation, consider a number of developments to the model. Firstly, we break up the model into its separate components: IS, project organization and stakeholders. Next, we reassemble the elements into a quite different, but familiar mode, whereby each of the components provides an axis in a three-dimensional cube (Figure 3). In doing so, we establish some differences in

Figure 3. The Implementation Cube

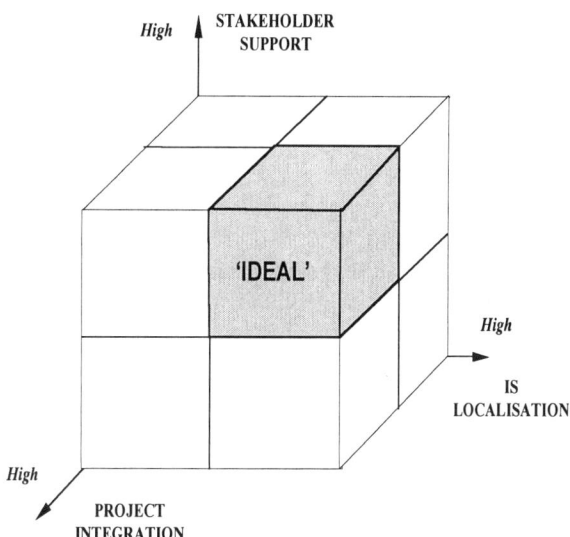

the reconfiguration of axes. Thus, the axes become three important influences on the implementation of CMIS: IS localisation, project integration and stakeholder support. A final element, context, is not shown, but, like in Sauer's model, provides an overarching influence on implementation.

In order to establish the importance of the new framework, let us consider its design. In doing so, we demonstrate how it fits the frame of our results. First, the x-axis, IS localisation, refers to CMIS, the extent to which it fits and serves the organization, and whether the central solution has been tailored to local needs. As such, this is subtly different to Sauer's original model (where Sauer concentrates on IS features rather than evaluation or objectives), pivoting on the finding that *local* evaluation is an important influence on projects. Prior research has underlined the importance of evaluation in successful implementation, here we suggest that local evaluation is important in terms of, for example, ownership. This axis approximates to the category Conditions for Implementing Case Mix, as given by the grounded theory. The y-axis refers to the project organization, and the extent to which efforts are directed to integrate the IS into the hospital, e.g., technical integration, communication, user involvement, training and so on. This relates largely to the Implementing Case Mix category in the grounded theory. Finally, the z-axis is associated with the Actions and Reactions to Implementation and Use of Stakeholders, particularly as they exercise their support or otherwise of the IS project. Important stakeholder groups were users (particularly clinical and managerial), top management, the RMI manager, the RMI team and vendors. As in the Sauer framework, these processes operate within the organizational environment. These are indicated by the grounded theory in terms of External Context, Organizational Context and RMI & IS Context.

The 'ideal' box, refers to a situation where a system has been planned and designed to fit the requirements of the organization, with clear and pertinent objectives. This is important for large-scale, cross-functional systems like CMIS (although for projects that differ from CMIS, other boxes may provide suitable alternatives, e.g., small, highly structured projects may not need significant user involvement – see McFarlan, 1981). In the 'ideal' box the IS has also been absorbed into the organization by way of strong project management, including attention to planning, vendor management, sensitive clinical coding solutions, technical integration and interfacing, control, communication, consultation and involvement of stakeholders, and education and training. As a result, stakeholders are supportive of the resultant system, and the system should be used productively as intended.

However, this utopian situation is difficult to achieve, at least in its entirety (the furthest most point from the origin in the ideal box). One or more flaws are likely to push a system from the origin to an adjacent box, and it may move several times before a project reaches an equilibrium (by project we refer to a phase of development such as a CMIS).

To illustrate the relevance of the framework, consider comments made by the RMI manager at Alpha Hospital in the last phase of the research, describing the environment for IS implementation:

> ...we are in an impossible situation. The [central] Case Mix idea is not a good one for Alpha. It doesn't meet the call of the medics, who fancy that it is a financial toy...this is made all the worse by the increasing importance of contracting and the changes that this has had on things. Medics find it hard to get enthusiastic about Case Mix, since it doesn't yet do anything that they want...it is restricted to the business side.
>
> I suppose the way that we have gone about things could be better...maybe medics could have been more involved in the process of defining the project. Teaching them about computers was not easy...older medics were simply not interested...it was difficult to get the time to teach them individually.
>
> ...those at the top don't want Case Mix and do not give the control and support we need. The system [as part of RMI] poses a threat to their control by the reins. Medics think Case Mix is a tool of management and sit on the other side. We sit somewhere in the middle."

The implications of such discourse surfaces clearly through the framework. Thus, using the Implementation Cube, we should be able to analyse the hospitals' experiences with Case Mix.

Analysing the Cases with the Implementation Cube

All of the hospitals studied had quite distinctive experiences with the implementation of the Case Mix strategic IS. In this section, we analyse and explore these experiences, drawing on pertinent aspects of the Implementation Cube to provide explanations and conclusions. Note that the names of the hospitals have been changed to provide confidentiality.

Alpha Hospital

Alpha Case Mix is perhaps the least successful of all hospitals studied. In this sense, it is perhaps a good case to begin with: Alpha demonstrates that there are a number of causes that may combine to restrict progress. At a fundamental level, the strategic IS project did not come from within the hospital and fit localised IS needs: the objectives and finance were delivered centrally, and were affected by the shifting priorities of the NHS. A more solid, localised justification and set of objectives would have been more likely to withstand the tides of organizational change.

The issue of aims created problems for stakeholder support, as many had difficulties coming to terms with the value and relevance of Case Mix. Neither was the issue helped by the poor integration of the Case Mix project within the hospital environment. The project lacked resources: although it seemed like a lot of money to stakeholders at the time, the relative IT content was high. The vendor, ABC, knew little about the problem and oversold an expensive, poorly developed and ill-supported system, which did not really provide a full and viable solution. Furthermore, the integration strategy lacked project management experience and rigour, the involvement of and communication to all stakeholders, and education and training were curtailed. Numerous technical and operational difficulties were also an obstacle to technical integration and use. The future clinical use of the strategic IS was uncertain, dependent upon whether technical and operational difficulties (coding, data issues) could be overcome. However, financial and business aspects were useful, and it was likely that such areas would be rolled out before those of clinicians.

Overall for the Alpha case, there were shortfalls in each of the implementation axes, and it struggled to provide a locally relevant solution and implement the strategic IS in a situationally sensitive manner without marginalizing key players. The hospital found it difficult to break out of the origin box. However, obviously some inroads were made in providing a solution, particularly in finance and planning. Hence, we place the hospital near the adjoining *low localisation, high integration, low support* box.

The other three hospitals found themselves in a variety of different positions. All of them attempted to provide locally relevant solutions, largely by increasing the clinical components of CMIS. Thus, in attempting to place them, we confine ourselves to the rightmost four boxes of Figure 3, which include the 'ideal' box. Let us consider each of them in turn.

Beta Hospital

Beta appears a more successful case than that of Alpha. The hospital attempted to create a system that met local objectives and requirements, assisting in organizational integration and in gaining support. Furthermore, the choice of a respected and able clinician as project manager was an extremely effective measure in gaining stakeholder (user, top management, team) support, and in providing a catalyst for CMIS integration within the hospital. Project and vendor management was efficient and formalised, and communication channels were clearly established. Where problems occurred these were largely via the centrally imposed organizational changes (which caused some confusion in the direction of the project), in technical integration and development (e.g., interfacing, and the inclusion of a clinical card) and through the lack of resources for training. Support and integrative activity began to fall with poor progress during the last phase of the research. Notwithstanding, Beta had the feel of a potentially successful case. Much of the ground had been laid for the future success of the system. Business and clinical use was growing, and with the development of additional clinical features and further training, the system would be likely to flourish.

Overall, Beta took an involved and clinically oriented approach, headed by a respected senior pharmacist. The work in achieving integration via user involvement and communication, and the positive responses of stakeholders pushes it just into a low position on the *'ideal'* quadrant. Clearly much work was still required in completing CMIS to further this position.

Gamma Hospital

The Gamma project appeared to approach many aspects in a positive manner. The project aimed to adjust objectives to the new hospital environment, and get clinical users involved in defining the project and breaking the standard CMIS binds, thereby presenting a locally relevant solution. Unfortunately, this period of procurement was so prolonged that it had serious implications on the availability of time and resources for the remaining tasks.

Embarking upon integrative activities, RM personnel were positive and communicative, and stakeholder perceptions were positively influenced by the respect and influence commanded by the project manager. Training for pilots was of a sufficient quality. However, the project was affected by technical development and integration difficulties, partly due to difficulties with vendors, and problems regarding the implementation of Read codes. In a sense, Gamma fell into the trap that it had most tried to avoid, that of an underdeveloped and unfit system. User involvement was also selective, and whilst there was support from clinicians and some senior management, this was less so with more distant stakeholders. Cultural barriers to IT were apparent, although being eroded, and structural and sub-cultural fragmentation caused political friction between some key stakeholder groups (i.e., Resource Management/Computer Services, coding clerks/medical secretaries and clinicians/managers). In the last phase of the research, the system was limited to clinical pilot use, but given funds and time, many potential benefits could be unleashed: there was a core of support which would be valuable to the project.

Gamma took a more conservative approach to integration, led by a respected senior nurse and focusing on a few key stakeholders. The responses of clinicians were positive for 'their' system, but this was less so for other users. Poor progress was likely to diminish support, much work was still outstanding in completing and integrating the system. The hospital can be placed in the *high support-low integration* box.

Delta Hospital

Delta attempted to provide a locally relevant system and objectives, tailored specifically to clinicians. Alongside, there was a high level of clinical involvement. Combined, these had a powerful effect on clinical support and ownership. However, support was not widespread. Senior management were opposed to the machinations of devolution, but forced into submission by the changing structure and politics at Delta. Similarly, business and finance users were more distanced and sceptical of CMIS.

In terms of integration, Delta had the benefit of strong project management from the manager, team, IS strategy and project plan, although vendor management and contractual arrangements were not strong. Integration suffered as a result of the externally imposed changes on the hospital environment, including the Trust split and the unpredicted slow system development. Thus, although progress had been made in Order Communications, other areas were less successful: the system needed more time and money to continue, whilst support began to fall with poor progress. Notwithstanding, the clinical focus of the project held significant promise for the potential success and benefits of the system in the future.

Overall, the Delta project was led from the front by clinicians who were highly involved and supportive, although at the expense of other users. Senior management were opposed to the project, "a tool of devolution," and the system sat uncomfortably between this group and clinicians. Progress was slow, and a great deal of work was required to complete CMIS and train users (although Order Communications was working successfully). Within Figure 3, like Gamma, Delta should be placed just inside the *high support-low integration* box, but fairly close to the high integration border.

In summary, we have seen that the Implementation Cube classification can be used, either ex ante or ex post, to explain, envision or appraise the organizational changes allied to Case Mix. For example, a centrally driven Case Mix development is likely to ill-fit a hospital, engendering poor support and difficulties in integration. Such integration requires acute attention to project management if it is to be successful, with education, communication and stakeholder involvement being particularly important. On the other hand, a hospital that pays attention to gaining support and providing for the local community is likely to integrate more easily and provide productive solutions. The next section considers these and other issues, exploring the implications of the framework.

IMPLICATIONS OF THE IMPLEMENTATION CUBE

The implications of the aforementioned framework may be divided into two areas: theoretical and practical.

Theoretical Implications

At a theoretical level, empirical validation and elaboration of concepts and the framework in additional environments is certainly required. The theoretical framework was produced by examination of four cases, albeit in depth. Further empirical grounding and comparisons will hone and enrich the concepts and framework generated here, and render a more involved understanding of the phenomenon. Three initial strategies for future research are suggested.

Firstly, it is necessary to investigate different contexts where Case Mix has been introduced. The four hospitals studied here had a number of common contextual characteristics, such as size, clinical specialisms and the area of study (i.e., Manchester in the UK). Similarity was also shared to some degree in hospital structure and NHS culture, although there were some differences. They still only represent a few organizational types. More organizations need to be examined to ascertain whether the proposed concepts and framework are relevant in other situations. In this way, the analytic generalisation posited here, that other hospitals' experiences with Case Mix will resemble the patterns detailed above, will be tested and elaborated.

Furthermore, in terms of wider generalisation, research into similar organizational IS developments in the health sector (e.g., hospital information systems or HIS) will give an indication of the broader applicability of the research. This is an important alternative to further CMIS research, particularly in consideration of the fact that, at the time of writing, very few CMIS projects were beginning. Thus, the opportunities for further longitudinal CMIS research are limited.

Second, some of the dimensions in the Implementation Cube may need to be elaborated or refined. While a tripartite categorisation was adequate for this study, it is possible that future empirical work will require extending the dimensions, or providing a different configuration. For example, we may consider incorporating a greater variety of concepts, or making more explicit use of context (e.g., Orlikowski, 1993).

Third, we note that the implementation cube results are limited to three boxes. In order to broaden our knowledge and understanding, other positions on the implementation cube should also be studied to find out the organizational consequences of such combinations. Empirical research into such experiences will help to establish the particular content, context and process associated with these alternatives.

Practical Implications

Moving on from theoretical issues, it is useful to consider whether the research has ramifications for IS implementation practice. In particular, we draw attention to three areas:
- *Understanding IS implementation.* The framework provides a useful resource for enhancing the understanding of a complex and dynamic situation.
- *A blueprint for planning.* The framework draws attention to a number of important areas of concern for IS implementation planning. Failure to address these can lead to later problems.
- *A tool for diagnosis.* The framework could be used to trace problems and pinpoint areas of deficiency in IS implementation.

The theoretical framework generated matches the qualifications of practical applicability posited by Glaser and Strauss (1967). First, it fits a substantive area of study. The concepts and relations posited as central are intimately related to (because they are derived from) the arena of Case Mix implementation. Second, the resultant theoretical framework is sufficiently general to be applicable to a range of situations around the implementation of Case Mix and other similar IS applications. Third, it is readily understandable by practitioners, and should accordingly serve as a useful direction in the change management designs of hospitals introducing Case Mix. By providing practitioners with some insight into the context, structure and process of CMIS implementations, the framework serves as a basis from which the IS practitioner can appraise and manage what is characteristically a poorly understood, complex and dynamic situation.

The framework developed and presented here has important implications for IS practitioners. It suggests that before the implementation of CMIS, or a similar technology, the project manager should pay explicit attention to: providing a system which fits *local* aims and objectives, ultimately with the involvement of stakeholders; clearly articulating such objectives and gaining the support of further stakeholders, particularly users; and assessing the full context of IS implementation. These items will significantly influence the change process and resultant organizational consequences. Having examined and articulated these issues, key players can more effectively plan the implementation of Case Mix, and facilitate the action required to enact the intended changes. Moreover, a clearly defined and supported project is more likely to "weather the storm" of the kind of externally imposed organizational changes experienced in the hospitals.

Managing integrative activity properly is a critical issue in achieving a fully implemented and supported IS, and will mediate its success and benefits. Here we need to consider social integration via education, training, communication and involvement, as well as other formal project management activity, such as procurement, planning, vendor management and technical integration and development, particularly in terms of clinical coding and IT standards (e.g., platforms, networks and so on). The ensuing process will further shape reactions, appropriations and consequences of the system. All of this occurs within context.

Critically then, in managing such projects, the implementers need to consider IS localisation, project integration and stakeholder support *together* and within *context*: the implementation cube provides a blueprint for planning the implementation of an IS. Inadequacy in any of these areas is likely to mean a loss of benefits or success of some kind, whether, for example, it is an inappropriate project or system, a poorly managed project which runs over time or budget or a loss of support and an unused system.

In addition to planning, the framework can easily be used as a means of assessment or diagnosis for implementation. If CMIS is unsuccessful, we can trace the antecedents of such problems using the framework, and come to some conclusions about the influences on such outcomes. On a more pragmatic level, reference against the framework during implementation can pinpoint areas of deficiency that may require attention in order to avoid significant shortcomings.

While these findings have been generated by only four organizational sites and require further investigation, they do have considerable face validity, and a number of documented instances of CMIS implementation have hinted at one or other such influence (e.g., Brown, 1995; Hackney and McBride, 1993).

SUMMARY AND CONCLUSIONS

This chapter has argued that the implementation of strategic IS within hospitals is a complex phenomenon, and that much can be gained by researching and managing it accordingly. The research has been useful in generating a set of insights, concepts and processes that address the critical organizational elements involved in implementing and using Case Mix. Generally, such elements have been largely overlooked in the IS literature, and have certainly not been examined in detail for RMI CMIS. The theoretical framework generated from the empirical findings suggests that the content of implementation, the change process, as well as the social context, critically influence what changes are associated with Case Mix. The framework also provides valuable insights for practitioners, detailing the important facets of organizational implementation that are associated with CMIS and how these might be assessed and managed. Thinking more broadly, such issues have considerable implications for achieving other strategic objectives for IS in healthcare, such as networking and standardization, both of which are explored in detail in later chapters.

REFERENCES

Anonymous (1993). MPs throw book at health chiefs over Wessex fiasco. *Computing*, vol. 13, 7.

Audit Commission. (1995) *For Your Information: A Study of Information Management and Systems in the Acute Hospital*. London: HMSO.

Beynon-Davies, P. (1995) Information Systems 'Failure': The Case of the London Ambulance Service's Computer-Aided Dispatch Project. *European Journal of Information Systems*, Vol. 4, pp. 171-184.

Beynon-Davies, P. (1995) "Information systems 'failure' and risk assessment: The case of the london ambulance service computer-aided dispatch system. *Proceedings of the Third European Conference on Information Systems*, Athens, June, pp. 1153-1170.

Black, N.A. and Moore, L. (1994). Comparative Audit Between Hospitals: The Example of Appendectomy. *International Journal of Health Care Quality Assurance*. 7(3), 11-15.

Brown, A. D. (1992) "Managing Change in the NHS: The Resource Management Initiative", *Leadership and Organizational Development Journal*, Vol.13, No. 6, pp. 13-17.

Brown, A.D. *(1995) Organizational Culture*, Pitman, London.

Collins, L. W. (1994) "CIOs Must Look Beyond the IS Horizon", *Computers in Healthcare*, Vol. 12, No. 5, pp. 39-40.

Cooper, R. B. and Zmud, R. W. (1990) "Information Technology Implementation Research: A Technological Diffusion Approach", *Management Science*, Vol. 36, No. 2, pp. 123-139.

Cross, M. (1992) "Computing the Cost of Health Care", *New Scientist*, Vol. 130, pp. 22-23.

DHSS (Department of Health and Social Security), *Health Services Management: Resource Management (Management Budgeting) in Health Authorities.* Health Notice (86) 34, HMSO, London, 1986.

Eisenhardt, K. M. (1989) "Building Theories from Case Study Research", *Academy of Management Review*, Vol. 14, No. 4, pp. 532-550.

Glaser, B.G. and Strauss, A..L. (1967) *The Discovery of Grounded Theory*, Aldine, Chicago.

Hackney, R. and McBride, N. (1993) "Interpreting Information Systems Strategy in the Public Sector", *Proceedings of the Third Annual National BIT Conference*, Manchester Metropolitan University, Manchester, May, 1993.

Health Economics Research Group. *(1991) Final Report of the Brunel University Evaluation of Resource Management*, Brunel University, Uxbridge.

HMSO (Her Majesty's Stationery Office), *(1993) Wessex Regional Health Authority Regional Information Systems Plan*, 63rd Report of the Committee of Public Accounts, HMSO, London.

Hockstrasser, B. and Griffiths, C. (1991) *Controlling IT Investments: Strategy and Management*, Chapman and Hall, London.

Holmes, A. and Poulymenakou, A. (1995) "Towards a Conceptual Framework for Investigating Information Systems Failure", *Proceedings of the Third European Conference on Information Systems*, Athens, June, pp. 805-823.

Jones, B. and Worsdale, G. (1993) "Can IT Help in Working for Patients?", *Health Services Management*, Vol. 89, No. 2, pp. 3-16.

Keen, P. G. W. (1981) "Information Systems and Organizational Change", *Communications of the ACM*, Vol. 26, No. 6, pp. 24-33.

King, W. R. and Grover, V. (1991) "The Strategic Use of Information Resources: An Exploratory Study", *IEEE Transactions on Engineering Management*, Vol. 38, pp. 293-305.

Kramer, A. K. and Ellertson, R. J. (1993) "Using PCs for Effective Case-Mix Based Budgeting", *Healthcare Financial Management*, Vol. 47, No. 6, pp. 52-58.

Land, F. (1976) "Evaluation of Systems Goals in Determining a Design Strategy for a Computer-Based Information System", *The Computer Journal*, Vol. 19, No. 4, pp. 290-294.

Lock, C. (1996) "What Value do Computers Provide to NHS Hospitals?", *British Medical Journal*, Vol. 312, pp. 1407-1410.

Lock, C. (1996) "The Assessment of IT in Healthcare and the Relevance of the Private Finance Initiative", *Proceedings of the Third European Conference on the Evaluation of Information Technology*, Bath, November, pp. 63-72.

Lyytinen, K. (1987) A taxonomic perspective of information systems development: Theoretical constructs and recommendations. in Boland, R.J. and Hirschheim, R.A. (Eds.), *Critical Issues in Information Systems Research*. Chichester: Wiley, pp. 3-42.

Lyytinen, K. and Hirschheim, R.A. (1987) "Information Systems Failures, A Survey and Classification of the Empirical Literature", *Oxford Surveys in Information Technology*, Vol. 4, pp. 257-309.

McFarlan, F. W. (1981) "Portfolio Approach to Information Systems", *Harvard Business Review*, Vol. 59, No.5, pp. 142-150.

Naude, P., Proudlove, N. and Bellingham, R. (1994) "Group Decision Support for IT Procurement", *OR Insight*, Vol. 7, No. 3, pp. 6-11.

Orlikowski, W. J. (1993) "CASE Tools as Organizational Change: Investigating Incremental and Radical Changes in Systems Development", *MIS Quarterly*, Vol. 17, No. 3, pp. 309-340.

Oz, E. (1994) "When Professional Standards are Lax: The CONFIRM Failure and Its Lessons", *Communications of the ACM*, Vol. 37, No. 10.

Pettigrew, A. M. (1990) "Longitudinal Field Research on Change: Theory and Practice", *Organization Science*, Vol. 1, No. 3, pp. 267-292.

Pettigrew, A.M., Ferlie, E. and McKee L. (1994) *Shaping Strategic Change*, Sage, London.

Rea, D.M. (1994) "Better Informed Judgements: Resource Management in the NHS", *Accounting Auditing and Accountability Journal*, Vol. 7, No. 1, pp. 86-110.

Richards, B. (1986) "Computers in Clinical Medicine", *Data Processing*, Vol. 28, No. 10, pp. 543-546.

Roberts, H. J. and Barrar, P.R.N. (1992) "MRP II Implementation: Key Factors for Success", *Computer-Integrated Manufacturing Systems*, Vol. 5, pp. 31-38.

Robinson, R. (1992) "Roll-call after Roll-out", *The Health Service Journal*, Vol. 102, pp. 18-19.

Sauer, C. (1993) *Why Information Systems Fail: A Case Study Approach*, Alfred Waller, London.

Schultz, R.L., Slevin, D.P. and Pinto, J.K. (1987) "Strategy and Tactics in a Process Model of Project Implementation", *Interfaces*, Vol. 17, pp. 34-46.

Strauss, A. and Corbin, J. (1990) *Basics of Qualitative Research: Grounded Theory Procedures and Techniques*, Sage, London.

Swanson, E.B. (1993) *Information Systems Implementation*, Irwin, Homewood, 1988.

Tate, P. Hunter, P., McPartlin, J.P., and Duffy, M. "London's Embarrassing Mistake", *Wall Street and Technology*, May.

Willcocks, L. and Lester, S. (1993) *Evaluating the Feasibility of Information Technology*, Research and Discussion Paper RDP93/1, Oxford Institute of Information Management, Oxford.

Yin, R. (1984) *Case Study Research*, Sage, Beverly Hills.

Yin, R. (1994) *Case Study Research: Design and Methods*, Sage, London.

Chapter III

Streamlining Operations in Healthcare with ICT

Reima Suomi
Turku School of Economics and Business Administration, Finland

Health care is an information-intensive industry. Its cornerstones are a research tradition of hundreds of years, and detailed understanding of each customer, patient. As compared to other industries, say banking, the data about the customer needs to be very detailed, and must include trend data to allow analysis of the development of things. When caring for a patient, even very special knowledge and know-how is often needed, and this compels the industry into a networked mode of operation, with a lot of communication needs.

With this background, it is astonishing to see how slowly the industry has adopted to new information and communication technology (ICT). Currently, however, a major revolution is under way, and the health care industry has become a key application area for ICT, and an object for both national and international programs to promote usage of ICT.

We want to understand these trends better. Our research questions are:
1. Which reasons led to the late adoption of modern ICT in the healthcare sector?
2. Why is the situation now changing fast?
3. Which seem to be the main application areas?
4. Which kind of progress can we now see?

To each of the research questions, we allocate one section in our chatper. This article is conceptual in nature, but argumentation is supported by concrete examples and field work done at the author's Institute in more than 10 projects in the health care sector. The main conclusions are that:
- Starting from "scratch" has made a fast development in the field possible when it comes to modern ICT.

Copyright © 2001, Idea Group Publishing.

- *Developments have been very fast; on the other hand demand for information and ICT has grown too enormously.*
- *ICT has been a total change agent for the industry, and a needed one.*
- *Fast introduction of modern ICT has been made possible through the simultaneous introduction of many modern management techniques such as quality assurance.*
- *The Internet was and is the "killer platform" in this industry too.*
- *The whole sector has turned from a handicraft industry to a knowledge industry.*

INTRODUCTION

As compared to many other industries, health care has been a late adopter of information technology. Individual clinical devices have been used as isolated islands of technology already for a long time, but integrated solutions to support total patient care have been late to arrive. One of the early signs of the change was the classical American Hospital Supply (Short and Venkatraman, 1992), which, even when limited to supply and demand on medicine and other hospital supplies, first opened our eyes to the huge improvement potential within the healthcare sector. Some less-known individuals saw the development trends already very early: *"Wholly new forms of encyclopedia will appear, ready-made with a mesh of associative trails running through them, ready to be dropped into the memex, and there amplified... the physical, buzzled by a patienst's reaction, strikes the trail established in studying an earlier similar case, and runs rapidly through analogous case histories, with side references to the classics for the pertinent anatomy and histology..."* (Bush, 1949).

Our view is that the healthcare industry, together with retail and tourism, are going to be major turnaround industries in Information and Communication Technology (ICT) usage in the next ten years. That's why we want to introduce the readers to the changing trends in the industry.

Our analysis focuses on the patient consultation and interaction level. How have the patient-related processes changed? This means that several important developments in the nearby disciplines have to be ignored. For example, in the more technical field, several telemedicine, image processing and computer modeling techniques exist. To take a more administrative point of view, we could long discuss process development initiatives in the healthcare sector. The management and resource allocation systems of the healthcare industry would also be of most interest. However, we see that the patient contact is the moment-of-truth in health services, and we should focus on that and the developments in that field because of modern ICT.

Major trends in the healthcare sector as such are too out of the scope of this chapter. The reader should be reminded of the major developments: the population is altering fast and life expectancy is growing. New diseases are being discovered all the time, and even small malfunctions of the human body are intervened with nowadays. Also the demand for services is growing very much because of several reasons. At the same time, in many countries the proportion of healthcare-oriented costs of the total Gross National Product is at its peak: no increase could be tolerated. So, without extra resources, ways to answer to the increased demand must be found. The key is increased effectiveness and efficiency, for which ICT applications are major tools.

Other main trends are those of privatization and increase in information intensity. Activities are turning from public hierarchies to private markets and networks. This means new cost-awareness. Information, often costly and difficult to gain, is a key to success in the market, instead or at least at the side of other production inputs.

Networking of the actors in the field is a key trend. The services needed are so complex that no organization can provide them alone. This means increased communication and control needs. Fortunately, modern ICT is a key enabling technology in this sense.

Our research questions are:
1. Which reasons led to the late adoption of modern ICT in the healthcare sector?
2. Why is the situation now changing fast?
3. Which seem to be the main application areas?
4. Which kind of progress can we now see?

To each of the research questions, we allocate one section in our chapter. The article is conceptual in nature, but illustrated through case-examples from the literature and from the research projects the author is involved in.

INHIBITING FACTORS FOR ICT INTRODUCTION

We have found the following reasons for the late adoption of modern ICT in the healthcare sector:
- Fragmented industry structure
- Big national differences in processes
- Strong professional culture of medical care personnel
- One-sided education
- Handcrafting traditions
- Weak customers
- Hierarchical organization structures.

Good competitors and customers are a key to success for any company and industry (Porter, 1990). Unfortunately, the healthcare sector has not been able to neither of them. For a long time healthcare has been considered as a faceless public service, where normal competitive forces are not in effect. Healthcare organizations have not felt as competitors, but neither have they documented productive cooperative behaviour. First, with penetrating privatization, the situation is starting to change.

As it comes to customers, most often they get into touch with the industry when in a critical and sensitive situation, where bargaining power is very low. Bad service has just to be suffered. First, during the last few years, the concept "customer" has started to substitute the word "patient." Regulative bodies have also become active in this respect, and for example in Finland, a special patient-ombudsman has been institutionalized and legislation on patient reclamation and insurance has been introduced. Customer power is too increased because of their increased knowledge. Through Internet and other means, it is nowadays easier than before to collect even detailed and professional medical information, and often the patients become the best experts in their diseases. In such a situation, it is clear that bad service and care is less tolerated than before.

Professional cultures can have a profound impact on organizational outcome Martin and Siehl, 1983). Within the healthcare sector, there are many strong professional cultures, the strongest of them being those of doctors and those of the nurses. People seeking these professions usually value human interaction, and are not much for abstract systems such as computers. Issues of power come into play: professionalism means power, and health care professionals naturally are uneager to share their power positions with new professional groups.

A part of hospital organization has always been a strong hierarchical, professional and specialized structure. Work on the computers, unfortunately, is low on the hierarchy list, especially of course in the activities of keying in patient data that would be a natural thing to do for the doctors. As The European Information Technology Observatory (1995) puts it: "*...for many healthcare applications, the most difficult obstacles can be social and cultural.*" It is well known that information system development and application can be very difficult or at least different from less bureaucratic organizations than healthcare (Middleton, 1999).

Even when we conclude that healthcare is a very information-intensive industry, it has not been considered as such one. A good doctor is valued because of his handcrafting skills, especially in surgery or dental care, and it is not understood that behind the handcraft operations, a vast amount of knowledge is needed. Some, anyway, have understood that the human body is the most complex entity in the world, and of which information and knowledge has been collected over thousands of years.

Finally, education of healthcare personnel has traditionally not focused on computer skills. Even the classical university tradition has kept medical and natural science (and thus computer) faculties apart from each other. Fortunately, during recent years, the drive for deeper cooperation between different science fields has begun to bear fruit.

Patient care is very culturally bound, and especially the administrative processes behind vary greatly from one country to another. This, of course, makes standardization very difficult and the industry a bad target for suppliers of standard software and platforms. Neither do we have any dominant players in the field that would behave in the market as strong customers and trend-setters.

CHANGE AGENTS IN THE INDUSTRY

Several pressures affect the healthcare industry too. Here are some, which we found to be of most importance and which we want to discuss:
- New networked way of handling patients and processes
- Increasing cost justification needs
- Advances in ICT
- Growing demand
- Better education of personnel
- More demanding customers.

As a whole, society is turning away from hierarchies and simple value chains to complicated networks and value systems. This is also the case for the healthcare industry. Increasing skill demands and cost pressures drive even this industry towards specialization, and an individual patient, the customer, is being circulated in a network of service providers. Mastering of processes in this network and catering for the needed data to follow the patient to different service points all necessitate heavy usage of information technology.

Even more, the boundaries between healthcare and other industries blur. This is especially true for the social sector. For example, elderly people need services other than just health-oriented services, their needs are many and intertwined. For example, providing electronic commerce services to them can be a major help (Heikkilä, Kallio, Saarinen and Tuunainen, 1999). A good example of a Finnish innovation is that by the Finnish Post. Their internal innovation prize was given in 1997 to a product, where postmen during their daily distribution rounds visit older people to see that everything is ok, and if needed help with minor tasks or call for further help.

Healthcare-related expenses grow in all modern societies. People live longer, and even severely handicapped or sick people can be offered quite normal living environments and conditions. New diseases are being discovered all the time, and even small malfunctions in the human body, that before went unnoticed, are being addressed by modern medical science (say plastic surgery). This all of course causes enormous costs for the society. If new extra resources are not available from other sectors of the society, the only way to answer to the increased demand is increased efficiency. A key to this efficiency is information technology, which frees healthcare professionals from routine tasks to patient care.

As in other sectors of life, modern information technology can offer very much. Note that we have constantly in this chapter used the term ICT, information and communication technology. Actually, at the moment, telecommunications-based systems are developing faster than traditional information systems. Keywords in this area are Internet and mobile communications, both to be integrated in the near future.

A new key technology is that of smart cards, which allow patient data to be stored efficiently. Advances in telemedicine and especially in graphical data manipulation should neither go unnoticed. Computer files are slowly beginning to substitute old media for x-ray picture storage. Computers, for example, can too very effectively scan vast amounts of pictures and select outstanding cases for further human inspection. Visualization techniques have also been a key for faster product development in the drug industry (Karjaluoto, 1999).

Education of healthcare staff is growing in intensity and coverage. Computers are essential tools for future doctors already in the education phase, and they get into interaction with them even in their private lives, say at homes. The Internet and other digital sources are substituting traditional books and journals as sources of knowledge in the sector.

Because of the more intensive care needs, customer groups have become more heterogeneous. *"Satisfaction with healthcare across Europe is thus relatively high at a general level, but variations inevitably occur as the services and groups of patients under consideration become more specific"* (European Health Care Reforms, 1996). Not all get into contact with the healthcare system in severe conditions, especially since healthcare has become more protective and proactive instead of just being reactive. Customers demand more, and so the quality of actions needs to be improved. Many, especially in the case of chronic diseases, became nearby experts in the area. Applications such as on-line patient communities provide mutual help. Actually, what would connect people better than a common disease, online patient communities fit well to the definition of Internet communities (Rheingold, 1993): *Virtual Communities are social aggregations that emerge from the Net when enough people carry on public discussions long enough, with sufficient human feeling, to form webs of personal relationships in cyperspace"*.

Even small mistakes and malfunctions of the system fast find their ways to the public knowledge and discussion. Mistakes in health care can be very dramatic, and so it is no wonder the media follows the industry very carefully. Everyone has some contact points to the industry, in opposition to many other industries, and so it is clear that the general human interest in the industry is very high.

Table 1. Differences between being a patient or a consumer (European Healthcare Reforms, 1996).

the role of patients	the role of consumers
patience	activity
dependence	integrity
weak position	equality
lack of freedom	mobility, freedom of choice
to be represented by experts	to represent oneself
unawareness of quality	awareness of quality
unawareness of costs	awareness of costs

The difference between being a patient and being a consumer is nicely put in Table 1.

A TENTATIVE CLASSIFICATION OF ICT SYSTEMS IN THE HEALTHCARE INDUSTRY

Classifications of ICT techniques in the healthcare sector are few. We propose the classification as shown in Figure 1.

The heart of our classification is in the interaction between the medical personnel and the patient. The systems support discussions in the interaction situation; we call the customer support and consultation tools. These tools become active as a relationship between the patient and care-taking personnel is established. Customers, the patients, as well as the medical staff, however, have the interaction needs to be established, timed and synchronized, and for these purposes we introduce the systems of interaction support tools and process support tools.

Interaction-related support tools address the situation from the viewpoints of the primary actors, patients and care-taking personnel, whereas process support tools take the viewpoint of the total value chain. Finally, the transactions have to be financially tracked, and for that purpose introduce the category of money-related support tools.

Medical care is very knowledge-intensive, and an important category of systems falls into the category of decision support provision. With this name we focus on the knowledge needs of each individual care-taking action, but of course knowledge is being produced and used in other connections too.

We feel that the distinction used in services, that of front-end and back-office systems, is usable in the healthcare sector too. Preparation tools support the customer, care-taking personnel interaction, but are not active in the actual transaction.

Figure 1. Classification of ICT tools in healthcare

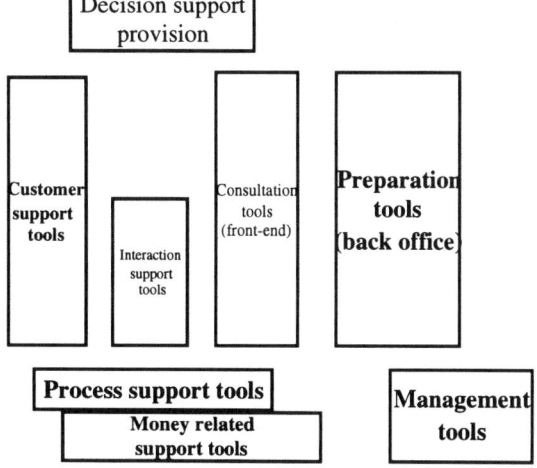

Finally, we have a category of management tools for the healthcare sector. In our classification, they are active at a general level, and not used in an individual consultation situation. Most likely they are of the same character as in any management activity.

All the components of this ICT infrastructure interact with each other, some more intensively, some hardly at all. However, as we are not able to go very deep into that topic in this chapter, we leave the presentation of the connections between the components out from the figure.

As we can see, individual system installations can be active in many of these categories. For example, basic patient data systems fall into many of these abstract categories. Next we have a closer discussion of all the system types.

Customer support tools

Information systems in this category are targeted at giving support for the customer, patient, in his or her daily coping with his/her health (sickness), as well as specifically in interactions with healthcare personnel or systems.

In the broad sense, all information systems contributing to the well-being of humans belong to this category. More specifically, however, we should focus on systems that help the patients in coping with health data. A simple spreadsheet where someone keeps track of his/her weight would belong to this category. More specific examples are tailored equipment to measure and keep track of different health-related data, such as the Finnish Wellmate concept for measuring and delivering blood pressure data. The concept has since then been commercialized and expanded through the Lifechart, brand (see http://www.lifechart.com/). Smart cards with patient data belong to this category too.

Interaction support tools

With these systems we mean mainly computerized reservation systems for consultation. They are often pioneering applications. With modern Internet-based techniques, these systems can be turned into self services. From the personnel point of view, different systems to keep track of consulting hours and other activities belong to this category.

As a further step, the whole consultation process can be conducted through information systems. Finally, whole hospitals can become virtual ones. To see an example, take a look at the Finnish Atuline (see http://www.atuline.com/).

Consultation tools

Consultation tools are there to help the care taking personnel in the customer interaction situation. This area is of key importance: "the doctor-patient relationship tends to be of primary importance to most patients"(European Health Care Reforms, 1996). Consultation tools deliver the basic patient data, and may direct the consultation situation through data input demands, and workflow and customer interaction process recommendations.

To give an example, surgeon operations are often a most critical point in a care-taking chain for a patient. However, current systems and work habits do not cater for proper information to be collected during them. Solutions that allow for fluent collection of data without disturbing the delicate actions or surgery are badly needed.

Decision support provision tools

Whereas the consultation tools deliver the basic patient data, with decision support provision, we refer to information systems that deliver general information that needs to be assessed and assembled for use in the specific consultation situation by the care taking personnel. It is well known that the amount of medical know-how is growing very fast all the time. For example, the known number of effects medical components have on humans is currently increased to 500 from 50 some 10 years ago, and very soon we will recognize some 5,000 effects. The Internet has been the tool that has suddenly made huge amounts of information accessible for every doctor.

Process support tools

Process support tools guide and escort the patient through different caring activities in the healthcare value system. They of course interact with the interaction support tools, but take a broader view on the process than just one consultation interaction. Here critical issues are among other the routing of the customer through different consultations, and taking care that needed data follows the customer. From the viewpoint of the service points, even and right-sized load is a key factor. Major cost benefits can be gained here through directing the customer to the right level of consultation, at the right time and place. These systems are among the most difficult to implement, because they are co-operative in nature (see Suomi, 1990). However, we have seen documents of even early success stories (see for example Ribbers, 1991).

Money-related support tools

Money-related support tools master the money flows in healthcare. They are used also by the customer, but the more they can be handled as back-office, functions, the better for the customer. Through these systems, the payer, say public administration and insurance companies, get involved in the processes. Because of the strong players in the field and the huge economical values at stage, even information technology innovations have traditionally born fruit there (see for example, Martin and Eckerle, 1991)

To emphasize the complexity of the area, for example in Finland, for a long time the budgeting system distributing state support for different healthcare organizations was one of the heaviest to use and maintain in the whole public administration (*Tietoja valtionhallinon atk-toiminnasta*, 1997). A key solution here will again be the smart card that will include payment data in addition to patient data.

Preparation tools

Preparation tools are systems at a service point that help the care taking personnel to prepare for the customer interaction, but are not self-active at the consultation time. Typical examples are different systems for handling laboratory activities and mastering x-ray pictures. Decision support provision of course heavily interacts with these systems too.

Management tools

Management tools support the management of healthcare. Most importantly, they collect statistical data for directing purposes from all other information systems. Management tools can be very classically divided into systems at operational, tactical and strategic levels. Especially strategic planning tools are badly needed. In our definition, strategic decisions are decisions that affect the total amount of resources available for a certain purpose (see Barney, 1991). For example, for years the Finnish political decision-makers have had difficulties in deciding how many doctors should be educated. Some years reductions in education are demanded; some years proof of doctor shortages is presented.

An alternative typology basis is that of classifying primary stakeholders in the process. For each stakeholder, a number of systems exist, but for space reasons we will not start a discussion on the systems per stakeholder category here. The stakeholders are summarized in Figure 2.

The figure separates five groups in the value chain. The patient is the primary caring object, but his/her well-being is of course in the interest of a group we call secondary customers, the family being the foremost, but shortly followed by his/her employers and the society as a whole, we hope.

With primary care we mean those parties that get into direct interaction with the patient. Here we of course have the responsible doctor, the other care taking staff and pharmacists. The secondary layer of care suppliers is already more vague, but in our classification stakeholders that produce direct inputs for the consumption of the primary care as their main business belong to this group. Administration refers to those stakeholders that provide the regulative and infrastructure basis for healthcare, but do not give any direct inputs to the consultation of the patient.

Figure 2. Stakeholder analysis of healthcare

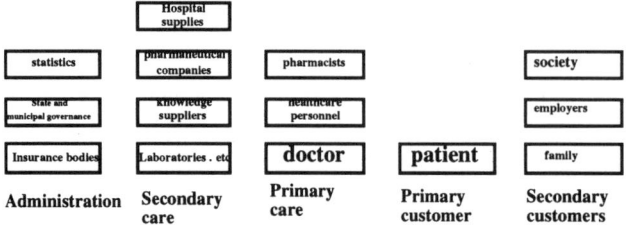

PROOF OF CONCRETE CHANGES

Not just are the pressures to take modern ICT into use in healthcare enormous, the accomplishments so far seem to be promising ones. We have been witnessing the following trends:
- Active research initiatives in the field
- Major scientific advancements because of ITC
- Major investments of hospitals into healthcare information systems
- Active regulative and infrastructure investments
- Boom of medical data on the Internet
- Cheap equipment for home usage
- New pharmacy products
- Functional food offerings.

Research on healthcare information systems has boomed during the last five years, this ECIS track being a good example of that. Both European Union and national research programs have allocated research funds into this field, the EU 5th Framework program discussion the theme under the title, "Improving the quality of life and management of living resources" with the following subtitles (Cordis, 1999):
- Food, nutrition and health
- Control of infectious diseases
- The "cell factory"
- Environment and health
- Sustainable agriculture, fisheries and forestry and integrated development of rural areas including mountain areas
- The aging population and disabilities.

Major improvements in medical science are there because of the research possibilities allowed by modern ICT. Maybe the biggest promise is the completion of the human gene map, made possible by extensive databases and modeling techniques unavailable still a few years ago.

Hospitals and other service providers in the area invest huge amounts of resources into ICT. For example, in Turku, a deliberate decision was made 1992 to abandon the building of one more health center and to invest the money into ICT in the sector, which was the start for--on the Finnish scale--a considerable project called Primus (see http://www.turku.fi/tervi). An average patient is maybe not at the first hand understanding the intensity of modern ICT usage in hospitals, as back-office functions are many times automated first (Klein and Schad, 1997).

Active regulative investments are also called for in the field of healthcare. Patient privacy seems to be a major problem area. "Care must also be taken to safeguard patient privacy and the confidence of medical records" (European Information Technology Observatory, 1995). A lot of activities already happen in the field. As it comes to the telecommunications infrastructure, many main links and techniques in this area have become feasible because of medical applications giving the basic load for the infrastructure.

On the Internet, the amount of medical data is booming. This is of course true for other areas of life too. In addition to bulk data, currently personal consulting in the form of virtual hospitals is available on the Internet too. Of course the Internet is a key technology for many activities eroding health too, say drug businesses. And finally we must remember that the demand for healthcare–related information is also growing very rapidly (Klein, Lee, Lei and Quereshi, 1996).

What we still seem to miss is a documentation of the benefits the customers have met. The trick is to separate which improvements are there because of modern information technology and which because of some other reason. As an integrated one, it should be safe to conclude that both the quality and efficiency of healthcare have improved over the last decades. It is also safe to assess that at least a part of this development is there because of modern information systems.

Large-scale production and cheap microchips have made it possible to build equipment for home usage with reasonable quality and price. A prime example is that of hearth rate monitors (see for example http://www.polar.fi/). Earlier we discussed the Wellmate concept. New products both in the traditional pharmacy as well as in more traditional nutrition category, the product groups that are fast integrating, have been witnessed. For new medicine development, computer simulations can speed up the process reasonably. An example is the emergence of new functional food stuffs such as Benecol®, with the fat-soluble plant, stanol ester, that effectively restricts the absorption of cholesterol from the digestive tract and thus reduces serum total and LDL cholesterol (see http://www.raisiogroup.com/group/products/index.html).

CONCLUSIONS

Many information technology professionals dream of starting something from the "green field." In the healthcare sector, this dream has come partly true. Sometimes starting from scratch is better than repairing old systems, as was documented in the case of the build-up of the ex-DDR telecommunications infrastructure (Tenzer, 1997).

ICT applications of healthcare are in many places not just modernized, but leapfrogged to the future. Actually, for example in more technical computing, many advantages are put forward by the hard demands from the medicine side in disciplines such as computer modeling and visualization techniques. ICT should be seen as a powerful change agent for the whole healthcare sector. The tradition-rich and conservative industry is not only suffering from the changes. We have already seen similar, almost radical changes in other traditional industries such as insurance (see Suomi, 1991) or the publishing industry. Most evidently, the changes have been positive as seen from the macro perspective.

It is not to be forgotten that the patient is a human. The old proverb "high touch–high tech" is getting new content in the case of healthcare information systems. Fortunately, nowadays ICT is seen as an extension of human capabilities, not as a substitute for them. Introduction of modern ICT has coincided with several other developments supporting it. For example, disciplines such as focus on business processes, quality systems and thinking, organizational learning and break-down of hierarchies – all topics active in the healthcare sector – support and actually necessitate the introduction of modern ICT.

Even in the healthcare sector, one cannot escape the power of the Internet. First the Internet has launched several critical applications to the field and made it possible to communicate efficiently and internationally. All too often the Internet is, however, still seen as an information distribution tool, and real interactive solutions in the healthcare sector still remain unseen. This is especially true for structured business/consultation transactions. Maybe the transactions between patients and the care-taking staff in healthcare are so complicated and human-oriented that structuring them to a computer screen are almost impossible. This means that growth-paths for usage of the Internet in healthcare remain there for a long time to come. When are we to speak of electronic commerce in the healthcare sector?

Finally, let us focus back on the strong professional culture of healthcare. The healthcare profession is turning from a handicraft to a knowledge profession. As diseases and their caring methods grow more complex, they are won through knowledge, not solely through experience. Handcrafting skills are needed in some areas such as surgery, but those activities become forums for specialized professionals, and the average staff is not always having material contact with the patient. As we speak of a knowledge profession, ICT is to be natural part of the total, not just some odd add-on.

REFERENCES

Barney, J. (1991). Firm resources and sustained competitive advantage. *Journal of Management.* 17(1).

Bush, V. (1949). As We May Think", *The Atlantic Monthly*, Reprinted in I.Greif, (editor) *Computer-Supported Cooperative Work: A Book of Readings.* San Mateo, CA. Morgan-Kaufmann, 32.

Cordis www-site. http://www.cordis.lu/fp5/src/t-1.htm. Read 12. November 1999.

The European Information Technology Observatory (1995).

European Health Care Reforms – Citizen's Choice and Patients' Rights (1996) World Health Organization Regional Office for Europe. Copenhagen.

Heikkilä. J., Kallio, J., Saarinen, T. and Tuunainen, V. (1999). EC of groceries for elderly and disabled - Comparison of alternative service models. *Information Technology and People*, 12(4).

Karjaluoto, K. (1999). *Knowledge Management in Customer Relationship on High-Throughput Screening Market: Case EG&G Wallac.* Master's Thesis. Turku School of Economics and Business Administration.

Klein, S., Lee, R., Lei, L. and Quereshi, S. (1996). Pharmatica- Supporting the Complex Information Needs in the Changing Healthcare Sector. *EM – Newsletter*, 6(2), 25-26.

Martin, J. and Siehl, C. (1983). Organizational Culture and Counterculture: An Uneasy Symbiosis. *Organizational Dynamics*, no. 2, 52-64.

Martin, J. and Eckerle, R. (1991). "A Knowledge-Based System for Auditing Health Insurance Claims. *Interfaces*, 21(2), 39-47.

Middleton, P (1999). Managing information system development in bureaucracies. *Information and Software Technology*, vol. 41, 473-482.

Porter, M. (1990). The Competitive Advantage of Nations. *Harvard Business Review* March/April, 73-93.

Rheingold, H. (1993). *The Virtual Community - Homesteading on the Electronic Frontier.* Addison-Wesley.

Ribbers, P. (1991), *"RHCNET - A Regional Healthcare EDI-Network in the Netherlands.* Commission of the European Communities, TEDIS Programme, Task B12, Information Campaign 3, Case studies and training material for management.

Short, J. and Venkatraman, N. (1992). Beyond business process redesign: redefining Baxter's business network. *Sloan Management Review*, 34(1), 7-20.

Suomi, R. (1991). "Alliance or alone - How to build inter-organizational information systems. *Technology Analysis & Strategic Management.* 3(3), 211-233.

Suomi, R. (1990). *Assessing the Feasibility of an Inter-Organizational Information System on the Basis of the Transaction Cost Approach.* Doctoral Thesis. Turku School of Economics and Business Administration. A-3.

Supply Chains: a Framework for Business Transformation. (1996). In P. Swatman, J. Gricar and J. Novak (eds.) *"Electronic Commerce for Trade Efficiency and Effectiveness, Proceedings of the Ninth International EDI-IOS Conference Bled, Slovenia, June 10-13.* Kranj: Moderna Organizacija, 28-53.

Tenzer, G. (1997) *"Statement Anlässlich der Pressekonferenz dum Aufbau Ost am 10. December in Neubrandenburg".* Deutsche Telekom AG.

Tietoja Valtionhallinnon Atk-Toiminnasta (1997). Valtionvarainministeriö.

Tuunainen, V. (1999) Different models of electronic commerce – Integration of value chains and business processes," *Helsinki School of Economics and Business Administration,* A-153.

Section 2

Standardization in Healthcare IS

Standardization Strategies
Nina Lundberg
Ole Hanseth

Standardization
Peter Lagendijk
Robert Stegwee

Electronic Patient Record
Pieter Toussaint
Marc Berg

Chapter IV

Standardization Strategies in Practice—Examples from Healthcare

Nina Lundberg, Gothenberg University, Sweden
Ole Hanseth, University of Oslo, Norway

This chapter explores some of the consequences of strategies used to develop electronic standards in healthcare, especially the consequences of electronic standards for communication work. The two standardization strategies explored are the prototype strategy used to develop intranet applications and the specification strategy used to develop Picture Archiving and Communication Systems (PACS) in healthcare. It was found that computer systems based on different electronic standards intervene in work in different ways, and that they do not always intervene in the ways they were initially intended. For example, the PACS based on the DICOM standard have primarily attained a local role, although its initial aim was to support universal image communication within healthcare. On the other hand the intranet application based on the Internet standards primarily not designed for this particular purpose has come to support communication of images and reports within the heterogeneous hospital network.

INTRODUCTION

During the past 15 years, international organizations and countless dedicated individuals have devoted great effort to the development of electronic standards for storage and transmission of radiological images (Jost, 1994). It is impossible to build large communication networks of people and things unless they are based on standards (Hanseth and Monteiro, in manuscript). As there is a great need for communication within healthcare, the need for standards is obvious. To support this large-scale communication, a number of technical standards have been developed within healthcare, such as Digital Imaging and Communications in Medicine (DICOM). Between 1983 and 1994 this standard was developed mainly by the American College of Radiology (ACR) and the National Electrical Manufacturers Association (NEMA). It is now also being developed in conjunction with JIRA/IS&C in Japan, and reviewed by IEEE, ASTM, HL7 and ANSI in the USA.

Different strategies are associated with the development of electronic standards. For instance, the European standards for healthcare, including DICOM, are based on a specification-driven approach, seeking more homogeneous solutions, presupposing a common design implementation in all medical units. Simultaneously, other electronic standards have been implemented in healthcare, such as the Internet standard. The Internet society has developed through a prototype-oriented strategy and is growing rapidly. It is based on the idea that there would be multiple independent networks of rather arbitrary design. The idea of the Internet was that any provider could freely design an application and make it work together with the other networks in the Internet. It emphasizes an underlying heterogeneous solution in work.

There has been little research focused on electronic standards in healthcare (Hanseth and Monteiro, in manuscript), although electronic standards are rapidly being introduced. For instance, Laurin (1998) reported that 60% of all radiology departments in Sweden were planning to introduce electronic standards within the next three years. It thus seems important for us to strive to contribute an understanding of some of the consequences of electronic standards in medical work.

We view standards as an agreement that establishes a framework within which to solve particular problems. An example of this is the rules for how many different medical actors should use the radiological examination order. Secretaries use the request to book examinations, radiographers to carry out examinations, radiologists to diagnose patients, archive staff to archive documents, clinicians to request radiological examinations and to carry out patient intervention and treatment, etc. The standard covers more than one local activity, and is applied in the context of making things work together over distance and heterogeneous metrics. Although its aim is to support cooperative work, it cannot guarantee interoperability between entities. Communication must take place according to shared, standardized protocols. Work must follow standardized practices. In the standardized radiological network, actors rely in their actions on other actors following the standards.

The empirical data has been collected from a larger ethnographic study that was initiated in October 1997 at the Radiology Department, Sahlgrenska University Hospital, Gothenburg, Sweden. It has been followed up by several additional studies at the Pediatric Radiology Department, Astrid Lindgren Children's Hospital, Stockholm, Sweden, and at the Radiology Department, Örebro University Hospital, Sweden. Ethnography has recently become widely recognized in the IS field (Hughes et al., 1994; Bowers et al., 1995; Bellotti and Bly, 1996; Button and Harper, 1996; Button and Sharrock, 1997; Suchman, 1998). The research approach is to investigate and understand the relevant work practice in context. Several different qualitative research methods were used: workplace video studies; interviews illustrated by video documentation; unstructured interviews; observations; discussions and interviews integrated with observations of diagnostic practice and social interaction. More than 40 hours of video documentation were recorded. More than 45 hours of observations and 28 interviews were conducted, each about an hour-and-a-half in length. Some participants were interviewed more than once over the period of study.

The aim of this research was to explore some of the consequences of different strategies used to develop electronic standards in healthcare. This was done by analyzing the implementation of different electronic standards, based on various standardization strategies, in work practice.

The remainder of the chapter is organized as follows. Section 2 presents the related research. Section 3 describes the electronic standards in healthcare at the hospitals we have studied. Section 4 presents the use of electronic standards in radiological practice. In Sections 5 and 6, the use of different standardization strategies are analyzed and discussed. Our conclusions appear in Section 7.

RELATED RESEARCH

The importance of standards for overlapping cooperative work between distributed units has produced a range of studies and analyses of standards in sociotechnical networks.

Important studies have centered on the design of technical standards. For instance, Hanseth and Monteiro analyzed the ISO (International Organisation for Standardization) and Internet 'association' supporting the creation of standards (Hanseth, 1996; Hanseth and Monteiro, 1996; Hanseth et al., 1996). They conducted a series of investigations into the interplay between stability and change. They highlight the tension between standardization and flexibility in the creation of communication systems as a key design factor.

This approach resembles those applied by Bowker and Star (1994, 1999) and Star and Ruhleder (1996). In their studies they analyze the evolution of the classification of diseases developed by the World Health Organization. They illustrate how the establishment of standards is anything but neutral; they are the results of political and social work.

In this chapter we seek to add to the current understanding of implementation and use of different standardization strategies in healthcare. We analyze and discuss two different standard strategies used to design electronic standards in healthcare. There are complementary studies to ours; for example, Berg (1997) explores empirically how universal standards, by means of medical records, are appropriated to local medical contexts.

The following section briefly describes the PACS in use (for more detailed descriptions of the film diagnostic process and the PACS diagnostic processes, see Lundberg, 2000).

PACS IN USE

PACS – Picture Archiving and Communication Systems – are the globally used applications for electronic storage, retrieval, distribution, communication, display and processing of medical image data. PACS date back to the early 1980s, when healthcare focused on information technology's ability to communicate, exchange and distribute image information in an accessible and fast format. Most PACS products are based on the technical standard "Digital Imaging and Communication in Medicine" (DICOM). With beginnings in 1995, some 8% of the radiology departments in Sweden have now (1999) implemented PACS. The initial aim of using PACS was to replace films or the entire film diagnostic process with electronic images based on PACS to improve the creation, distribution, communication and exchange of medical images between physically distributed actors, and hence to make the healthcare practice more effective and efficient. A number of references provide a historical presentation of PACS and the DICOM that standard PACS products are based on (for example, Hindel, 1994; Jost, 1994; Parisot, 1994; Donizelli and Giachetti, 1998).

The central role of PACS is to store and distribute images. However, PACS are also designed to support other functionalities in radiological work. For example: 1) in image production, users can manipulate images' gray scale, size and orientation (rotate or invert the images); 2) in image saving and archiving, users can create "electronic lists" (desktop folders) that support the organization and management of work; 3) in image distribution, PACS support the communication with other nodes in the network; 4) in image prefetching, display of old images, image analyses and diagnosis, radiologists can measure angles and areas on the image and display images in stacks by scrolling between them; and finally 5) in clinical image demonstration, PACS are used to fetch and display images.[1]

PACS are closely linked to RIS in most activities in radiological work, for example: 1) In the administrative activity, when the patient is scheduled in the RIS, a message is automatically transferred from the RIS to the PACS. This message triggers the automatic retrieval in advance of relevant examinations from the long-term PACS archive. 2) In the image production, quality and evaluation activity, the radiographer uses a hand scanner to scan the barcoded ID sticker attached to the paper request. This triggers retrieval of the patient's digital data and images on the workstation, from RIS as well as PACS. 3) In the diagnostic activity the radiologist retrieves patient data and images on the workstation in the same manner as the radiographer did. Three monitors are situated side by side, in front of the radiologist. On the left-hand one, the PACS and RIS are integrated into one interface, while the middle screen displays the new images and the right-hand screen displays the old images. When the radiologist browses through various new images, the corresponding old image will automatically be displayed on the right-hand screen. 4) Both PACS and RIS are also essential during the ad hoc discussions between radiologists and clinicians as well as during the daily interdisciplinary meetings. During these sessions, medical staff use PACS and RIS as they do in the diagnostic activity.

Therefore, in order to understand the use of PACS, we also need to understand the role and use of RIS.

A hospital can introduce PACS at different levels of use. The radiology department introducing a *"first-level PACS"* (Tellioglu and Wagner 1996) works with many "unconnected" modules for local production of digital images in the different laboratories. This means that the radiographer views and selects electronic images, adjusts the density level to produce the optimum image, and performs any reorientation and annotation. She thereafter prints the electronic images as analog films (on laser printers). Radiologists then diagnose the analog films. At what we could call the *"second level,"* PACS use includes a local network connecting the different image production modules, the archive, the hardcopy machine, and the diagnosis and reporting workstations. In this environment the radiographer carries out image production and quality control of images in the same way as in the first-level PACS. Images are electronically distributed and radiologists retrieve patient data on workstations. The radiologist zooms and uses the tools to magnify and change the contrast of images. Manipulation of the images on the workstations allows a range of densities to be seen in the image, just as it allows the instant measurement of various findings. Images are compared, for example, by switching between images showing different views of the patient's chest. All images are stored in the PACS archive. If clinicians request images, these are printed either as analog films or as an image on paper and manually transported to the requesting clinical unit. A *"third-level"* large-scale PACS functions in a hospital-wide electronic network, not only connecting the entities listed in second-level PACS, but also connecting to workstations in clinical units within the hospital. This means that clinicians in practice receive and retrieve electronic images via workstations linked to the PACS archive.

To the best of our knowledge, there are no PACS and RIS systems integrated with any hospital Information Systems (HIS) at a hospital in Sweden so far. This means that the radiology departments always receive "paper" examination requests, and always need to deliver the diagnostic answer manually as a paper document. In order to access the information electronically within the radiology department, many departments scan the received paper request.

To add to the understanding of standardization strategies in healthcare, in the next section we will briefly describe the different strategies used to develop and implement the PACS (Picture Archiving and Communication Systems) and intranet applications in healthcare.

ELECTRONIC STANDARDS IN HEALTHCARE

According to Bowker and Star (1999) standards are any set of agreed-upon rules for the production of (textual or material) objects. Legal bodies often enforce standards. There is no natural law that the best standard will win. Once a standard has been adopted by a large number of users, it is very difficult and expensive to change.

An important feature of a technical standard is that it has a social dimension in addition to the technical one. For instance, medical data must be written in a way that medical staff understand, data must be consistent with standardized shared (Latin) concepts. The technical standard itself has limited influence on either the medical data written into it or the way that the medical information is understood and used by medical groups. It is therefore important to develop a social standard for the use of a new technical standard. In practice, these two dimensions of standards are inseparable.

The DICOM–Based on the Specification Strategy

The CEN/TC 251, which is developing the DICOM standard, has divided up its work into seven different subfields within healthcare: terminology, semantics and knowledge bases; information modeling and medical records; communication and messages; imaging and multimedia; medical device communication; security, privacy, quality and safety; and intermittently connected devices. DICOM was initially designed as one single universal standard, or one coherent set of standards, covering any need for medical imaging and multimedia exchange. At the outset, it focused on radiological imaging.

The DICOM is based on several service classes: DICOM store, DICOM query, DICOM retrieve, DICOM print, Ethernet and TCP/IP Networking. To claim that one is following the standard, one must document and specify what service classes this is related to in a conformance statement. Moreover one must in the conformance statement specify in which way this service class is used. Without a conformance statement, a system does not comply with the standard. The DICOM standard does not specify the overall set of features and functions to be expected from a system. There are a number of compulsory computer attributes that have to be included in the system. There are also a number of volunteer attributes, that the users can choose among themselves. In sum, conformance statements should confirm that all compulsory attributes are included in the system, in addition all volunteer attributes used should be specified as well. It will be specified in what way data is communicated by the service class user (the digital images retrieved from the PACS) and what way the service class provider communicates data (the way digital images are sent out from the PACS database). This means that a valid response to all of the optional data elements must be incorporated in the application to comply with the DICOM standard.

As illustrated, the specification-driven approach seeks a more homogeneous solution, presupposing a common design implementation in all medical units. It is based on the idea that there will be one homogeneous technical network of uniform design. It is designed for one application, PACS. The conformance statements impose stringent restraints. Under these 'regulations,' DICOM was developed on the assumption that there would be a single universal network for image communication within healthcare.

PACS technology is based on DICOM conformance statements. Its main function is to create a shared electronic unit where radiological images can be saved. PACS facilitate the sharing of the image data across organizational and professional boundaries (Tellioglu and Wagner, 1996). Images may be archived and organized in central units, and be accessed and used in cooperation by locally distributed actors.

In 1995, a proposal for the installation of a second-level PACS at the Thoracic Section, Radiology Department, Sahlgrenska University Hospital (SU) was put forward and accepted. This proposal was linked with a relocation of the Radiology Department. The new department was built and equipped by May 1996.

PACS are built around a central archive to which all workstations are connected through fiber distributed data interfaces (ATM/fiber optic network) and a Fast Ethernet. PACS have an interface to the Radiological Information Systems (RIS) that support the transmission of data from these systems to the connected workstations at the Radiology Department.

Similar, second-level PACS implementations were installed in April 1998 at the Pediatric Radiology Department, Astrid Lindgren's Children's Hospital (ALB), and at the Radiology Department, Örebro University Hospital. These two sites have implemented the same PACS application. This is a system bought from a vendor.

The vendors offer training in connection with all PACS implementations. In addition, there are radiological 'superusers' that support the training of new users.

The PACS implementation process

Various design approaches can be applied in the development of computer systems. The vendor developing the PACS at Astrid Lindgren Children's Hospital and Örebro Hospital has developed its own design approach. Once a year the vendor meets with all its users from different hospitals in a joint meeting. The aim of these meetings is to specify the requirements of the next PACS version. The meetings start out with a 'brainstorming session' in which all users can put forward specifications of new and improved PACS functionalities. The vendor then quotes a price for each specified improvement to the functionality. When all costs have been specified, the vendor states the total amount of money to be spent on the new PACS version. A voting session is started. Users have a number of votes proportional to their investment in the PACS. Specified functionalities will be implemented according to users' priorities. For example, in last year's version users gave priority to the ability to illustrate images in a stack. The possibility to tag one or several images in a stack, as well as to swap images in two stacks simultaneously, was also given priority. This is useful, for instance, in a tumor case where there may be about 20 radiological examinations: X-rays, ultrasound, CT, MRI, etc., and some 1,000 images may be included. Of all the images, there may be about 10 that the radiologist wants to save in a stack. The next radiologist who needs to examine this patient may retrieve the saved stack.

In next year's PACS version, users have specified and given priority to the implementation of pointers between desktop folders. This can eliminate storage of the same image in multiple electronic locations. A copy may currently be saved in 7-10 different desktop folders in the short-term archive, which in turn fills the short-term archive much faster than had been expected.

According to the radiologists, this process of specifying the PACS design is too slow. As one radiologist put it, "It takes such a long time just to organize these large user meetings. We have ideas, but the vendor has limited scope for making changes, it is a bit difficult. We are used to working with technology and fixing problems ourselves as they arise. With PACS we have to work together with the vendors. We are stuck with them, the PACS and its standard." He continued, "The PACS design process does not encourage quick thinking; it is a less dynamic way of working. I do not think this design philosophy will last for long. It just takes too much time."

The team designing the PACS system at Sahlgrenska consisted of a senior radiologist as project leader and three computer technicians. In addition students from the departments of Informatics and Computer Science have been working in the project for periods ranging from half a year to one year, focusing on the design of the PACS system and various gateways linking the system to its environment.

Due to the fact that a senior radiologist has been in charge of the project, there has been a strong focus on existing work practice within the Radiology Department.

The image production applications have been purchased from different retailers. The computer technicians have done the modeling and programming of the gateways between various image production applications and the PACS system in close collaboration with the project leader. The graphical interfaces were specified by the project leader on the basis of discussions with the computer technicians, taking cautious consideration of the heterogeneous work practices in the Radiology Department. The system has become a most important and appreciated technology among the radiological users. However, as the system has become larger, it has become more and more complex and expensive to create new versions. Several new features are wanted, although it has shown to be difficult to both identify technicians that can develop the system and raise financing for the implementation of new features. To overcome the system support problems concerning the PACS database, the project leader is planning to hire a company to externally manage this.

According to one of the technologists, the complex structure of the DICOM conformance statements in combination with the size of the PACS is problematic. It requires extensive technical knowledge and finances to redesign, and promotes a development process that is designed in a formal 'specified' fashion. For example, the estimated cost of four lines of code in the PACS was around SKr 180,000. It was related to formal meetings and 'endless negotiations with the vendors,' as the radiologist put it. The four lines of code were never implemented. The high cost was due to dependencies between these lines and several other PACS functions that would also have to be changed.

The Intranet – Based on the Prototype Strategy

The Internet has revolutionized the computer and communication world like nothing before it (Leiner et al., 1997). Since 1985, the Internet has been growing rapidly. The Internet is set to be the underlying basis of new services and products within healthcare, electronic commerce, education, etc.

The Internet is based on the idea that there would be multiple independent networks of rather arbitrary design. It is designed for many different applications, such as e-mail, information transfer, remote logins, synchronous communication, disk sharing and packet-based voice communication. As illustrated, the Internet was not designed for one application alone, but as a network on which new applications could be based. The idea of the Internet was that any provider could freely design an application and make it work together with the other networks in the Internet. It has so far proved remarkably flexible, adaptable and extendable (Hanseth and Monteiro, pp. 84, in manuscript).

In an open-architecture network such as the Internet, the individual networks can be designed separately. Each application can have its own unique interface, which it can offer to users. Each network can be designed in accordance with its specific environment and user requirements. There are generally no constraints on the types of network that can be included or on their geographic scope, although certain pragmatic considerations will dictate what makes sense. In this way the Internet was developed on the assumption that there would be not one single, universal network, but rather any number of heterogeneous network technologies.

After the PACS had been in use for a while at Sahlgrenska Hospital, both clinicians and radiologists wanted to extend the system with functions enabling the clinicians to access the images from PCs at the clinical departments. As the PACS were tailored for complex radiological use and was running on a Unix platform, the software could not simply be installed on the PCs. Instead, an application was tailored to convert the images 'on the fly' to a format readable from the hospital intranet. This was a simple solution developed by a master student within three months. It enabled the clinicians at the hospital to access all images at hard-disk level from the PACS at any time from any PC connected to the intranet.

The team that designed this so-called intranet one application included students from the Department of Informatics and Computer Science. They have been working in the project for periods ranging from half a year to one year each.

A similar intranet application, referred to as Intranet Two in this chapter, was implemented at the Pediatric Radiology Department, Astrid Lindgren's Children's Hospital, as well as at the Radiology Department, Örebro University Hospital.

There is a difference between the two intranet applications. Instead of converting images on the fly, Intranet Two has developed plug-ins to Web browsers, converting both the RIS reports and PACS images to a format readable from the hospital intranet.

News of the implementation of intranet one and two spread through hearsay.

The clinicians referred to the electronic access of radiological text and images as a top-priority request. They stressed the need for these images in clinical work, research and teaching, as well as for explanations for patients.

The intranet implementation process

This section describes how the intranet changed in an evolutionary process as it was implemented in work. As it started to change, the social and technical links associated with the intranet application also started to change.

The intranet application started out as a very simple technology, including the following functionalities: search for a patient; retrieve, zoom and rotate images; display responses from the RIS. It offered access only to the short-term archive (with the 1,500 latest examinations). Clinicians used it for research. This meant that clinicians had to collect their images regularly so that they did not lose any data. As a clinician put it, "If you are away for a few days, the information is lost." According to the vendors, access was restricted to the short-term archive in order to avoid clashes between queries from radiologists and clinicians.

After the system had been implemented for half a year, the clinicians contacted the vendors. They asked if they could use this intranet application to access the long-term archive. Clinicians also need access to images and requested answers that are more than three months old. Perhaps the intranet application could give them access to the radiological images and texts from home? Could changes to the X-ray images be saved in the short- or long-term archive? Could annotations to the X-ray images, inserted by the radiographers, be retrieved from the intranet applications? As images were sometimes retrieved upside down and there was no way of telling whether it was the right or left part of the body that was displayed on the screen, radiologists requested images to be displayed correctly.

The first request was fulfilled; medical staff can now access X-ray images from both the short- and long-term archive. The second was not: the intranet application could not be used from home, since there was no immediate technical solution that could guarantee compliance with legislation regarding the confidentiality of the X-ray images. The third request was not fulfilled either, since it is not possible to update low-resolution images (such as JPEG images) with high-resolution DICOM images. The fourth request was fulfilled. It is now possible to retrieve annotations that the radiographers have made to the X-ray images. This works well now and has also contributed to the use of the intranet application for diagnostic work, when a radiologist gets a call to his office from a clinician, he retrieves the information for the clinician's patient on the PC and discusses the case over the phone. The final request was fulfilled immediately. It had been possible to mistake a left arm for a right one, there was no way to tell from the X-ray image whether surgery was to be conducted on the right or the left arm. As one of the radiologists put it, "There was no control in the system, causing serious risks for the patient." For this reason, the intranet application was withdrawn for a few months from early 1999. In spite of these problems, users were very positive towards the intranet application, its benefits in practice and its theoretical potential, which they discussed readily.

The clinicians contacted the vendors again. This time, they asked whether the intranet application could give them access to the scanned paper request sent by the clinician. This was fulfilled; medical staff can now view the clinician's request from the intranet application. This version also included the possibilities to change the brightness and the contrast of the image. This request was not made by this particular radiology department, but most likely came from another user.

With all these improved functionalities, one of the technicians said, "It is not the functionalities that are the main limitation of this application any more instead it is the rather slow server that converts DICOM images to a format accessible to the intranet application (JPEG)." However, no user has been rejected access to the intranet application yet. Users are completely free to decide whether, when and how to use this application. There have been very few formal decisions relating to its use.

As a radiologist discussed the potential of the intranet application, he commented: "I understand why the vendors are scared of this new technology, it enables us to design and develop our own technical solutions. The need for this kind of technology among clinicians is unlimited." He continued: "Everyone should have access to this kind of technology, it is obvious."

As the intranet application started to change, many new actors became central in the design process, for instance, the act relating to the protection of personal privacy, the DICOM standard and the patient. The process also illustrated that when the intranet application started to change, so did its social and technical links. Just as the technology started to change, new application areas were established for the intranet application – surgical work, teaching, diagnostic work, research, etc.

In the next section, we describe the use of the DICOM standard in radiological practice.

THE USE OF ELECTRONIC STANDARDS IN RADIOLOGICAL PRACTICE

In order to understand the consequences of different standardization strategies, we need to understand how each one of these has become embedded in medical practice. More specifically, we need to know how, for what purpose and in which contexts they are used. This understanding can allow a comparison of the consequences of the two strategies.

The radiology department is mainly a diagnostic service unit, carrying out radiological examinations for clinical departments inside the hospital, other hospitals and primary care units (general practitioners). The radiology department provides interpretations of radiological images, and the results are delivered to clinicians by means of reports and meetings. The radiological examinations and reports form a basis for the correct diagnosis and treatment of patients.

The examinations offered to clinicians by the radiology departments are usually classified in relation to the body's organ system, such as the skeleton and chest: mammography; odontological, gastrointestinal, genitourinary and vascular examinations. The classification may also relate to the type of equipment used: ultrasound, CT (computer tomography) and MR (magnetic resonance).

Medical Work Practice

In this section we will describe the radiological practice as well as other clinical activities linked to it in radiology departments operating with PACS and intranet applications.

For a radiological examination, patients are usually sent from clinical wards, outpatient clinics, primary care units, etc., to the radiology department. The examination request is created manually by a paper-based system. When the examination request is received in the radiology department, it is scheduled by assigning an examination room and a radiographer or a radiologist to the examination in the RIS. When the patient is scheduled, a message is automatically transferred from the RIS to the PACS. This message triggers the automatic pre-fetching of relevant examinations from the long-term PACS archive after midnight on the night before the patient examination. Retrieval time is kept to a minimum because the next day's images are retrieved during the slack hours of the previous night, and the process does not compete with the archival of new images. The retrieved images are available from the information storage unit, and can be viewed on the screen within a half second to five seconds after the radiologist has clicked on them. Images that are not automatically retrieved must be retrieved from the permanent long-term archives, which usually takes from three to 10 minutes, but may take longer if the system is busy. The instruments generating the images are nowadays all based on digital technology. This means that when the radiographers produce the images, they are stored directly in the database of the PACS.

During examination of the patient, the radiographer uses a hand scanner to scan the bar code, which is attached to the paper request. The patient's electronic request is thereby retrieved on the workstation. She then positions the patient and takes the images. The radiographer views and selects the PACS images, adjusts the density level to produce the optimum image, performs any reorientation and annotation that is necessary, and then verifies the examination. When the images have been verified, PACS automatically transfers the images to a folder, which contains about 1,500 examinations for reporting. To diagnose the patient, the radiologist sits down at one of the PACS workstations. All workstations are provided with infrared barcode readers. The radiologist retrieves patient data to the workstations by "swiping through" a barcoded ID sticker attached to the paper request. When all barcodes have been swiped through, a work list has been created in PACS. With the paper at hand, the radiologist clicks on the first patient in the work list. He reads the patient name and ID in the written request and checks it against the patient data in the electronic request.

Three monitors are situated side by side. On the left-hand one, PACS and RIS

Figure 1. Radiologist reading images

are integrated into one interface, while the middle screen illustrates the new images and the right-hand one illustrates the old images (in this examination).[2] When the radiologist browses through various new chest images, the corresponding old image will automatically be displayed on the right-hand screen. The radiologist zooms and uses the tools to magnify and change the contrast of images. Manipulating the images on the workstations allows the radiologist to view a range of densities in the image, just as it enables the instant measurement of various findings. He switches between images showing different views of the patient's chest to compare them. After the diagnosis has been made, the radiologist must decide whether the examination should be brought up on the ward round or not. If so, he must drag and drop the electronic request to the relevant 'meeting list.'

At the daily meetings at the radiology department, when the radiologists and clinicians discuss the patient examinations, electronic images are fetched from the meeting list in the PACS. The radiologist zooms and filters the images to highlight findings.

The importance of various kinds of lists as a resource in work was also confirmed at ALB and Örebro Hospital. Not only do they support the organization of work, but also, as a senior radiologist put it, they make it possible to work in new ways. For instance, during the meetings the patients' images may be placed in a 'stack' of perhaps 120 images; these can be displayed as a video in which images may be 'clicked' forward. It is possible to 'tag' images in the stack in advance in order to stop the display at these images. As the senior radiologist put it, "It is possible to make most flashy presentations during meetings, if you want to and have the time.'

In a cooperative project, an electronic network was set up between the

Figure 2. Meeting at the Radiology Department

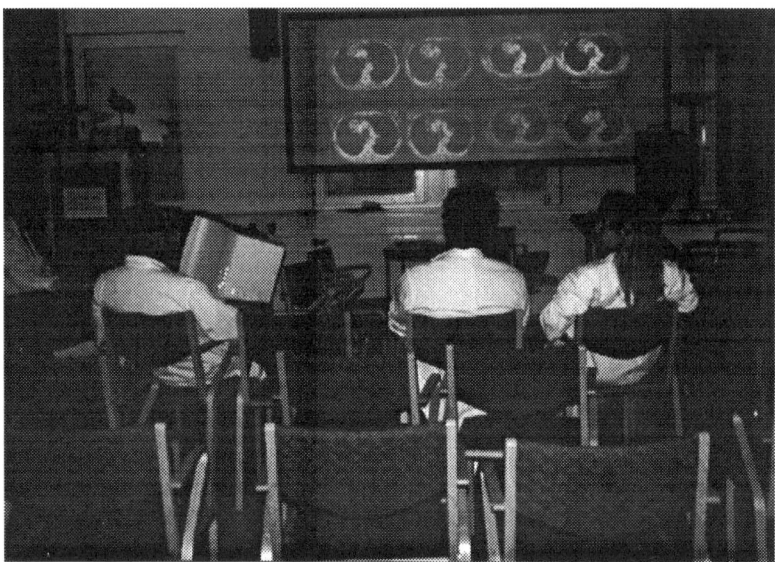

respective radiology departments of the Sahlgrenska University Hospital and Skövde Hospital in Sweden. The aim of the project was to send CT (computer tomography) images of the skull from Skövde to Sahlgrenska for specialty consultation and in complex emergency situations. The idea behind the emergency procedures was that radiologists at Sahlgrenska would be able to evaluate, from a distance, whether the patient should be sent to Sahlgrenska for specialized treatment. The communication was based on a technical link between two different computer tomography workstations at the respective departments. Both these workstations converted data from the image acquisition system into data conformant with the DICOM standard. However, since all the data elements of the pixel module are machine-related and constant for a particular CT system, and CT images in visual non-binary coding are also fixed and unique to a particular CT display system, incompatibilities between these systems occurred, creating many technical problems. It was possible to send images, but there was too much information loss in the image received at Sahlgrenska. This project became very expensive. In all, it cost about SKr 1 million. It was used for half a year, and 10 patients were diagnosed during this period. As the radiologist in charge put it, "There was too much technical trouble, and it cost too much. We ran out of motivation to continue the project."

Intranet One and Two are essential during the ad hoc discussions between radiologists and clinicians. To access patient reports and images, the radiologist enters the patient ID numbers into Intranet One and Two. The system responds by displaying a list of patient examinations. The clinician clicks on an examination in the examination list. The clinician zooms and retrieves further images. Images are compared by switching between images showing different views of the patient. During clinical work, images are retrieved in the same manner.

Each radiological report is distributed to each requesting clinic by 'transporters.' The clinician reads it and writes a summary of the radiological report into the HIS. All clinicians that have requested and obtained a pass to an intranet application have full access to all images, even before the radiologist has diagnosed them. According to the clinicians, these images are frequently used. They support the clinical work and research work as well as the discussions with the radiologists over the phone, in which both parties of medical staff can view the images simultaneously.

Medical staff at ALB said that the clinical PACS-based systems cost around SKr 150,000 for every PC installation. Simultaneously, ALB has paid a license for SKr 150,000 that covers an unlimited number of Wiseweb licenses at the hospital. As the clinical PACS are quite complex in functionality and use, while the Wiseweb is considered to be quite transparent, it has been more convenient to implement and use the Wiseweb for the medical staff. In addition, a project is to be started between the central Radiology Department, Karolinska Hospital, and the Radiology Department, Haukeland Hospital in Bergen, Norway. This project will evaluate the extent to which the Wiseweb fulfills radiologists' requirements for image quality during remote consultation.

The intranet application was to be implemented in the entire Örebro region in Sweden, in the second half of 2000, to support the communication of radiological text and images between all the medical units in this area. Radiologists expect this application to strengthen the relationship between the medical units at a modest cost.

HOW DO STANDARDIZATION STRATEGIES INTERVENE IN WORK PRACTICE?

This section explores the consequences of different strategies used in the development of electronic standards in healthcare. This has been done by analyzing how different electronic standards, based on various standardization strategies, are designed and applied in work.

The Specification Strategy

It is important to emphasize that when the PACS were developed in the early 90s there was no well-established and well-tested Internet technology. Designers of digital documents and images within healthcare were more or less forced to build large and complex standard solutions, as these were based on complex electronic medical standards. The development and application of PACS has been an important step for the use of technology within healthcare. The PACS and RIS provide a starting point, there are image and text databases that can be opened up for a larger number of people in various contexts when linked to the Internet technology.

Electronic standards based on different standardization strategies intervene in work in different ways, as we have illustrated in this study. They do not always intervene in the ways in which they were intended. For instance, the aim of the DICOM standard was to support universal image communication in healthcare. To do this, the specification-driven approach presupposed a common design, where one single universal standard was to be implemented in all medical units. However, this study illustrated that DICOM-compliant computer systems were not entirely identical (see Section 3). This made data exchange between computer systems difficult, because it is a prerequisite that all technical nodes in large and complex networks are compatible. Thus, checking the DICOM conformance statements of two computer systems may not be sufficient to establish communication that functions well between different socio-technical networks. This means that the initial objective of PACS, to support interdisciplinary communication between various medical units, has not been realized. Instead, PACS have enhanced a more local role. They have become most important tools in the local radiological context.

A problem with the specification-driven approach is that, since it is so formal, it results in slow and complex design processes and systems (see section). The system complexity resulted in slow adaptation to the technology. Users need extensive training to be able to retrieve and manipulate the images appropriately and accurately in a PACS. As the system is complex, they usually require an advanced technical platform, for example workstations connected by fiber distributed data interfaces (ATM). In addition, the extensive and formal specifications have made these systems very complex and expensive to develop (see section).

Another problem with the specification strategy is that it is based on the principles of large-scale production, in which large volumes of a single common system are considered important for cost efficiency. This is why each PACS bought from a vendor is used as one coherent common system among different users in various contexts. In practice, this means that each PACS is a compromise for all its users from a local work practice perspective. Therefore, the results of this study indicate that great emphasis is placed on the development of a common standard solution designed according to large-scale production principles. It has been hard to demonstrate cost efficiency related to large-scale production principles of computer systems supporting work practice in heterogeneous organizations such as healthcare.

The aim of the specification strategy is to embed all components into the computer system when it is implemented the first time. This is a process in which designers try to develop a system that is as complete as possible in one step. This study supports Hanseth and Monteiro's recent criticism (in manuscript) of the specification process as all too slow and complex. It also supports Hanseth and Monteiro's (ibid.) suggestion that the more formal the standardization process is, the slower its adoption becomes.

The Prototype Strategy

Electronic standards based on the prototype strategy intervene in work in different ways, as we have seen. The intranet applications were initially designed and implemented as a step towards the 'filmless' hospital. The objective was to support clinicians with electronic images, if images were requested, when this was a problem for the PACS. Both of these systems started out on a small scale with functionality limited to retrieving and zooming into images. The fact that the intranet applications by their nature are quite seamless and transparent meant that no user training was needed to use the standard technology. In spite of being very small-scale applications, both of these systems quickly became embedded in medical practice.

These technologies rapidly intervened in new areas of use. For instance, they served as an important tool during telephone discussions between radiologists and clinicians, just as they served as an essential tool in surgical work, medical teaching and conferences. These electronic standards quickly enrolled different meaning and roles in different social worlds, but their structure was common enough to make them universally recognizable. They supported communication of images and reports within the heterogeneous hospital network and therefore became most important in this network. The ease with which images could be distributed via intranet applications was very important, because it affected the users' acceptance of these applications. As new features are planned to be implemented in the system, the communicative role of the intranet application may be strengthened. For example, in September an intranet application will be introduced to support sharing of all radiological image and information within the entire Örebro healthcare region in Sweden, including five hospitals, all the primary-care units and private practitioners.

Introducing flexible and inexpensive Internet standards has changed the prerequisites for developing and using computer systems. It opens the way for new design strategies such as the prototype strategy, with the emphasis on the development of tailored solutions based on local knowledge.

The prototype strategy is based on an evolutionary process where the application is developed through a series of versions. Each version is in use for a period, and experience with it is used as the basis for developing the next version. It simultaneously evokes a de facto process where there are fewer regulating, institutional arrangements influencing the process (Schmidt and Werle, 1998). This opens up many possibilities, such as developing systems well adapted to users' needs, starting with simple and clear functionalities. Another advantage is that the Internet technology is fairly cheap. It is a flexible system that has the potential to grow according to the organization's needs.

SUMMARY AND CONCLUSION

The study suggests that striving for communication solutions with maximal potential for application in a heterogeneous world has implications for the standard strategies applied. In this chapter, we have illustrated the advantages of the prototype strategy in the development of communication technologies in large and heterogeneous organizations, such as healthcare. It is important to stress that we are not choosing between two strategies and technologies. It is a great advantage and almost a prerequisite to have the PACS and RIS databases from which integrated sections of information can be retrieved and presented in a browser interface. What we suggest is that the PACS and Internet technologies complement each other. The time has come to apply Internet technology much more extensively in healthcare: among other things it has the potential to open up PACS and make it more available for more users in different contexts. The Internet technology has clear functionalities and is less expensive than other electronic standards. It has the potential to grow and meet the challenges of interoperability and collaboration between heterogeneous networks of people and things. This standardization strategy has the potential to facilitate an evolutionary process where the application is developed through a series of versions, with each version in use for a period; experience with the version is used as the basis for developing the next version. There are no regulating, institutional arrangements influencing the process. This opens up many possibilities in which bits and pieces of technical components are linked to the technology over time. This is contrary to the specification-driven standardization strategy that results in a formal, long and complex design process. As a result these systems are rather expensive, and need a more complex technical platform. Users have to learn the programs, and take much longer than Internet applications to become embedded in work.

This study has also illustrated that the intranet applications have quickly developed into an essential part of medical work practice. The ease with which images could be distributed via intranet applications was very important, because it affected the users' acceptance of these applications. The planned deployment of these technologies between entire healthcare regions in Sweden is an example of this.

In sum, it was found that computer systems based on different electronic standards intervene in work in different ways, and that they do not always intervene in the ways in they were initially intended. For example, the PACS based on the DICOM standard have primarily attained a local role, although its initial aim was to support universal image communication within healthcare. It has developed into an important tool supporting the production, retrieval, processing and archiving of radiological image data. On the other hand the intranet application based on the Internet standards primarily not designed for this particular purpose has come to support communication of images and reports within the heterogeneous hospital network.

The focus of the study reported is information systems used in relation to radiological examinations, i.e., RIS and PACS. We believe, however, that our findings and analysis are valid for a larger collection of information systems like Electronic Patient Records (EPRs) and the communication between EPRs and information systems used within other laboratories and service departments. All these systems are, or should be, supporting practices having the same character as those described here. This fact is illustrated by the relative success of the HL7 standard compared to those worked out by CEN TC/251. The HL7 standards are developed by following an approach sharing important aspects with a prototype-oriented strategy. The HL7 effort has since its birth been pragmatic with a strong focus on early implementations. Just a few messages were defined and standardized in the first phase in order to satisfy the immediate needs within a limited domain. The limited numbers of actors involved soon implemented these messages. From this time on, the standards have been improved based on extensive practical use, and new ones have been defined as needs and opportunities appeared.

ACKNOWLEDGMENT

We are most grateful to Erik Stolterman, Tone Sandahl, Bo Jacobsson, Staffan Gustavsson, Håkan Jorulf and Torbjörn Andersson for generous support, comments and discussion. We are also very grateful to Magnus Bergquist for prior cooperative research. This work was partly supported by the Swedish Transport & Communications Research Board (Kommunikations-Forskningsberedningen) through its grant to the «Internet Project».

REFERENCES

Bellotti, V. and Bly, S. (1996). Walking away from the desktop computer: Distributed collaboration and mobility in a product design team. *Proceedings of the Conference on Computer-Supported Cooperative Work CSCW'96*: 209-218.

Berg, M. (1997). *Rationalizing Medical Work. Decision Support Techniques and Medical Practice*. MA: MIT Press Cambridge.

Berg, M. (1998). *Rationalizing Medical Work – Decision-Support Techniques and Medical Practices*. MIT Press Cambridge, Massachusetts London, England.

Berg, M. (1999). Accumulating and coordinating: Occasions for information technologies in medical work. *Computer-Supported Cooperative Work (CSCW): The Journal of Collaborative Computing*. 8(4), 373-401.

Bowers, J., Button, G. and Sharrock, W. (1995). Workflow from within and without, In H. Marmolin, Y. Sundblad, and K. Schmidt (Editors): *Proceeding of the Fourth European Conference on Computer-Supported Cooperative Work ECSCW'95*. Stockholm, Sweden. 51-67 (September).

Bowker, G. and Star, S. L. (1999). *Sorting Things Out. Classification and its Consequences*. MIT Press Cambridge, Massachusetts, London, England.

Button, G. and Harper, R. (1996). The Relevance of 'Work-Practice for Design', *Computer Supported Cooperative Work (CSCW): The Journal of Collaborative Computing*, vol. 4: 263-280.

Button, G. and Sharrock, W. (1997). The production of order and the order of production: possibilities for distributed organizations, work and technology in the print industry. In J. Hughes et al. (Eds.), *Proceedings of the Fifth European Conference on Computer-Supported Cooperative Work ECSCW'97*: 1-16.

Collin, M. (1995). *A History of Medical Informatics in the United States, 1950 to 1990*. American Medical Informatics Association.

Greinacher, C. F. C. (1994). Informations systeme fur die bildgebende Diagnostik, Teil 1. MTA, 9(12), 1000-1002.

Hanseth, O. (1996). Information infrastructure development: Cultivating the installed base. *Studies in the Use of Information Technology,* No. 16. Department of Informatics, Göteborg University.

Hanseth, O. and Monteiro, E. (in manuscript). *Understanding Information Infrastructure.*

Hanseth, O., Monteiro, E. and Hatling, M. (1996). Developing information infrastructure: The tension between standardization and flexibility. *Science, Technology and Human Values,* 21(4) Sage Periodicals Press: 407-426.

Hanseth, O. and Lundberg, N. (1999). The Radiological information infrastructure. *Informatics in the Next Millennium,* Studentlitteratur, Sweden: 255-281.

Heath, C. and Luff, P. (1996). Documents and professional practice: 'bad' organizational reasons for 'good' clinical records. *Proceedings of the Computer Supported Cooperative Work CSCW'96*: 354 – 363.

Hughes, J., King, V., Rodden, T. and Anderssen, H. (1994). Moving out from the control room: Ethnography in System Design. *Computer Supported Cooperative Work (CSCW): The Journal of Collaborative Computing*: 429-439.

Jost, G. R. (1994). The role of electronic radiology laboratory at the mallinckrodt institute of Radiology. *Implementation of the DICOM 3.0 Standard. RSNA –Radiological Society of North America Founded in 1915*: 10-12.

Laurin, S. (1998). Civil beredskapsplanering inom röntgendiagnostik: Andrade förutsättningar genom digital bild och PACS (In Swedish). *Report, Socialstyrelsen,* Sweden (March).

Law, J. (1992). Notes on the theory of the actor-network: Ordering, strategy, and heterogeneity. In J. Law, Eds. *Systems Practice,* 5(4), 379-393.

Leiner, M. B. (1997). The past and Future History of the Internet. *In The Communication of The ACM*, 40(2), 102-108.

Lundberg, N. (2000) *IT in Healthcare – Artefacts, Infrastructures and Medical Practices.* Dr. Scient Thesis, Department of Informatics, University of Gothenburg, Sweden.

Monteiro, E. and Hanseth, O. (1995). Social shaping of information infrastructure: on being specific about technology. In Orlikowski, W.J, Walsham, G. and Jones, M. R. and DeGross, J. I (Eds). *Information technology and changes in organisational work.* Chapman & Hall: 325-343.

Nagy, A., Nyúl, L., Kuba. A., Alexin, Z. and Almási, L. (1997). Problems and solutions: One year experience with the SZOTE-PACS. *Proceedings of the 16th EuroPACS Annual Meeting.* Barcelona, Spain: 39-43 (October).

Schmidt, S. K. and Werle, R. (1998). *Coordinating Technology: Studies in the International Standardization of Telecommunications (Inside Technology).* MIT Press.

Star, S. L. and Ruhleder, K. (1994). Steps towards an ecology of infrastructure: Complex problems in design and access for large-scale collaborative systems. *Proceedings of the Computer-Supported Cooperative Work CSCW'94.* 253-264.

Suchman, L. (1995). Making work visible. *Communication of the ACM*, 38(9), 56-64.

ENDNOTES

[1] For a more technical description of PACS functionalities, see Greinacher (1994).

[2] In other examinations it could very well be that old and new images are integrated in the same monitor and interface.

Chapter V

Healthcare Information and Communication Standards Framework

Peter J.B. Lagendijk and Robert. A. Stegwee
University of Twente, The Netherlands

Standardization in healthcare is a rapidly growing field. To prevent proliferation in standardisation, good coordination in both the development and usage of standards is necessary. In this chapter we propose a framework to analyse the fit between the proposed purpose of the standard and the perceived needs of the applications using the standard. An available standard can be characterised by the level of acceptance, the application area, the object of standardisation and the kind of user a standard is aimed at. The same aspects can be determined for the kind of standards needed for a specific application of information interchange. In a practical sense this will help in determining which standards to use. Also, it may provide a better perception of the supply and demand of healthcare information and communication standards in general.

INTRODUCTION

Within healthcare organisations most of the work is information-based. The professionals have to agree upon the content and the meaning of the information to realise effective communication. To achieve the desired quality of work, it seems that communication is one of the major issues. Basic training of healthcare professionals prepares them to put the fundamental communication agreements into practice. However, advanced research and the extensive use of information and communication technology has led to numerous vocabularies and procedures. To realise effective communication within a specific healthcare organisation or throughout the healthcare network, a certain degree of standardisation is necessary. On one hand a lot of progress has been made in developing standards, like LOINC (Forrey et al., 1996) or SNOMED (de Bruijn, Hasman and Arends, 1997) for terminology or CEN (European Committee for Standardisation Technical Committee for Health Informatics) and HL7 (Heitmann, Blobal and Dudeck, 1999) for digital messages. On the other hand there is the danger of misuse of the developed standards. When the necessity to apply standardisation arises in healthcare, one can choose either to use existing standards or to create a new standard. In order to make an informed choice for an existing standard, it can be useful to know what standards are available for the specific application. A framework for health information standards can provide a helping hand in identifying the appropriate standard. With this framework, both health information standards as well as the application that needs to use standardisation can be categorised in order to achieve a meaningful fit between the two.

WHY CATEGORISE A STANDARD?

During our research, standardisation is viewed as a process to develop, implement and maintain a standard. When a standard is developed, it can concern several different areas, such as concrete objects (like the kind of implant to be used or the type of medication to be administered), subjective observations (like the diagnosis or the findings of the radiologist), as well as activities or procedures (like standard treatment or the unit of measure). Because of the different application areas of standardisation, the standards can be specified on a number of different levels. Within healthcare organisations multiple standards for different application areas and of several levels have to be used simultaneously. This can lead to conflicts in communication. Categorising the standards and the applications that use these standards can lead to several benefits to the healthcare organisation.

- *Supporting the choice of a standard.* By categorising the applications that have the need to use a standard, a healthcare organisation will minimise the risk of choosing the wrong standard or misusing a standard. When there is the possibility to categorise the standards, there will be more clarity about the standard.
- *Supporting the combination of standards.* When a single standard is not

Figure 1: Communication with Immediate Use Interaction

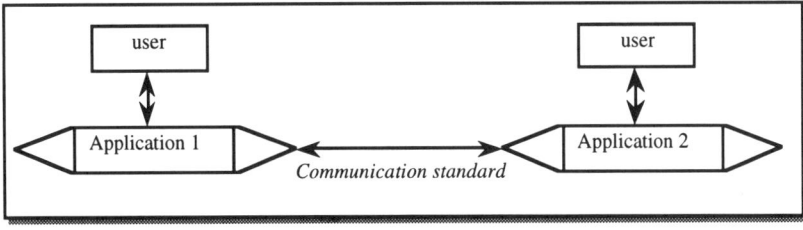

enough to fulfil the needs of an application, the categorisation of standards will support the combination of standards because the overlap of standards will become clear.
- *Improve the development of standards.* By categorising the applications that show a need to use standards, a long-term perspective can be developed for the focus of standardisation efforts.
- *Resolving present conflicts.* Because of the use of several standards in a healthcare organisation, conflicts can appear. By categorising the standards in use and the applications using them, mismatches can more easily be identified.

However a communication standard will always affect a number of applications (they don't necessarily have to be the same). Within the healthcare chain there are numerous applications that have to communicate. Obviously, using one common overall standard seems to be an illusion, but why? Just the applications are used at several different levels. There are applications in use that are in direct contact with the physicians or nurses (like an appointment planning system or systems to communicate test results from the lab). Figure 1 portrays such a setting, in which the two applications communicate directly with each other and interact with the user to obtain the desired result.

Several applications, however, don't contact the employees directly at all, but are supporting other applications to realise the necessary result (like a PACS-system that operates basically between modalities, an archive and several viewing stations). Figure 2 shows such a situation, in which applications need to communicate through communication subsystems that allow the applications to perform the necessary functions for their users.

In a more general sense, one can think of the two communicating parties as consisting of three components each: the human component, the process component, and the technological component. Some standards are developed to support the communication between humans, irrespective of process and technology. Language in general is such a standard, but more specific to healthcare, one can think of the distinct vocabularies in use by different specialised healthcare professionals. Other standards may aim specifically at computer-computer interaction, thereby support-

Figure 2: Communication Without Immediate User Interaction

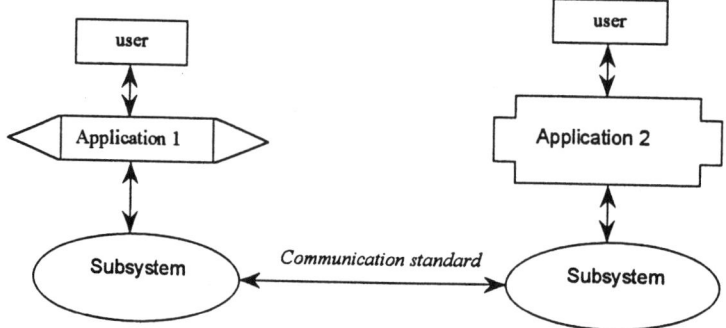

ing the technological components of the communicating parties without any consideration for the processes or humans involved in the interaction. Such purely technical standards, like TCP/IP or ASCII, are well known, but fall outside the scope of healthcare standards. In general, healthcare standards presuppose a certain context within which the exchanged information is to be used, hence the process component plays a definite role. Figure 3 shows the different types of communication between parties, when viewed from the perspective mentioned above.

In addition to this broad differentiation, standards will be focussed on other dimensions as well. Depending on the specific kind of healthcare process or the knowledge of the humans involved in the process, different kinds of standards will be needed. For example, a technological standard in the context of a test ordering process can be a simple message, stating the code for the test to be ordered, along with patient identification and additional information. This message is constructed on the basis of a user interaction, but it doesn't necessarily communicate in a legible format. The communicating systems may each have their own way of translating this message onto the screen or some other display. However, the same standard will not be able to handle the same information in the process of medical record exchange, as the structure of a medical record is fundamentally different from an order message. A similar example can be found in the direct communication between healthcare professionals. For instance, when talking about a specific patient, a doctor may use a well-known phrase to describe the patient's illness to a fellow-doctor, but more precise codes are needed when the same information is recorded for epidemiological studies. These examples show the day-to-day necessity of standards and the range of standards needed to cater to the needs of different processes, human communicators and technological platforms. In order to coordinate the development and use of these standards, some form of categorisation is needed. In the next paragraph we propose a set of dimensions that can be used to

Figure 3: Communication Without Immediate User Interaction

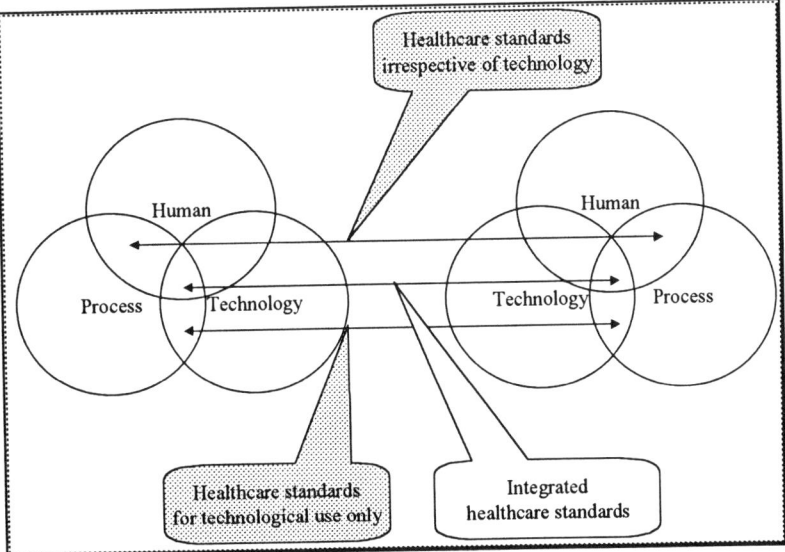

categorise healthcare information and communication standards.

DIMENSIONS OF STANDARDISATION

Choosing or adopting a standard has to be done in a clever way. Several elements, like end-users and environment, are important to address in the standardisation process. By choosing the right standard, the reach of information systems and their degree of integration can be improved significantly. The characterisation of a standard on a number of distinct dimensions can support the adoption process. The dimensions we define are the following:

Level of Acceptance

A standard can be accepted at several levels: institutional, regional, national and international. It refers to the range where the standard is *known and agreed upon*. An institutionally accepted standard cannot directly be used beyond the walls of the institution because the agreements of the standard are made inside the walls. A standard defined in a bilateral relationship between two institutions could be termed 'local' standard, but we prefer to consider it as part of institutional acceptance, as it is uncertain whether the same standard will be used in communication with other parties. When there is an agreement between several institutions to use the same method to communicate, a regional standard is born (assuming the institutes are in the same geographical region). Beyond the agreement nobody uses (and knows) the standard. The national and international levels are self-explanatory. However, it is important to understand that an internationally accepted standard can be available everywhere, but is not necessarily used for worldwide communication. The latter refers to the application area of the standard, to be discussed below. According to McDonald et al. (1998), a model with a high level of acceptance requires a high degree of abstraction.

Application Area

The levels we differentiate within the application area are the same as the level of acceptance: institutional, regional, national and international. The application area refers to the organisational scope within which the standard has to operate, i.e., the organisational extent of communication supported by the standard. It is only slightly related to the level of acceptance. When a standard is used in a specific area, it will automatically be accepted in this area, but not vice-versa. The level of acceptance of a standard has to be greater than (or equal to) the application area where the standard will be used. For example, in the Netherlands an international standard like the ICPC code (to index diseases in primary care) is used at the general practitioners' offices, but is not used for communication on an international level, not even on a national level. This is quite alright, but the other way around would be insane: to have all GPs use their own standard codes for international statistics on primary care. The level of acceptance is particularly interesting when looking at technological standards: with technology vendors operating on an increasingly international scale, they will prefer a high level of acceptance of the standards incorporated in their systems, even though the application area is on a much lower level. It means that they can limit the efforts to be spent on developing and maintaining the interfaces for different countries or regions, as they will all be based on the same (inter)national standard.

Object

The object that is standardised is the third and maybe most important dimension of standardisation. In the international arena there seems to be a lack of agreement about what values are to be discerned in this dimension. One may look at the division of labour within the larger standards organisations. The European Committee for Standardisation (CEN) distinguishes working groups on information models, terminology, security and technology for interoperability (Klein, 1998). The International Standards Organisation (ISO), however, has established working groups on health records and models, messaging and communication, health representation, security and health cards (ISO homepage). Finally, Treseder and Williams (Treseder and Williams, 1998) support the ISO categories and divide it into six fields: information models, records and functions, privacy and security, content and structure, representation (including vocabulary) and message communication. While taking the different fields into account, we have tried to come up with a set of values that covers the different views and that also keeps it simple to categorise. We think that the object of standards for health information and communication can be characterised as messages, procedures, terminology and vocabulary, and authorisation and authentication. Within the 'messages' object we distinguish message structure (the elements included in the message and their internal relationships), message intention (what is the purpose of the message) and message representation (what is the format of [parts of] the message). Standard procedures are usually established by scientific associations and are meant to be employed by the professionals to increase the quality of care. Other uses of standard procedures can be found in the area of managed care, balancing the quality and cost of care by prescribing authorised medical behaviour. Standard terminology and vocabulary is used to minimise the chance of a definition problem. As discussed above, these definition problems are more of an issue in the statistical processing of information than in human information interchange. However, when medical professionals from different institutions or different professions communicate, the definition problem may arise as well. Finally authorisation and authentication are a fairly recent object of standardisation. The introduction of the electronic patient record (EPR) has been on the agenda for quite some time, and the booming proliferation of the Internet must be recognised as the driving force. Standardisation of authorisation is necessary to grant relevant parties access to the EPR from outside the institution, as is authentication to avoid the impersonation of medical professionals.

User

When objects are standardised, the question is whether people have to know the standard or not to make it work. Therefore, we define the user as being either a human or a machine. The impact of a standard that is aimed at a human end-user can involve such issues as (a lack of) acceptance and education. When the intended user is merely a machine, and the human user never comes in contact with the standard, it can have an impact on, e.g., the information infrastructure or the technical platform.

The dimensions of standardisation and their respective values are shown in Table 1.

LIMITATIONS

To make proper use of the framework outlined above, standards have to be put into the framework. Based solely on the dimensions identified in the framework, it is still not possible to choose a standard for a specific application. Take, for example, the situation in which a physician wants to standardise the referral letter. The object will be 'message' and the user will be human. The application area will be regional or national, hence the level of acceptance should be at least national. However none of the dimensions will tell the physician that a standard is suitable for a referral. The fact that a standard is valid for the 'message' object does not mean it automatically covers every possible topic of a message. Therefore it is necessary to identify limitations of the standard. It is extremely difficult to define a set of values for the limitations of a standard, because there are just too many possibilities. Examples of limitations are the following:

- a specific group of patients, such as diabetics or renal patients;

Table 1: Framework for Health Information Standards

		Dimensions		
	Level of acceptance	*Application area*	*Object*	*User*
Values	Institutional	Institutional	Message *structure* Message *intention* Message *representation*	Human
	Regional	Regional	Procedure	Machine
	National	National	Terminology and vocabulary	
	International	International	Authorisation/authentication	

- the context of care, such as clinical or ambulatory care;
- a specific group of healthcare professionals, such as general practitioners or dieticians; and
- a certain field within the medical profession, such as radiology, pathology or nuclear medicine.

The limitations are in certain ways related to the dimensions described, but can also be influenced by several environmental factors. As an example, Table 2 shows a number of standards categorised along the lines of the presented framework.

THE USE OF THE STANDARDISATION FRAMEWORK

When there is the need to use standards to increase the quality of communication, the specific application has to be the starting point (and not the standard). By using the framework for health information standards from the viewpoint of the *user's need,* corresponding standards can easily be found. Practice proves that conflicts appear when standards are used for objects that do not correspond with the target of the application. This can happen when several interested parties are involved in the development of a standard or when the scope of the standard doesn't fully fit to the scope of the application. This last conflict can be solved by developing a local (relatively small) standard for the missing part. Another method can be the combination of several (already existing) standards.

It seems that on several occasions various standards are needed to achieve the purpose of the application. The main reason is that after categorising the application, there is no perfect standard according to the standardisation framework. First of all, the limitations are an important cause of this. A second problem is that standards are usually focussed on one specific object and one kind of user. However, the majority of applications cover a much broader scope of objects and kinds of users. To solve

Table 2: Examples of Standards in the Framework

Standard	Dimensions				Limitation
	Level of acceptance	*Application area*	*Object*	*User*	
SNOMED	*International*	*Institutional*	*Terminology*	*People*	*Clinical care*
HL7	*International*	*Institutional*	*Message*	*Machine*	*Hospital processes*
DICOM	*International*	*Institutional*	*Message*	*Machine*	*Images*
LOINC	*National*	*Regional*	*Terminology*	*People*	*Orders*
PACS	*International*	*Institutional*	*Message*	*Machine*	*Pictures*
ICD10-CM	*International*	*International*	*Terminology*	*People*	*Clinical care*
X12	*National*	*National*	*Message*	*Machine*	*Insurance*

this problem there is the possibility to use a combination of standards. However, a source of conflict among standards can be traced to an overlap of the standardisation object or the application area. Combining standards can be effective when the objects of the standards used do not have an overlap, and when the standards make use of references to each other. HL7 is a good example of a standard that incorporates references to other standards. Many elements within an HL7 message can be coded with an explicit reference to the terminology standard used in coding this element. On the other hand, the combination of DICOM and HL7 is a good example of overlapping standards. Both are message standards, but especially in the message intention--they overlap--as both standards describe, among others--messages that intend to communicate the schedule of appointments for patients in a given time period. The recent demonstration of DICOM/HL7-based interoperability has caused a number of major decisions on the part of the implementers (Sippel Schmidt, 1999).

To clarify the use of the framework for health information standards, some relatively simple examples are discussed below.

Hospitals are rapidly trying to make use of the 'Picture archiving and communication system' *(PACS). To realise this, communication has to be carried out.*

Lets presume that a radiology department wants to improve the information flow of (digital) pictures between professionals within the department. The application used is called PACS. It is the underlying application to archive digital pictures (like X-rays or MRI-scans). Therefore the application is connected to other 'machines' to deliver the input (the pictures) and the output (archived pictures on a screen) result. As screen viewing and manipulation is supported by the radiologists' workstations, the user of the standard will be the machine. The objects that are involved in PACS are all the three message elements. First PACS needs a kind of *structure* to process the pictures to be archived, together with relevant information

Table 3: Match Between PACS Application and DICOM Standard

Application	Dimensions					Limitation
	Exp. need for acceptance	Application area	Object	User	
PACS	Regional	Institutional	Message • structure • intention • representation	Machine	Pictures
DICOM	International	Institutional	Message • structure • intention • representation	Machine	Images
Standard	Level of acceptance	Application area	Object	User	

on the patient, the kind of picture, the assistant taking the picture and the radiologist responsible for formulating conclusions. PACS also needs to be able to convey the *intention* when sending or receiving a message, like STORE or PRINT the picture, or RETRIEVE a specific picture or set of pictures. Finally PACS contains the representation of pictures, like picture size, and the way of coding the individual pixels (grayscale) of the picture. The area where PACS is applied is institutional (or even departmental). The expected need for acceptance is hard to say, but it has to be at least the same as the application area. If communication of digital pictures outside the institution is foreseen for the near future, the expected need for acceptance rises to the regional level. The limitation for PACS is the matter of pictures.

When several applications want to communicate with a PACS, the system has to use a standard that meets the need. By using the framework, the DICOM standard appears to match the categorised PACS application, as it is an international standard with institutional applications, covers messages to be exchanged between different machines and has images as its limitation. The match between the need and the standard is shown in Table 3.

A more complicated example is the transmission of lab-orders and results. The lab-results are used directly by professionals, but the machine always has to process the data. On the one hand, it has to interpret the lab-orders in order to calculate, for example, the necessary bloodsamples. On the other hand it has to interpret the results and match them with relevant reference values in order to provide emergency signals. The transmission of lab-results is limited to medical content. The objects concerned are the message structure, message intention, message representation and the terminology in specifying lab-tests. The area where the application is needed

Table 4: Match Between Lab Application and a Combination of Standards

Application	Dimensions				Limitation
	Exp. need for acceptance	Application area	Object	User	
Lab	Regional	Regional	Message • structure • intention • representation Terminology	Machine and Human	Medical content
HL7	International	Institutional	Message • structure • intention	Machine	Hospital processes
LOINC	National	Regional	Terminology	People	Orders
metric	International	International	Message • representation	People	Measurements
Standard	Level of acceptance	Application area	Object	User	

is restricted to specific healthcare regions. The specified characteristics of the application will help to find an appropriate standard. However the characteristics seem to be too broad for one standard, therefore a combination has to be found.

By combining the LOINC and the HL7 standard, the application can be sufficiently standardised. Both the standards can be applied on a regional level. The HL7 standard covers the message intention and the message structure with a 'machine' as a user, while the LOINC standard covers the terminology applied by human users. In addition, the metric system for measurements can be used as a representation for the results. This is an important addition, as the needs specify a message representation standard in order to generate emergency alerts automatically. However, even though the match seems reasonable, some problems may occur, as LOINC is not accepted outside the USA and HL7 has not yet been applied on a regional scale. Table 4 summarises the combination of standards needed to fill the needs of a lab application.

RECOMMENDATIONS

On the one hand the use of information systems in healthcare is growing rapidly. On the other hand the explosion of Internet development cannot be stopped. If the link between healthcare information systems and the Internet cannot be established, the two worlds will grow away from each other. This is definitely not in the interest of the patient and the quality of care. Communication and therefore standardisation must be seen as a main topic in healthcare. Whether standardisation is necessary in healthcare communication is not an issue. *Which* standards are needed seems to be a more difficult problem. A decision-support tool for standardising applications in healthcare has been described in this chapter. By putting four disparate dimensions and their values in a framework, the applications as well as currently known standards can be categorised. The tool can be used by first categorising the application that needs to employ a standardised form of communication, then categorise and select the standards that can be considered appropriate in this context. Finally compare the supply and demand and apply the most suitable standard(s). The framework therefore can be useful in comparing the demand with a determined criterion and the possibility to combine several standards to satisfy the demand.

Standardising healthcare communication applications may bring complications if there are no (adequate) standards, according to the specified dimensions, or when objects of combined standards appear to have overlaps. However, the lack of an appropriate standard for a certain application can trigger new standard development efforts. Also, the identification of definite overlaps between standards can guide future developments of these standards.

REFERENCES

de Bruijn, L.M., Hasman, A. and Arends, J. W. (1997). Automatic SNOMED classification—A corpus-based method, *Computer Methods and Programs in Biomedicine,* 54(1-2), 115-122.

European Committee for Standardisation Technical Committee for Health Informatics: http://www.centc251.org/.

Forrey A.W., McDonald, C. J., DeMoor, G., Huff, S. M., Leavelle, D. Leland, D., Fiers, T., Charles, L., Griffin, B., Stalling, F., Tullis, A., Hutchins, K. and Baenziger, J. (1996). Logical observation identifier names and codes (LOINC) database. A public use set of codes and names for electronic reporting of clinical laboratory test results, *Clinical Chemistry* 42(1) 81-90.

Heitmann K.U., Blobel, B. and Dudeck, J. (1999). *HL7 Communication Standard in Medicine, Short Introduction and Information,'* Cologne.

ISO homepage: http://www.iso.ch/.

Klein G.O. (1998). Standardization strategy from a European perspective, *International Journal of Medical Informatics* Vol. 48, 67-70, Elsevier, Ireland

McDonald C.J., Overhage, J. M., Dexter, P., Takesue, B. and Suico, J. G. (1998). 'What is done, what is needed and what is realistic to expect from medical informatics standards', *International Journal of Medical Informatics* 48, 5-12

Sippel Schmidt, T. (1999). *"Integrating the Healthcare Enterprise, The IHE Technical Framework"*, Presentation at IHE Vendor Orientation Workshop, May. http://www.rsna.org/IHE/iheyr1wkshp/may3_4/2_ihetf.pdf.

Treseder P. and Williams, P. (1998). "The common principles of health informatics standardisation that require exchange of information between the standardisation bodies of different countries", *International Journal of Medical Informatics* vol. 48, 39-42, Elsevier, Ireland

Chapter VI

The Electronic Patient Record As An Organizational Artifact

Pieter Toussaint
Leiden University Medical Centre, The Netherlands

Marc Berg
Erasmus University Rotterdam, The Netherlands

The research effort on Electronic Patient Records (EPRs) has rapidly increased in the last decade. Much of this research focussed on standardisation and technical realizations. We will describe such a research effort in this chapter and evaluate its success. Our main finding is that the lack of success of this specific research effort is mainly due to its technological bias. Although standards (both conceptual and technical) are important prerequisites for the realisation of an EPR, organisational issues are decisive for success. The role played by these organisational issues will be illustrated by analysing the findings of the case study presented in the chapter. We will argue that research on EPRs should be more focussed on the role of an EPR as an organisational artefact that coordinates the work of healthcare professionals, in order to lead to successful implementations.

INTRODUCTION

Healthcare changes. In Berg (1999), the authors discuss both internal and external reasons for this change. External stakeholders, such as insurance companies and the government, want more influence on the process of providing care to patients. Their objective is to increase the efficiency and effectiveness of the care process. Internal reasons for the change of healthcare are the further specialisation of the medical profession and the more frequent occurrence of chronic diseases due to the increase of average age. These internal reasons imply a more intensive cooperation between healthcare professionals in the process of delivering care. This cooperation requires co-ordination of activities in time and place.

The Electronic Patient Record can play a major role in enabling and shaping these changes. In Berg (1999) two main functions that an EPR can play are discussed: accumulating and coordinating. The EPR accumulates information on patients. That is, it stores and aggregates patient data, and as such provides an overview of the care history related to the patient. It must be stressed that in doing this the EPR is an active artefact, because it constructs a view (or multiple views) of the patient record in the process of accumulating. The EPR also coordinates the work of different healthcare professionals. It enables the sharing of knowledge on a patient, and can passively (by making knowledge accessible for all healthcare professionals) and actively (by notifying or alerting professionals) influence their work processes.

This coordination function can result in a change in the cooperation between healthcare professionals. Because of this effect the EPR is often claimed to enable the emergence of 'virtual' healthcare teams. This claim is evaluated in this chapter against the results of implementing an EPR in order to support shared care for diabetes patients, which was done as a pilot of a European R&D project on EPRs called Synapses (Grimson et al., 1996).

The Synapses project ran from 1995 until the end of 1998. It involved 26 partners from 14 different European countries. The budget for Synapses was 5.2 million ECU. The project set out to solve problems of sharing medical record data between autonomous information systems, by providing generic and open means to combine healthcare records or dossiers consistently, simply, comprehensibly and securely, whether the data passes within a single healthcare institution or between institutions. The Synapses project developed the specifications of a server, acting as a mediator between information systems keeping parts of medical records (the so-called feeder systems) and client applications, used for viewing medical records.

Currently, the electronic and paper records used by healthcare professionals are mostly held in islands of information. Therefore, sharing information across systems is very difficult and time consuming. Often, non-automated and non-efficient means of communication are used for sharing information. This is hampering the progress towards shared care and cost-containment.

These problems are clearly illustrated in the case of diabetic patients. The treatment of diabetic patients involves the general practitioner (GP), a nurse specialised in the treatment of diabetic patients and several healthcare professionals at the outpatient clinic, and various departments within the hospital. At the different stages of this process, several flows of information occur between the healthcare professionals involved. In the Academic Medical Centre, it was felt that the the efficiency and the effectiveness of communication between the healthcare professionals involved in this process was far from optimal, and therefore a re-engineering of the shared care process for diabetic patients was considered within the scope of a Synapses pilot. A major objective of the Academic Medical Centre was to adhere to the so-called St. Vincent declaration, a document compiled in 1989 with diabetes organisations, healthcare professionals and people with diabetes. Based on the objectives formulated in this declaration, and some local objectives, a number of goals were formulated for reorganising the diabetes care process (Synapses Consortium):

1. Increasing the self-regulation by the patient.
2. Increasing involvement of the treatment by first-line healthcare professionals, such as general practitioners. In particular, patients suffering from diabetes mellitus type II must be treated and monitored as much as possible by their general practitioner.
3. Diminishing the complications of diabetes mellitus. Some of the specific objectives are: 50% less amputations, 33% less blindness and 33% less kidney insufficiency caused by diabetes.

In order to achieve these objectives, intensive coordination of the treatment of diabetic patients is required. The goal of diabetes management is to keep blood glucose levels as close as possible to the normal (non-diabetic) range. The patient is responsible for day-to-day care. In addition, an endocrinologist monitors their physical condition and checks for complications. Also, people suffering from diabetes often see other specialists, such as: the ophthalmologist for eye examinations, podiatrists for foot care, dieticians for meal planning guidance and diabetes educators for instructions on day-to-day care.

In principle diagnosis, treatment and monitoring patients suffering from diabetes mellitus type II can be performed by general practitioners. It requires no knowledge to the degree of a specialist. However, this is not common practice, because most general practitioners feel uncomfortable with their knowledge, skills and policy of treating diabetes patients.

The basic requirements that followed from these objectives are that information on the physical condition of a diabetes patient can be shared by all professionals involved in the care process, and that guidelines on treating these patients are exchanged between endocrinologist and general practitioners. A number of Dutch Synapses partners (software company HISCOM at which one of the authors was employed, Academic Medical Centre in Amsterdam and two general practitioners practices in Amsterdam) cooperated in the development of a record server that is compliant with the Synapses specifications, in order to enable the sharing of the medical entities included in the DiabCare dataset between these healthcare providers. The DiabCare dataset is a set of data elements, agreed upon at the European level, encompassing all information relevant for monitoring the stage of illness, the therapy and secondary complications in the case of diabetes patients (Diabcare Q-net). Furthermore, the record server provides access to a database with guidelines or protocols for treating diabetes patients.

In [6, 7] the technical solution has been reported and discussed. In this chapter we will focus on the evaluation of the use of the system. First, we briefly describe the Synapses solution using the five viewpoints advocated by the Open Distributed Processing (ODP) standard. Then, we evaluate the system use and discuss the findings.

SYNAPSES SOLUTION

The Synapses solution can be seen as the realisation of a distributed healthcare record system, constructed out of different heterogeneous component systems. The ODP standards initiative defines five perspectives, called viewpoints, from which distributed systems can be described. These five viewpoints are:

- the *enterprise viewpoint* is concerned with the business environment in which the system has to operate;
- the *information viewpoint* is concerned with the information to be stored and processed by the system;
- the *computational viewpoint* is concerned with a description of the system as a set of *objects* that interact at *interfaces*;
- the *engineering viewpoint* is concerned with the mechanisms supporting system distribution;
- the *technology viewpoint* is concerned with the detail of components from which the distributed system is constructed.

In this chapter the Synapses server, as developed for supporting shared care for diabetes patients, is described from each of the five ODP viewpoints. We will start with a description from the enterprise viewpoint, and work from there all the way down to the technology viewpoint.

The Enterprise Viewpoint

The enterprise viewpoint describes the distributed system to be developed in the business environment in which it will operate. The main focus of such a description is the relations between the participants in the business process to be supported. Our model from this viewpoint will be illustrated by means of a small number of scenarios exemplifying four typical cooperative activities taking place within the realm of diabetes care.

1. The general practitioner consults the internist on the correct diagnosis.
2. The general practitioner consults the internist on the choice treatment to provide.
3. The general practitioner consults the internist on an issue related to conducting the treatment chosen.
4. The general practitioner refers the patient to the hospital (transfers the care to the internist and the diabetic nurse).

In the following figure these scenarios are depicted graphically. We have divided the care activity into five sub-activities: taking the anamnesis, performing some examinations, diagnosing, planning a treatment and conducting a treatment.

The arrows between the sub-activities are labelled with a number indicating to which scenario the arrow belongs. This figure does not advocate a strict ordering of phases, with clear transitions between them, as the model of medical care. It is only included to indicate the different stages of the care process at which communication and coordination between different healthcare providers takes place in the four scenarios.

We have deliberately formulated these scenarios without reference to technology. Only human actors participate in the process of communicating and (as a result) coordinating behaviours. Our aim in developing the Synapses server was to enable communication and coordination by means of information and communication technology. So, the Synapses server would be an actor in itself, enabling, but also constraining, the interworking of the human actors in this specific network. This role of the FHCR is in line with the ideas on the role of EPRs as expressed in Berg (1999).

The Information Viewpoint

Enabling the communication of information between human actors is the key role played by the FHCR. As noted before, this information comes in two types: information on the physical condition of diabetes patients, and information on guidelines or protocols for diabetes treatment. The last type was exchanged as free texts, and is therefore not detailed here. The first type of information was structured according to the prescriptions coming from two complementary standardisation results: a standard on Electronic Health Care Records (Hurlen, 19959), and a specification of the dataset required for diabetes treatment and monitoring (Diabcare

Figure 1. Four scenarios that can be distinguished in the process of shared care for diabetes patients

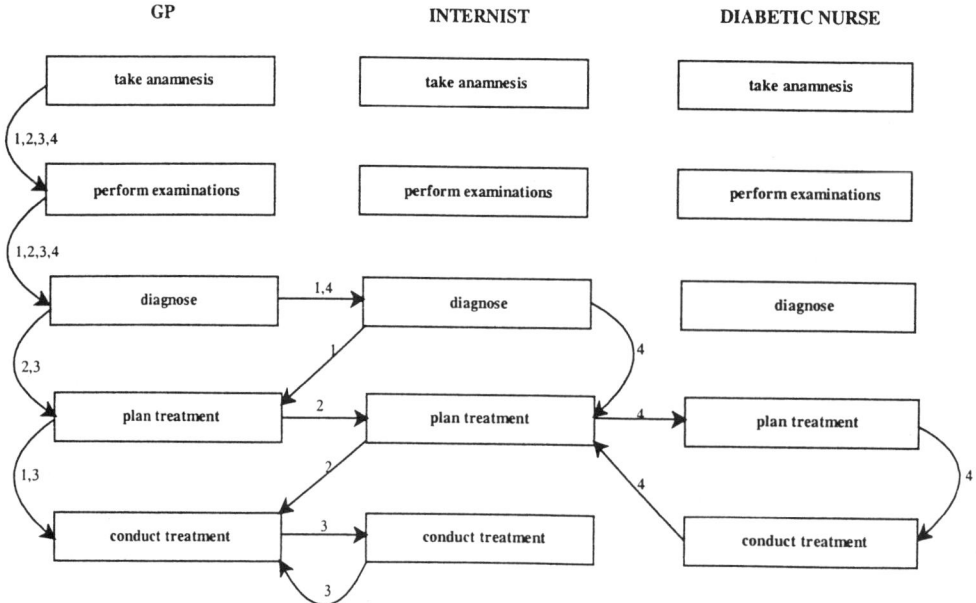

Q-net). Information coming from different sources was integrated into this structure, and presented to the different healthcare providers, giving them a uniform and integrated view of the diabetes record of a patient.

In the figure below a simplified version of the model is described as an object model, using the UML notation (Booch, Rumbaugh and jacobson, 1999). A RecordFolder (record of one patient) consists of one or more episodes of care. Each episode of care consists of one Episode_of_Care_Description and zero or more Episode_of_Care_Entries. An episode of care entry specialises into an element of the Diabcare dataset. Both description and entry inherit from the ENV 12265 class ComRIC, which represents the smallest meaningful, autonomous set of information that can be communicated.

The Computational Viewpoint

The integrated information model is distributed over the computational components making up the distributed system. We distinguish between three types of components: client applications, feeder systems and middleware components. The instances of these three types encountered in our pilot study are discussed below:

1. **Client application**: This component offers healthcare providers involved in the process of providing shared care for diabetic patients, a uniform view on the distributed patient record, as well as access to the repository containing the guidelines or protocols.
2. **Feeder system:** This component stores (parts of) the patient record.

Figure 2. The Object Model of the Synapses Server

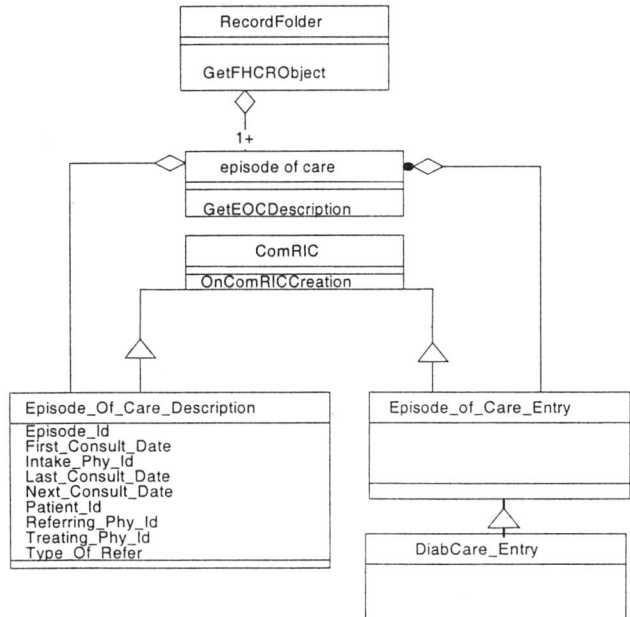

3. **Synapses server**: This middleware component is responsible for making the distributed character of the FHCR transparent to client applications. The view offered on the patient record must be compliant to the object model presented in the section on the information viewpoint.
4. **Client adapter**: If non-Synapses-compliant client applications are used, information flows between the client application, and the Synapses server must be syntactically and semantically converted. This is the function of the client adapter.
5. **Feeder adapter**: Currently a number of information systems are in use for registering parts of the medical record. In our pilot study diabetes-related information is stored in systems used by the general practitioners and in a hospital information system. These systems are not Synapses compliant. Their data is structured differently, they use different keys for patient identification, different security rules and different services for accessing the data. These differences are to be dealt with by the feeder adapters. These adapters wrap the feeders in such a way that they become Synapses compliant.

The components have well-defined interfaces. We have described these interfaces using OMG IDL (Siegel, 1996).

The Engineering Viewpoint

The engineering viewpoint further details the computational viewpoint. It specifies how the computational components are connected using a CORBA-based integration solution. It is the last step in the specification before technologies and platforms can be selected for realising the distributed system.

With regard to the client application and the feeder system components distinguished in the computational viewpoint, we also indicate which specific instances of these components will be chosen for the pilot study. So, the engineering viewpoint marks the transition from the generic Synapses solution to the specific pilot study. We have two instances of the feeder system component: a GP system and the HISCOM/HIS. They are wrapped by means of an adapter in order to make them

Figure 3. The Engineering Architecture for the Synapses Solution

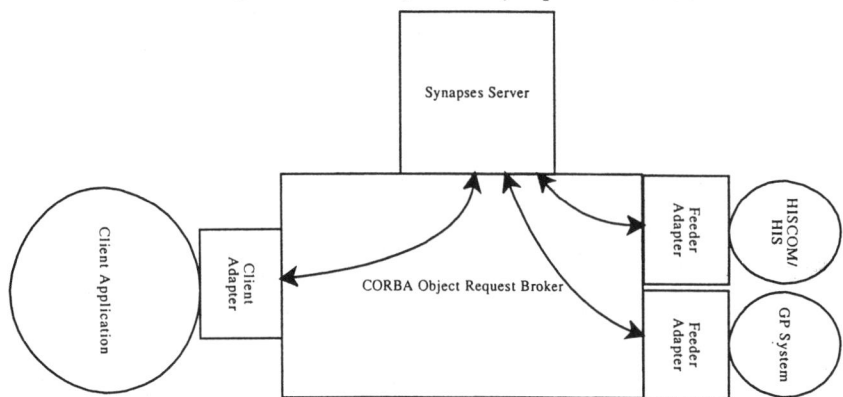

Synapses compliant. Requests from the client application are translated in the client adapter and passed via the **O**bject **R**equest **B**roker (**ORB**) to the Synapses server. Here the request is interpreted and translated into requests for the feeder systems. These requests are passed to the appropriate feeders via the ORB. Responses follow the same route in the opposite direction.

The Technology Viewpoint

The components distinguished in the engineering viewpoint are realised using several technologies and hardware platforms:

- *Client application*: Each of the healthcare providers involved in the process of shared care for diabetes patients has his own client application for accessing the patient record. Two clients were used in the pilot:
  - an application developed in Delphi, running on a PC under Windows95, already in use in the hospital;
  - an application developed in Java, used by the GP.
- *The Synapses server*: The server was developed in Visual C++ and runs on a PC under windows-NT 4.0.
- *The adapters:* The adapters were also developed in Visual C++, and run on a PC under Windows-NT 4.0.
- *The ORB:* For the CORBA Object Request Broker, we have chosen ORBIX 2.0 from Iona Ltd. This product offers an extensive implementation of the CORBA 2.0 specification. It uses a TCP/IP-based network protocol for supporting communication.
- *GP feeders:* One of the GP feeder systems runs under Windows95 on a PC and the other GP feeder system runs under UNIX.
- *HIS:* The HISCOM HIS runs under UNIX.

EVALUATION AND DISCUSSION

In the second half of 1998, the system was implemented at the validation site, and its use was evaluated. In this section we will present and discuss the main findings. A more extensive report on this can be found in the final report on the Synapses project, available at http://www.cs.tcd.ie/synapses/public/.

As stated above, the main objective of the FHCR was that it would act as a co-ordinator of cooperation between different healthcare professionals involved in the shared care for diabetes patients. The most important functions to be offered were enabling the sharing of medical records between the healthcare professionals, and the sharing of guidelines or protocols on diabetes treatment. These functions were realised, along the lines discussed in the previous section. Two major design constraints were central to the Synapses approach:

- (Inter) national standards had to be used if possible. As can be seen in the brief description of the Synapses solution in the previous section, this led to choices for technological standards, such as CORBA, as well as conceptual standards,

such as the European standard on record architectures and the Diabcare dataset.
- Legacy systems already in use by the cooperating actors had to be integrated into the FHCR as autonomous components. This led to the development of the adapters, which act as wrappers, turning legacy systems into CORBA/Synapses components. This loosely coupled strategy reflects the nature of the professional network in which the healthcare professionals cooperate.

So, the FHCR, as developed in the Dutch pilot, adhered to international standards on medical record structures and distributed technologies. Furthermore, it was structured as a loosely coupled system, a structure that reflects the nature of the professional network of healthcare providers cooperating in shared care activities. However, the system was not a success. It was not used in clinical routine, and even worse, the healthcare professionals involved did not conceive it as a promising solution for their problems. The main reasons for their dissatisfaction were:

- Small number of patients involved makes record useless.
- The records that are available are not complete. Only diabetes-related sub-set is accessible.
- FHCR clients were not integrated with legacy system clients.
- FHCR is a passive coordinator. Active means of communication are not implemented.

At first glance these reasons seem to relate to contingent features of the implementation. However, in our opinion these features are not that contingent at all. We will discuss each of the features below, and motivate that these relate to common problems encountered in Electronic Patient Record implementations.

First of all, the number of patients on which medical record information could be shared was very limited. Only 10 patients were involved. This limitation surely affects everything we want to say about the effects of the system as a coordinator of care, but it also highlights some problems with the implementation of these systems that are not incidental. The first reason for this limited set of patients has to do with the privacy regulations in the Netherlands. In fact, no medical information may be shared or exchanged between healthcare professionals without explicit consent of the patient. How does one handle this constraint in the realm of these types of systems that are aimed at enabling the sharing of medical information? In the Synapses pilot we decided to protect ourselves from legal problems by using a small group of patients, that were explicitly asked if they agreed with the pilot. The second reason for the size of the patient group was the fact that the endocrinologist was in the middle of a migration process from paper-based record keeping to electronic record keeping. Only a limited number of his patients were already 'in' his record system and from these patients only a selected part of their history had been included. So, the view on patient records that could be constructed from the electronic record system used by the endocrinologist was by no means comparable to the view contained in his paper-based archive.

The second reason relates to the completeness of the records. In the pilot we choose only to include information that was included in the Diabcare dataset.

Especially the general practitioners involved considered this to be a severe limitation. They encountered patients suffering from diabetes that were often visiting the hospital for non-diabetes-related problems. They wanted a complete update of the things that happened to these patients in the hospital, and not an update restricted to the diabetes-related activities only. In relation to this, they considered the restriction to a specific patient group artificial. This touches upon the problem of views, or professional specific aggregations of patient data. Each professional often needs a different view on the patient record--a view that relates to his or her specific role in the care process. Two important questions to be addressed here are: how can such a view be constructed from the fragments stored in the different feeder systems, and which data must be registered by the different healthcare professionals in order that such a view is constructable. But why should healthcare professionals register data with the sole purpose of facilitating the work of others. How can 'return on investment' be defined in this context? In the context of the Synapses pilot discussed in this chapter, it was clear that both the hospital and the hospital professionals involved were not inclined to change work processes or speed up record implementation efforts in order to increase the quality of communication with general practitioners.

The third reason for the limited usefulness of the FHCR developed was that client applications were not integrated with the client applications already in use by the general practitioners, the endocrinologist and the diabetic nurse. Again, this may be seen as a strong indicator for the limitations of the evaluation presented here, but also in this case this limitation is not a mere incident. Strong integration of the record systems of the different professionals by means of integration of their client applications jeopardises the autonomy of these record systems, and as an effect also the autonomy of the healthcare professionals. This contradicts the very nature of the professional network in which the healthcare providers are participating. Client applications are closely intertwined with the activities a healthcare professional performs, and therefore, changes to these clients will only be acceptable if the incentives to change a way of working are clear to the professional. So, we may conclude that this is in general a difficult thing to achieve.

The last reason is that no active communication functions were implemented in the system so the system did not actively submit reminders or requests to participating healthcare professionals. The coordination role was passive. Implementation of a more active role requires a more thorough understanding of the process of knowledge sharing between healthcare professionals, and is as such not systematically addressed in the literature on medical informatics. There are still a lot of open questions in this field of study, and as a result all implementations of electronic patients records will have to deal with this lack of essential knowledge.

So, we may conclude that the disappointing result of the FHCR implementation, within the Dutch Synapses pilot, is not the result of not using standard technology or standardised concepts, but the result of a lack of insight into important characteristics of the legal and organisational environment in which this systems was realised. The effects of the privacy legislation and the migration process towards an electronic record system taking place in the hospital were only noticed later on in the pilot project, and still the question how to address these issues properly is an open one. The issues of completeness of the record and the integration of FHCR clients with local record system clients relate to the trade off between autonomy and interdependency between the healthcare professionals being part of a shared care network. And the last point on the active role of the FHCR in the coordination of activities pushes this issue even a little further. Extended with this functionality, the FHCR becomes an active actor in the network, therewith changing its structure. Is this acceptable for the healthcare professionals involved, and will they trust the FHCR as such?

The work within Synapses presented here can be seen as a typical example of the work done within medical informatics in the last decade (see for example Masys, 1997) for an overview of current research). In the context of electronic patient records, there has been a lot of attention for technical and medical informational issues, but hardly any for the organisational issues around the patient record. In our view the electronic patient record is mainly an organisation artefact that accumulates patient data and helps in coordinating the work activities of healthcare professionals. So, in order to design and implement such an artefact properly, we must thoroughly understand the characteristics of the healthcare professional network and the role of the electronic patient record in such a network. This research objective has been taken up in a three-year research project funded by the Dutch government that will run from the end of 1999 to the end of 2003. Both authors will participate in this project. In close co-operation with a number of hospitals, we will analyse healthcare processes and derive design guidelines for electronic patient records.

REFERENCES

Berg, M.(1999). et al., *De Nacht Schreef Rood: Informatisering van Zorgpraktijken*, Rathenau Instituut, Den Haag.

Berg, M. (1999). "Accumulating and coordinating: Occasions for information technologies in medical work", *Computer Supported Cooperative Work (8)*, Kluwer Academic Publsihers, 373-401.

Booch, G., Rumbaugh, J. and Jacobson, I. (1999). *The Unified Modeling Language User Guide*, Addison Wesley.

Diabcare Q-net information can be found on the world wide web at: http://www.diabcare.de.

Grimson, J. et al. (1996). "SYNAPSES - Federated Health Care Record Server", in: *Medical Informatics Europe'96*, J. Brender, J.P. Christensen, J.-R. Scherrer, P. McNair (Eds.), 695-699.

Hurlen,P. (1995). *Electronic Healthcare Record Architecture*, CEN/TC 251/WG 1 N95-38.

Masys, D.R. (Ed.) (1997). *Proceedings of the 1997 Annual Fall Symposium of the American Medical Informatics Association*.

ODP, ISO/IEC DIS 10746, *Part 1-4*.

Siegel, J. (1996). *CORBA Fundamentals and Programming*, John Wiley & Sons, Inc.Synapses

Consortium, *Synapses ODP specification*, to be published at IOS press.
Toussaint, P.J., Kalshoven, M. Ros, M., van der Kolk, H. and O. Weier. (1997). 'Supporting Shared Care for Diabetes Patients: the Synapses solution', in: [12], 1997, pp. 393-397.
Toussaint, P.J. (1998). *Integration of Information Systems: a study in requirements engineering*, Ph.D.-thesis Leiden University.

Section 3

Transformation in Healthcare Chains

Business Transformation
Stefan Klein
Heike Schad

Telecommunication as a Medicine
Peter Lagendijk
Roel Schuring
Ton Spil

Transforming Healthcare
Elizabeth More
Mike McGrath

Chapter VII

The Introduction of EDI Systems in Healthcare Supply Chains: A Framework for Business Tramsformation

Stefan Klein
University of Muenster, Germany

Heike Schad
CapGemini Ernst & Young

While it has become commonplace knowledge that the benefits of an EDI introduction depend on organizational adaptations, there is an obvious lack of research on the related issues of inter-organizational process innovation (ioBPR) along the supply chain and business network redesign (BNR) which emphasizes strategically motivated changes in the value chain. Based on a review of the literature on BPR, ioBPR and BNR, we will develop a framework for business transformation which integrates the different redesign approaches and perspectives into a comprehensive analysis and change process. The framework is illustrated by using the example of a redesign process in the healthcare industry.*

INTRODUCTION

In recent years the awareness is rising that EDI, the computer-mediated exchange of structured business messages, based on standards like X12 or EDIFACT,

An earlier version of this chapter was published as Klein, Stefan and Schad, Heike. "The introduction of EDI systems in healthcare supply chains: A framework for business transformation," in the *International Journal of Electronic Commerce*, 2(1), ©1997, 25-44 (reprinted by permission from M.E. Sharpe, Inc. Armonk, NY, 10504).

among companies, has to be regarded as an embedded technology: its successful implementation is contingent on internal integration and organizational adjustments. Furthermore, the redesign of inter-organizational processes and relationships, and in some cases even adaptations on an industry level, e.g., standardization of product codes, are prerequisites for EDI benefits. Companies that want to exploit the potential benefits of EDI therefore need to focus on internal organizational adaptations as well as on adaptations along the supply chain.

Based on a project in the medical diagnostics industry, we are reconstructing the process of framing of EDI in a situation where the rationale of the EDI usage is questioned. In a brief literature review, we are comparing the perspectives of BPR, ioBPR and BNR, and are relating them to the set-up of EDI. In the third step, a framework for business transformation is developed that integrates BPR, ioBPR and BNR into a comprehensive analysis. The framework is illustrated by using the example of the supply chain for reagents in medical diagnostics.

THE CASE: THE SET-UP OF EDI IN MEDICAL DIAGNOSTICS

While a number of EDI projects in the healthcare sector are focusing on the procurement of pharmaceuticals, the project described here, INTHES, looks into extending and applying these results to the area of reagents for medical diagnostics. The distribution of reagents is influenced by a limited shelf life, few production sites and a high specificity. Instead of just implementing an EDI link between the participants, a thorough analysis of the distribution and replenishment cycle, including internal processes, has been conducted in order to identify the specific requirements of the message exchange and to prepare the participants to better integrate the results of the message exchange into their internal operations.

In order to reduce the complexity of different organizational settings and interests, it has been decided that the group of pilot partners should be restricted to only one company for each role that represents the interests of the industry:

- As hospital: Hospital Vall d'Hebron, Barcelona.
  Vall d'Hebron (VdH) is one of the largest hospitals in Catalunya, Spain, and is very active in setting up EDI links and in implementing innovative organizational solutions.
- As logistics company: Bomi SPA, Segrate, Italy.
  Bomi is actively developing new service strategies for logistics in the healthcare sector.
- As supplier: Hoffmann LaRoche Diagnostics Systems (RDS).
  RDS is currently developing new logistics strategies and is considering development of logistics solutions in cooperation with competing suppliers.

Building on these experiences, steps have been undertaken to evaluate and further disseminate the findings with other leading industry players.

Process Analysis and Suggested Improvements

Within the project, the macro design of the process, procurement of reagents,' i.e., the process chain between the supplier, the logistics company and the customer, has been analyzed. Moreover, the internal processes of the partners have been scrutinized, as the procurement process of the customers (labs) can only be changed radically if also the processes of the suppliers (diagnostics companies) and the intermediaries (logistics companies) are changed.

The customers, namely laboratories, rely on a continuous delivery-on-demand, as a stock-out of reagents will inevitably interrupt their ability to run tests. Currently the hospital labs send their paper-based orders to a central procurement department from where the orders are transmitted to the suppliers via fax. After the control of the order in the supplier's finance department, the order confirmation is written. The confirmation is sent to the hospital and the delivery of the reagents is initiated at the same time. Warehousing and distribution has been outsourced by RDS to BOMI. A shared database enables RDS to coordinate deliveries as if they owned the warehouse. While outsourcing of logistics is an initial step to ensure a Europe-wide delivery of small quantities within 24 hours, a close communication link between the three parties (supplier, logistics company and customer) is advantageous in order to gain the requisite lead time to reduce distribution costs.

Based on the process analysis, the message and information flow among and within the participating organizations has been scrutinized. Particular emphasis has been put on the sharing of information so that the participants can make use of advance information, such as forecast of demand or advance delivery notes, in order to improve their internal operations.

The participants started to negotiate interaction patterns in terms of mutually providing forecasts and advance information, and building incentives for compliance into the process: according to these agreements the hospital, for example, provides detailed specifications of monthly orders approximately two weeks before shipments are due and expects in exchange advance delivery notes no later than two days before the actual shipment. In addition, it is expected that only few errors occur during the distribution process (less than 5%) so that a limited number of messages, such as quotes, orders and invoices, would be sufficient to coordinate the entire supply chain.

EDI and Changes in Inter-Organizational Relations

While these actions contribute to a significant simplification of existing organizational routines, more profound changes in the distribution structure may be necessary to improve the inter-organizational coordination even further and to reduce redundancies in the process. EDI is regarded as an enabling technology for the improvement not only of the message exchange but also of the cooperation along the supply chain. For this reason different scenarios, like consolidated shipments for the hospitals, have been evaluated.

The analysis shows that it is imperative to study the processes first, because the set-up of EDI links is embedded in a set of inter-organizational assumptions, arrangements, and rules about the process flow, and action-response patterns among partners that require a thorough understanding of their internal processes and a high efficiency of operations.

One of the results of the project was the design of a simplified procurement/distribution process that is based on the three pillars of EDI solutions:

- standardized UN/EDIFACT business messages (*syntax*: structure of the messages);
- standardized product identification based on EAN-128 (*semantics*: content of the messages);
- an interchange agreement, specifying the sequence and timing of messages as well as business rules referring to pitfalls and frictions in the process (*pragmatics*: action-response patterns).

The rationale of this procedure was to start with an organizational analysis in order to identify areas for improvement before setting up EDI links. By this means, EDI becomes part of a combined organizational and technical innovation. The potential improvements through EDI are leveraged.

LITERATURE REVIEW: BPR, IOBPR, BNR AND EDI

While there is a rich body of literature and methods for BPR and IT (Hess and Brecht, 1995; Davenport and Short, 1990; Earl, 1994) less focus has been put on inter-organizational BPR or even business network redesign (BNR). The following overview shows perspectives on BPR and EDI in an inter-organizational context. In particular, papers have been selected that put emphasis on the inter-organizational aspects and that link (io)BPR and BNR to EDI.

BPR: The Success of EDI Depends on the Integration into Internal Applications

Anecdotal evidence suggests that in numerous cases, incoming EDI orders are printed and re-keyed into an internal IS because a seamless integration is too costly to implement. In these cases EDI systems are little more than expensive fax machines and do not provide any integration benefits (Emmelhainz, 1987, 1993; Sokol, 1989). Riggins and Mukhopadhyay (1994) underscore the interdependence between technological and process innovations: the integration of data transmitted via EDI into internal information systems is the basis for subsequent process changes within the receiving organization. Cox and Ghoneim (1994) have collected empirical evidence that the benefit of EDI depends on the level of its integration into internal business processes and on the centrality of the EDI application for the respective business.

This first group of authors emphasizes the link between benefits from EDI and its integration into internal IS and subsequent adaptations of the internal processing of incoming EDI messages. They argue primarily from the perspective of companies that receive EDI messages.

ioBPR: The Success of EDI Depends on a Redesign of the Inter-Organizational Processes

While the first group focuses on the redesign of internal processes, authors like Swatman, Swatman and Fowler (1993, 1994), as well as Clark and Stoddard (1996), emphasize that the potential of EDI to improve the performance of a value chain can only be realized by reengineering business processes among organizations: "... technological and process innovations are interdependent and both are needed to capture the potential benefits of EDI implementation through inter-organizational process redesign" (Clark and Stoddard, 1996). While an isolated implementation of EDI may not provide sufficient benefits for all the partners involved, a business-driven solution which attains a simultaneous and interdependent organizational and technological innovation will more likely yield incentives and advantages for the involved business partners.

Wagenaar and van der Heijden (1994) summarize a set of generic opportunities of EDI:

... to decouple information flows from physical goods or financial flows;

... to exchange the messages more frequently and timely, which means in the end the enabling of a tighter coordination between organizations;

... to share the data among different organizations without re-keying them.

These potential benefits are contingent however on industry structures and industry-specific business drivers.

This second group links EDI and process improvements along supply chains; it focuses the interfaces and coordination among the different players. These innovations usually involve changes of several partners at a time and require a certain level of cooperation among the different players.

BNR: The Capabilities of EDI Will Change the Industry Structure

Kambil and Short (1994) state that firms are using EDI "to transform business processes and relationships, the business network or the firm's business scope." They use the roles-linkages model to depict the relationship and governance changes among the EDI partners. Business network redesign targets more profound changes in supply chains and other forms of company networks such as redefining the firms' roles and relationships or redesigning the pattern of exchange through outsourcing or (dis-)intermediation. In an earlier article, Benjamin, DeLong and Morton (1990) argue that EDI can facilitate the restructuring of partnerships, and that in the long run EDI can change the structure of an industry as a whole and is thus becoming a prerequisite for competing successfully in those markets.

Davidson (1993) proposes a broader process of business transformation based on new IT capabilities and innovative business ideas. "This three-phase transformation process starts with structured automation and re-engineering efforts, builds on new infrastructure and capabilities to enhance and extend the original business, and then redefines it to create new businesses." He argues that driven by the redesign of business activities, transformation focuses first on business processes and infrastructures and second on organizational structures and systems. Organizational change is seen as a response to new business requirements and realities, and the transformation begins by focusing on core activities in the current business. He also discusses how to overcome possible barriers of the transformation process.

Venkatraman (1991, 1994) defines a framework, which proposes a hierarchy of five levels of IT-enabled business transformations. On the one hand he differentiates between evolutionary levels, like "localized exploitation" and "internal integration" and on the other hand revolutionary levels like "business process redesign," "business network redesign" and "business scope redefinition." The last two levels of transformation provide potentially greater benefits, but they also require a correspondingly higher degree of changes in organizational routines. Furthermore, Venkatraman (1994) points out that EDI is *not* equivalent to BNR, but BNR is more than the choice between common versus proprietary interfaces, and benefits of BNR are broader than efficient transaction processing.

While it is the aim of the business process redesign level to optimize the processes within an organization from a process-oriented point of view, the reorganization process spills over the boundaries of the firm and integrates the value chains of the suppliers and the customers on the business network redesign level. On

Table 1. Organizational and EDI scope of BPR, ioBPR and BNR

Level of analysis	Organizational scope	EDI scope	Reference
BPR	Internal processes	Integration of EDI into internal systems and processes	[10, 15, 16]
ioBPR	Inter-organizational processes, • e.g., simplification of processes based on bilateral agreements or (re-) allocation of tasks • redesign of bilateral transactions or within a supply chain	Selection of messages, interchange agreements: message flow and responses	[8, 34, 38]
BNR	Business relationships (governance structures) • industry solutions • new industry structures, e.g., direct sales or new forms of intermediation	Standardization and implementation issues, EDI as enabler for new organizational models	[12, 22, 36, 37]

the level of business scope redefinition, strategic adjustments, like the concentration on core competencies as well as the expansion of business functions (new products or services), are redefined.

The third group of authors extends the scope of analysis beyond the primarily organizational perspective of process innovation towards changes in the value chain and strategic implications for the respective players. Moreover, in BNR the scope is often widened to include numerous industry players. Table 1 summarizes the mentioned approaches.

Based on the literature review, a framework for business transformation is proposed that integrates the different perspectives and levels of analysis.

A FRAMEWORK FOR BUSINESS TRANSFORMATION: IMPROVEMENTS IN THE SUPPLY CHAIN FOR MEDICAL DIAGNOSTICS

BPR, ioBPR and BNR each cover different, yet interrelated aspects of process redesign. Using the example of a supply chain in medical diagnostics, we want to illustrate the specific requirements of ioBPR and BNR, and show how the different redesign approaches can be integrated into an analysis and design process.

The task in our case is to identify feasible and sustainable benefits through changes in inter-organizational processes and relations (with linkages to intra-organizational changes). For this purpose we have chosen a generic four-step model of:
- contingency analysis,
- requirements engineering,
- identification and evaluation of alternative scenarios,
- management of the change process and implementation.

Within each step, the specific requirements of inter-organizational redesign result from the necessity to distinguish and align not only the perspectives of the different players but also strategic, organizational and technical aspects.

Step 1: Analysis of Contingencies

The analysis of the impact of IT on governance structures, i.e., business relations as well as coordination mechanisms, has emphasized the embeddedness of IT in a broad framework of business decisions. Holland and Lockett (1994), Reekers and Smithson (1995) and Klein (1996) have developed multidisciplinary frameworks for the analysis of contingencies on the impact of IT. Table 2 summarizes the different dimensions which will, however, not be discussed in detail in this chapter.

The result of this first step is an initial assessment of the strategic position of the players in their industry and in relation to each other, as well as an inventory of inter-organizational systems (IOS) and related IT. The identification of the core business areas is crucial not only in order to assess the benefits of particular IOS applications but also to delimit potential areas of cooperation and outsourcing.

Step 2: Requirements Engineering

The goal of this step is the identification of requirements for improvements and key benefit areas. It is therefore mandatory to conduct this analysis as open as possible. Based on individual analyses of the respective players, a process of participatory requirements engineering has to be initiated.

Individual analysis

The individual analysis covers five phases: the identification and selection of a process (1), the scrutiny of the relevant context, in particular process interdependencies (2), the identification of contingencies for improvements (3), the modeling of the process and information flow (4), and an analysis of bottlenecks and potential areas for improvement (5).

(1) Identification of an inter-organizational process

Once companies start to look at inter-organizational processes, they find a dense web of interrelated processes which together are far too complex to be examined at the same time. It is therefore necessary to identify a process chain which

Table 2. Contingency Dimensions and Operationalizations

Dimension	Operationalizations	Medical diagnostics
Industry structure (environmental context, market complexity)	Competition, dynamics, complexity, uncertainty, degree of intermediation	Fragmented industry (numerous suppliers and customers), strong influence of government regulation in some segments, increasing price competition, stable demand
Inter-organizational relationships, (dependence, network theory, governance structure)	Interdependence, power, culture, asset specificity	Life cycle of test units approx. 5 years, trend towards closed systems, unit-specific investments by labs (training and interfacing), limited trust
Procedural arrangements (efficiency)	Intensity of interaction efficiency level of IS support for operations, (scope of) EDI use	Limited use of EDI, primarily for the exchange of test results, medium efficiency of distribution, weak ties among supplier and customer
Competencies	Identification of core business(es)	Suppliers: production of reagents; goal: providing system solution to customer; customers: running tests efficiently; logistics companies: forwarding, distribution and warehousing

can be dealt with separately before a further look is taken at the interdependencies with other processes. Criteria for the selection of inter-organizational processes are e.g., the degree of interdependency, coordination requirements, importance and level of internal integration, strategic position of the process (a peripheral process might be a candidate for outsourcing, a core process needs to be well linked with the business partners).

In the diagnostics case, we chose the supply chain for reagents, starting with the identification of needs at the customer side and finishing with the receipt of the invoice by the customer. This process covers different companies and within them different departments as well as different flows of information and physical goods. It raises a number of relationship issues as well as coordination requirements. The choice of this process has been motivated by recent discussions about distribution strategies on the supplier side and EDI pilot projects for the procurement of medical supplies from the hospital side.

(2) The relevant context: Analysis of process interdependence

Once a process has been identified, the challenge is to delimit the relevant context. For every process there are numerous linkages to other processes that might need to be considered in a later phase. The relevance of related processes depends on the required changes and whether these will have effects on other processes or will be affected by them. For example, changes in the distribution of products might affect production planning or procurement logistics.

Examples of related processes in our case are:
- Reagents are replenishable products, but besides the test units spare parts are also included in the diagnostic system. Their distribution however has a different frequency and is governed by different decision-making processes. The result is that a different process design is required.
- From the supplier side, procurement and production of reagents together with planning and controlling activities are related processes.
- From the customer side, processes for the procurement of other products might be affected in a situation where the entire procurement operations are streamlined.

(3) Identification of contingencies for improvement

The requirements for improvement reflect general strategies of the players in response to their respective competitive (or regulatory) environments. It is thus related to Step 1.

Increasing cost pressure and shrinking margins in the diagnostics sector combined with an intensifying competition with enhanced quality demands on the customer side pose contradictory requirements to the suppliers: they have to improve their responsiveness, which is often interpreted as time between order and delivery, and at the same time reduce logistics cost which depends on the lead time for deliveries.

Given the suppliers' requirements, the logistics companies need to organize the distribution efficiently. They need information about their tasks as early as possible and try to build some economies of scale by consolidating shipments whenever possible.

The customers want the information and physical flows to be integrated into their own internal processes in order to gain administrative benefits and, at the same time, prices being lowered.

The general requirements are a need for quality improvements and cost reductions throughout the supply chain.

(4) Process modeling

Based on a preliminary analysis of the contingencies, a detailed process and information flow analysis is conducted. Tasks and messages as well as IT support are described. The resulting process description comprehends organizational rules, timing and rhythm of activities, quality issues and responsibilities.

(5) Process analysis: Bottlenecks and key benefit areas

The process descriptions represent quantitative information, e.g., frequency and duration of processes, as well as subjective perceptions. The interview partners have been asked to identify bottlenecks and to suggest process improvements. In addition, the processes are checked for redundancies, potential areas for simplification, improved coordination and synchronization (see Table 3). Although this is still done by the players individually and they may come up with purely internal measures, the analysis aims to cover the entire process and looks in particular at inter-organizational interfaces. Options like re-allocation of tasks, implementation of EDI or inter-organizational arrangements that improve the process flow have to be taken into consideration.

Participatory Requirements Analysis

Although the before-mentioned analysis has been conducted by the different players individually, the requirements of inter-organizational process coordination have been taken into account. However, a further step is needed in order to bring the players together, discuss the respective requirements and match the different perspectives and interests. The process of describing and modeling is a crucial part of the participatory requirements engineering, it raises the awareness of the process flow, interfaces and requirements towards and on behalf of the other players (Cavaye and Cragg, 1994). The goal of this step is to uncover inconsistencies between the different perspectives and expectancies, and to develop a comprehensive and shared picture of the entire (distributed) process. Furthermore, (inter-)dependencies among the players' processes shall be identified.

Apart from the objective need to align the different perspectives in order to come up with a solution, it is assumed that the awareness of the respective and mutual interests will make the negotiation process more open (Fisher and Ury,

1981). This step also reveals the partnership uncertainty among the different players which has a strong impact on the development of inter-organizational relations (Bensaou, 1993).

There were two major findings in our case:

1) A significant discrepancy between the expectations of customers and suppliers: while suppliers were competing on time between order and delivery, customers said they had a pretty stable demand and could accept a delivery time of three working days for routine deliveries.

2) There was little trust among the players (Webster, 1995). The relationship was mainly based on an institutional rather than on a personal level. The quality of the supplier's services was rated as mediocre by the customers, while the supplier feared specific and expensive demands by the customers.

Step 3: Identification of Possible Solutions

The focus of the third step is to identify measures that require the collaboration of several players and that will affect inter-organizational processes. We distinguish between two different levels of solutions:

1) first-order changes cover procedural and technical improvements within the framework of existing relationships, i.e., within a supply chain;
2) second-order changes comprehend more profound changes in the relationships among the players, with possible impacts on a wider group of suppliers or customers.

Table 3. Examples of Bottlenecks and Benefit Areas

Player	Bottleneck	Benefit areas
Supplier	Time-consuming order management, high cost of urgent deliveries	- Delivery contract with customer - Enhanced order lead time will reduce cost of warehousing and distribution and improve the forecast of demands as well as production and distribution planning
Intermediary	Consignee order information arrives too late	- Use of bar codes will improve inventory management and control - Enhanced order lead time will improve coordination of transports and reduce costs
Customer	High administrative costs because • products are not bar-coded • invoices are not sent electronically • there is no advance delivery notification • shipments are fragmented	- Suppliers bar code their products - Suppliers send delivery note and invoice via EDI in advance which then can be compared automatically - Advance delivery information and consolidated shipments facilitates the streamlining of materials management operations

First-order changes are related to ioBPR, while second-order changes represent the results of BNR. However, the analysis of preconditions for the first-order changes, which initially are focused on a single supply chain, show that industry solutions are imperative in order to realize the potential benefits and to justify the required investments.

Building blocks of a first-order change: Procedural and technical improvements

The rationale of the first-order change is to improve the coordination of the processes and to simplify the process flow. In our case, this refers to order, delivery and administrative procedures. The measures we are proposing represent the pragmatic, semantic and syntactic level of communication (Kubicek, 1992).

(1) The pragmatic level: Interchange agreement

More efficient coordination requires mutual agreements among the trading partners with respect to quality, responsiveness and trust (Bakos and Brynjolfsson, 1993; Sabel, 1994). In order to simplify and improve the coordination of the process flow, the parties have to develop interchange agreements which specify the responsibilities, response patterns and time. The interchange agreements can be seen as inter-organizational rules that are more specific than the terms of trade. If IOS are in place, they comprehend rules for the exchange of messages, response time, security mechanisms and legal issues. Numerous documents have the sole function to confirm the receipt of another document and to specify the response (e.g., *when* will *which goods* be delivered *to where*?) Most of the confirmations are superfluous and can be turned into exception messages once the parties have agreed on response patterns. However, given the different regulatory frameworks and types of customers, the interchange agreements have to be kept customizable to different organizational and regulatory needs. One size does not fit all.

(2) The semantic level: Product identification

A unified product identification facilitates the coordination along the supply chain. Bar codes enable the usage of scanners that are linked to inventory control systems. However, the requirements vary among the participants, e.g., whether the bar code should be attached to a single item or to a box or other shipment units. In some cases they are subject to governmental regulations, i.e., they are due to the admission statements of the national drug agencies for particular product identifications.

In our case, the customer prints and attaches bar codes that contain the detailed information for inventory management and control, and uses scanners on various stages of the internal delivery process. For the customer, a clear benefit would be if the suppliers could attach the labels beforehand. Given the fragmented structure of the industry, a solution like this is only acceptable and viable if the same type of bar codes are used throughout the industry, ideally on an international basis.

In medical diagnostics, the required adaptations on all sides are considerable; the suppliers are hesitant to cover the extra cost of labeling their products unless they recognize a consensus of their customers in terms of need for bar coding and the type of bar codes. Such a consensus seems unlikely in a situation where, even within Europe, different types of bar code standards exist.

(3) The syntactic level: EDI messages

Numerous publications and empirical examples show the benefits of EDI message exchange along the supply chain, such as speed of message exchange and processing, administrative cost reductions and quality improvements (Heijden, 1995; Mukhopadhyay, 1995).

We have proposed an exchange of EDIFACT messages along the supply chain. Only a reduced set of messages is required if an interchange agreement, that specifies the obligations and response patterns of the trading partners, can be reached. Even though the frequency of exchanged messages is relatively low, the process coordination can be improved, and related processes like the procurement of other medical supplies on the customer side can be covered as well. However, only if the various players succeed in agreeing on standardized solutions will they be able to reap the benefits of the EDI-installations.

The benefits of introducing EDI reflect the rationale of BPR. They depend on the scale, i.e., the number of trading partners that use EDI; the scope of its usage, i.e., the number of related application areas that can be covered (Ebers, 1992); the coverage of the entire process, i.e,. all process steps from the offer to the invoice, or even payment, are covered by EDI messages so that automatic control procedures can be established (Cathomen, Klein and Kuhn, 1995); the level of integration into internal processes; and the centrality of the underlying application (Cox and Ghoneim, 1994).

(4) Interdependencies among the organizational and technical measures

The three considered measures are highly interdependent: the introduction of EDI presupposes the usage of standardized product codes and an interchange agreement. Although it might enhance the complexity of an EDI introduction, it is advisable to scrutinize the related processes first and not simply *EDIfy* the paper-based message exchange.

The choice and content of the bar codes depend on the application areas and related IS, e.g., databases that match external product codes with internal codes for storage, etc. The design of interchange agreements is related to technical issues like the introduction of EDI. Even beyond objective procedural interdependencies, the parties will establish a linkage between different measures in order to balance gains and compromises in the negotiations.

(5) Individual and systemic benefits

The various players look for their own benefits, which in cases of interdependency can only be achieved through mutual agreement on the necessary changes as well as on the division of costs and benefits (see Table 4). Axelrod (1984) shows the superiority of a 'Tit for Tat' strategy in a non-zero-sum situation. In addition to an evaluation of the individual costs and benefits, we have tried to appraise the systemic benefits, i.e., the net benefits of the process improvements.

While this step has emphasized ioBPR with a focus on the vertical supply chain, we have shown that the overall benefits that can be gained depend on extending the solution in two directions:
* internally, the achievable benefits depend on an enhanced procedural and technical integration (BPR), and
* externally, an industry solution is imperative in order to reach the critical mass which is indispensable to ensure efficient and sustainable solutions (BNR).

Table 4. The evaluation of proposed changes from different perspectives, costs are indicated by italic types

Appraisal / Changes	Supplier	Intermediary	Customer	Systemic
Interchange agreements specifying lead times for orders and delivery notes	*Contracting cost,* order lead time	*Contracting cost,* lead time, opportunity to consolidate shipments	*Contracting cost,* advance information about physical delivery, transparency, influence on delivery time and mode	Win - win situation as long as contractual obligations are met, trust building
Bar-coding	*Standardization cost, system investment and additional operational cost,* competitive necessity	*System investment,* beneficial for inventory control and delivery process	*Adaptations to supplier system,* beneficial for inventory control	Depends on the diffusion of bar code-based inventory systems
EDIFACT	*Standardization cost, system investment,* benefit depends on internal integration and volume of transactions, application in non-core area, competitive necessity	*System investment,* benefit depends on number of communication partners on the shipper and consignee side, volume of transactions & internal integration, application in core area	*Standardization cost, system investment,* benefit depends on volume of transactions and internal integration	Closing the cycle and gaining a high proportion of EDI exchange depends on the diffusion of EDI-based systems throughout the industry (economies of scale and scope)

The rationale behind the involvement in an ioBPR project with a limited number of partners is to develop solutions for electronic linkages between suppliers and customers that have the potential to become industry-wide solutions. A kernel of innovative industry players (early movers) may be able to initiate a process which leads to the development of an industry solution.

Within our project, we have tried to initiate the design of an industry solution with a core group of industry players and customer representatives.

Second-order change: BNR scenarios

While the proposed measures contribute to a significant simplification of existing organizational routines, more profound changes in the distribution structure may be necessary to improve the inter-organizational coordination even further and to reduce redundancies in the process. This step aims at the development of alternative scenarios which depict new roles and linkages for the players ([Kambil and Short, 1994, for different levels of organizational interconnectivity see also Clark and Schiano, 1996).

The scope of scenarios covers different types of governance structures among the players, from vertical outsourcing to horizontal partnerships, and the degree of mediation affected by the introduction of new roles, such as distributors (Teng, Grover and Fiedler, 1994 focus their analysis on the degree of mediation and the degree of collaboration). These options, even though they are focused on logistics, have significant implications on other functional areas like marketing and therefore have to be aligned with business strategy (see Figure 1).

(1) Outsourcing

As IT lowers the cost of control and coordination across the boundaries of companies, it facilitates the outsourcing of non-core functions to specialized service providers. [9, 18] The rationale for logistics outsourcing from the suppliers' point of view is to improve the efficiency of logistics.

RDS has outsourced their warehousing and distribution activities in Spain to BOMI and has established an EDI link for the exchange of shipment orders and for updates in the inventory database. Since this is a closely linked bilateral relationship, a proprietary solution has been implemented.

(2) Coordination among suppliers

On an organizational level, logistical coordination among the suppliers can yield considerable benefits:

* the customers would receive fewer, consolidated shipments;
* logistics costs for the supplier and eventually for the consignee could be reduced by increasing the scale of the shipments.

The given distribution structure with relatively few, small shipments warrants a coordinated solution. On a limited scale it is already in place since BOMI has succeeded to win several customers within the diagnostics industry. Beyond that, the existing distribution systems are so different that a compromise is difficult to reach.

(3) Regional partnership among customers

A partnership among customers (hospitals/laboratories) could improve the bargaining power in relation to the suppliers (procurement alliance) and/ or improve the scale and efficiency of logistical operations. As size and scale of operations are critical factors for the efficiency of hospital procurement operations, several hospitals in a region could join to run a regional warehouse. Pooled operations would justify investments in EDI solutions that would link the hospitals to the warehouse and the warehouse to the suppliers (or logistics companies).

Again, the main issues are whether consensus can be reached among the hospitals, which have a limited scope of action due to regulation, and whether the potential benefits of pooling can be realized.

(4) New roles - new players

While (2) and (3) focus on different ways to achieve consolidation and scale economies throughout the supply chain, a new intermediary like a distributor might also provide this function. Distributors or wholesalers are part of the supply chain in pharmaceuticals and apart from warehousing functions, they possibly take over customer order management.

The diagnostics industry currently tries to avoid the establishment of distributors as they fear the loss of the direct contact with their customers and the power that is often exerted by distributors.

(5) Industry solutions

Most of the sketched scenarios require either a contractual arrangement among a limited group of industry players ((3) and (4)) or an even broader consensus in terms of EDI and product identification standards. However, one has to bear in mind that even EDI solutions require bilateral agreements among the trading partners.

Figure 1. Distribution chain and options for cooperation

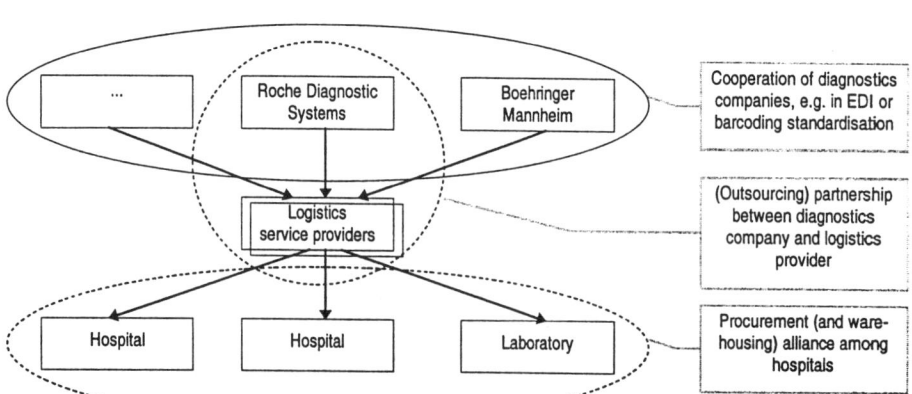

As for now, it is not clear, whether the pressure of the market is sufficient to motivate the suppliers to develop the required standards or whether groups of customers will be powerful enough to convince the suppliers to do so.

Synopsis

Table 5 gives a synopsis of the described analysis steps which comprise strategic, organizational and technical issues. During the different steps the perspective is broadened from an individual to an industry scope.

CONCLUSIONS

This chapter explores the interrelationship between organizational changes and the initiation of EDI linkages.

Table 5. Organizational and technical scope of the steps of change process

Steps	Organizational scope	Technical scope
1 Contingency analysis		
1.1 industry structure	Fragmentation, competition	Usage of IOS in the industry
1.2 inter-organizational relationship	Interdependence, power, trust	Governance of IOS
1.3 process and technology	Efficiency, intensity of interaction	EDI applications in related areas, existing standards that can be (re-)used, IS with external interfaces or process linkages, level of IS support for operations
1.4 competencies	Strategic evaluation of business segments and functions	Technical competence
2 Requirements engineering		
2.1 Individual analysis	Identification of processes and their relevant contexts, process modeling and analysis	External interfaces, links to internal systems such as order management or inventory control
2.2 Participatory requirements analysis	Inter-organizational process modeling and analysis, key benefit areas	Specification of technical requirements
3 Identification and evaluation of alternative scenarios		
3.1 First-order changes: ioBPR	Interchange agreements, evaluation of the systemic and the individual process improvements, impact on internal processes (BPR)	Improved informational representation of supply chain: bar-coding, EDIFACT, preconditions of EDI benefits, standardization on industry level required
3.2 Second-order changes: BNR	Scenarios related to coordination strategy: structural changes along the supply chain (outsourcing and intermediation), models of horizontal cooperation	Standardization issues

(1) The case

The case illustrates the preconditions and obstacles of implementing EDI. It underscores the different, often conflicting perspectives, needs and interests of the trading partners in a supply chain. However, major individual as well as systemic benefits can be identified through participatory requirements analysis. The introduction of EDI is thus primarily motivated and driven by organizational changes and it becomes embedded into a broader framework of inter-organizational arrangements, in this case improvements in the supply chain. An isolated assessment of EDI in this case would not yield a sufficient rationale for its introduction.

(2) BPR, ioBPR, BNR and EDI

We propose a distinction between BPR, ioBPR and BNR, because each approach has a different focus on EDI and its implications (cf. Table 1). BPR and ioBPR aim at internal or inter-organizational processes, while BNR focuses on the entire value or supply chain and discusses changes of roles and governance structures among trading partners. Moreover the combination of organizational and technological changes on several levels requires dynamic adaptations: new organizational models require, e.g., intensified communication among business partners, the subsequent use of IT enables further organizational adaptations.

(3) Framework for business transformation

The framework for business transformation underscores the complexity of inter-organizational changes. It integrates the different redesign approaches and perspectives into a comprehensive analysis and change process, and reveals thus the interdependencies between BPR, ioBPR and BNR.

Procedural and structural adaptations within the supply chain and in some instances even among a group of industry players are prerequisites for an efficient integration of EDI into the internal information systems as well as into existing procedures. If no consensus can be achieved within the industry, efficiency gains through EDI are lost by the multiplicity of arrangements and processes that have to be maintained for different business partners.

Because of the different scopes of changes, individual, participatory and systemic benefits have to be taken into account and aligned with each other.

The industry structure, i.e., the degree of fragmentation, intensity of competition, product characteristics as well as procedural arrangements and regulations, has a strong influence on the viability of improvements. Because of different national and regional healthcare regulations, any standardized solution also has to be adaptable and customizable.

Since there are different areas and levels of agreement that need to be achieved, the management of the change process becomes increasingly complex. The number and background of participants varies and with them the mandate of the representatives. In most cases, the process manager has no sufficient formal mandate. The analysis emphasizes the specific challenges for the management of inter-organizational redesign projects where sources of power have to be found which are different from traditional hierarchies. It thus explains at least indirectly why EDI has not spread further: the perceived benefits of EDI are not sufficient to justify the complexity of the change process and to overcome conflicts of interest. Process improvements might help to justify the effort, they add however at the same time considerable complexity and diversity of interests among potential EDI partners.

EPILOG

The core of this chapter has been published in the *International Journal of Electronic Commerce,* (Vol. 2, No. 1, 1997, pp. 25-44). Since then, our message that the introduction of EDI should be coupled to an analysis on the interorganizational and the network level has been confirmed in many ways: the proliferation of the Internet and specifically the World Wide Web (WWW) has highlighted the need and has provided a low-cost technical infrastructure to set-up business networks and to streamline supply chains as well as distribution chains (Peterson et al., 2000). Different approaches have been suggested to design business networks and interorganizational systems: Österle et al. (2000) have suggested a method for the design of business networks which covers vision, business models and technologies as well as the design of interorganizational processes. Gaugler (2000) takes an information management perspective on designing interorganizational systems and scrutinizes the effects of IOS on business relations and governance structures.

While this is true for almost any industry, the healthcare sector requires special attention as it is highly regulated and in many countries a mixed system of public and private institutions. Technology, combined with economic pressures, is intensifying structural changes in healthcare.

On the one side, the models of division of labor in the primary healthcare areas are revised and internal processes in hospitals are streamlined (Gförer, Raup and Schober, 2000; Heinzl and Güttler, 2000). Technology is facilitating a trend of specialization in medical knowledge and expertise, which as high-tech telemedicine or via the Web can be made available at remote locations, be it the household or remote medical facilities. The number and breadth of medical Web sites give clear evidence of the appropriation of a new technology in an industry. Despite all shortcomings and risks of online medicine, thousands of patients have become empowered in their pursuit of health and many times have found tangible help over the Web. A new role is that which in other areas is referred to as prosumer, i.e., a consumer who takes an active role in defining or even producing products and services.

On the other side, the trend towards outsourcing and other contractual arrangements which affect procurement and materials management is increasing. Projects are under way which mimic the idea of demand pooling which has become popular and successful in the retail consumer goods segment (see, e.g., http://www.letsbuyit.com): hospitals are joining forces to improve the efficiency and bargaining power in their procurement activities.

The discussion about dis-, re- or cybermediation reemphasizes the idea of business network redesign. Again, technology provides business opportunities and has led to the invention and emergence of new business models to create and add value. In many industries, cybermediaries or infomediaries have mushroomed which claim to act as the customers' agents and provide services like information retrieval, online consulting, price and product comparisons, privacy protection and efficiency in electronic transactions. The full extent to which this will affect the healthcare sector will only become apparent once the cautious steps to deregulate and open national healthcare systems will take place. The Commission of the European Union is carefully moving towards a European healthcare market which will, especially for pharmaceuticals, diagnostics products and replenishables, in the short term provide arbitrage opportunities and in the long term will diminish the opportunities for price discrimination.

In the 1980s and early 1990s, the introduction of EDI required huge efforts to create an (international) communication infrastructure which facilitated the (varying) needs of the networked business partners (More and McGrath (2000) give an example of the subsequent transformation in healthcare in Australia). In a remarkable contrast, the WWW has since then emerged as an affordable and powerful infrastructure for information exchange in the healthcare sector. EDIFACT is still the only global message (syntax) standard, however, it is increasingly implemented in the extensible markup language (XML, see http://www.xmledi.com) or even substituted XML-based forms or messages which are being developed by industry consortia.

Altogether, the linkage between IS and healthcare is drawing more and more attention in either field and we are expecting profound, IT-initiated, facilitated enabled changes in the healthcare sector.

REFERENCES

Axelrod, R. (1984) *The Evolution of Cooperation.* New York: Basic Books.

Bakos, J. Y. and Brynjolfsson, E. (1993) Why information technology hasn't increased the optimal number of suppliers. Nunamaker, J. F. and Sprague R. H. (Eds.) *Proceedings of the 26th HICSS*, Vol. IV: Collaboration Technology and Organizational Systems & Technology. Los Alamitos, CA: IEEE Computer Society Press, 1993, 799-808.

Benjamin, R. I., DeLong, D. W., and Scott Morton, M. S. "Electronic Data Interchange - How Much Competitive Advantage. *Long Range Planning*, 23 (1), 1990, 29-40.

Bensaou, B. M. (1993) "Inter-organizational Cooperation: The Role of Information Technology: An Empirical Comparison of U.S. and Japanese Supplier Relations. DeGross, J. I., Bostrom, R. P. and Robey, D. (Eds.) *Proceedings of the 14th ICIS*. Orlando, FL, 117-127.

Cathomen, I., Klein, S. and Kuhn, C. (1995) *Partizipative Anforderungsanalyse und Perspektiven des Netzwerkredesign am Beispiel der EDI-gestützten Abwicklung von Speditionsaufträgen,* Arbeitsbericht 24 des Kompetenzzentrums Elektronische Märkte am Institut für Wirtschaftsinformatik der Hochschule St. Gallen, April.

Cavaye, A. L. M. and Cragg, P. B. (1994) *"User Participation in the Development of Inter-Organizational Systems."* Baets, W. R. J. (Ed.): *Proceedings of the Second European Conference on Information Systems.* Breukelen: Nijenrode University Press, 655-675.

Clark, T. H. and Schiano, W. T. (1996) "Seven levels of inter-organizational connectivity: An examination of the U.S. grocery distribution channel." Nunamaker, J. F. and Sprague R. H. (Eds.): *Proceedings of the 29th HICSS*, Vol. IV: Information Systems Organizational Systems and Technology. Los Alamitos, CA: IEEE Computer Society Press.

Clark, T. H. and Stoddard, D. B. (1996) Inter-organizational business process redesign: Merging technological and process innovation. Nunamaker, J. F. and Sprague R. H. (Eds.): *Proceedings of the 29th HICSS*, Vol. IV: Information Systems - Organizational Systems and Technology. Los Alamitos, CA: IEEE Computer Society Press.

Clemons, E. K. and Reddi, S. P. (1994) "The impact of I.T. on the degree of outsourcing, the number of suppliers, and the duration of contracts." Nunamaker, J. F. and Sprague R. H. (Eds.): *Proceedings of the 27th HICSS*, Vol. IV: Collaboration Technology, Organizational Systems and Technology. Los Alamitos, CA: IEEE Computer Society Press, 855-864.

Cox, B. and Ghoneim, S. (1994) "Benefits and barriers to adopting EDI in the UK - A sector survey of british industries." Baets, W. R. J. (Ed.): *Proceedings of the Second European Conference on Information Systems.* Breukelen: Nijenrode University Press, 643-653.

Davenport, T. H. and Short, J. E. (1990) "The new industrial engineering: information technology and business process redesign". *Sloan Management Review*, 31(1), 11-27.

Davidson, W. H. (1993) "Beyond re-engineering: The three phases of business transformation." *IBM Systems Journal*, 32 (1), 65-79.

Earl, M. J. (1994) "The new and the old of business process redesign." *Journal for Strategic Information Systems*, 3 (1), 5-22.

Ebers, M. (1992) "Transaction scale and scope: How organizations get hooked on inter-organizational systems." *Paper prepared for the ESF Planning Workshop*, May.

Emmelhainz, M. A. (1978) *The Impact of Electronic Data Interchange on the Purchasing Process.* Working Paper 87-3, The University of Dayton, School of Business Administration, The Center for Business and Economic Research, February.

Emmelhainz, M. A. (1993) *Electronic Data Interchange - A Total Management Guide.* New York: Van Nostrand Reinhold.

Fisher, R. and Ury, W. (1981) *Getting to Yes - Negotiating Agreement Without Giving In.* Boston.

Fitzgerald, G. and Willcocks, L. (1994) "Relationships in outsourcing: Contracts and partnerships." In: Baets, Walter R.J. (Ed.): *Proceedings of the Second European Conference on Information Systems.* Breukelen: Nijenrode University Press, 51-63.

Gaugler, T. "Interorganisatorische informationssysteme" Wiesbaden: DUV, 2000.

Gförer, S. G.; Raupp, M. and Schober, F. (2000) "Restructuring the german outpatient healthcare system: An economic and IT perspective" Hansen, H. et al. (Ed.): *Proceedings of the 8th ECIS*, Vienna, 1261-1268

Heinzl, A. and Güttler, W. (2000) IT induced healthcare reconfiguration: German hospitals in transition" Hansen, H. et al. (Ed.): *Proceedings of the 8th ECIS*, Vienna, 1237-1244.

Heijden, H. G. M. van der (1995) *"Towards Organizational Redesign in EDI Partnerships."* Delft: Eburon.

Hess, T. and Brecht, L. (1995) *"State of the Art des Business Process Redesign."* Wiesbaden: Gabler.

Holland, C. P. and Lockett, G. (1994) "Strategic choice and inter-organisational information systems." Nunamaker, J. F. and Sprague R. H. (Eds.): *Proceedings of the 27th HICSS*, Vol. IV: Collaboration Technology, Organizational Systems and Technology. Los Alamitos, CA: IEEE Computer Society Press, 405-413.

Kambil, A. and Short, J. (1994) "Electronic Integration and Business Network Redesign - A Roles-Linkage Perspective." *Journal for Management Information Systems*, 10(4), 59-83.

Klein, S. (1996) *Unternehmungsnetzwerke und Inter-organizationssysteme - Organizatorische Und Technische Wechselwirkungen*, Gabler: Wiesbaden.

Klein, S. (1996) "The configuration of inter-organizational relations." *European Journal on Information Systems*, 5 (5), 92-102.

Konsynski, B. R. (1993) "Strategic control in the extended enterprise." *IBM Systems Journal*, 32 (1), 111-142.

Kubicek, H. (1992) "The Organization Gap in Large EDI Systems." Streng, R., Ekering, C.; Heck, E. V. (Eds.): *Scientific Research on EDI*. Samson Publishers: Alphen aan den Rijn.

More, E. and McGrath, G. M. (2000) "Transforming healthcare in Australia: The PeCC initiative" Hansen, H. et al. (Ed.): *Proceedings of the 8th ECIS*, Vienna, 1219-1226.

Mukhopadhyay, T., Kekre, S. and Kalathur, S. (1995) "Business Value of Information Technology: a Study on Electronic Data Interchange." *MIS Quarterly*, 19(139).

Österle, H.; Fleisch, E. and Alt, R. (2000) "Business Networking - Shaping Enterprise Relationships on the Internet ,, Berlin et al.: Springer.

Peterson, R.R.; Smits, M. and Spanjers, R. (2000) "Exploring IT-enabled networked organisations in healthcare: Emerging practices and phases of development" Hansen, H. et al. (Ed.): *Proceedings of the 8th ECIS*, Vienna, 1253-1260.

Reekers, N. and Smithson, S. (1995) "The impact of electronic data interchange on inter-organizational relationships: Integrating theoretical perspectives." Nunamaker, Jay F.; Sprague Ralph H. (eds.): *Proceedings of the 28th HICSS*, Vol. IV: Collaboration Technology and Organizational Systems & Technology. Los Alamitos, CA: IEEE Computer Society Press, 757-766.

Riggins, F. J.; Mukhopadhyay, T. (1994) "Interdependent benefits from interorganizational systems - Opportunities for business partner reengineering." *Journal for Management Information Systems*, 11(2), 37-57.

Rockart, J. F.; Short, J. E. (1991) "The networked organization and the management of interdependence." Scott Morton, M. S. (Ed.): *The Corporation of the 1990s - Information Technology and Organizational Transformation*. New York; Oxford: Oxford University Press, 189-219.

Sabel, Charles F. (1994) "Learning by monitoring: The institutions of economic development." Smelser, N. and Swedberg, R. (Eds.): *Handbook of Economic Sociology*. Princeton NJ.

Sokol, P. K. (1989) *EDI - The Competitive Edge*, New York.

Swatman, P. M.C. and Swatman, P. A. (1993) "Business process redesign using EDI - An Australian success story." Gricar, J.; Novak, J. (Eds.): *Strategic Systems in the Global Economy of the 90s*, Proceedings of the EDI & IOS Conference. Bled, 116-137.

Swatman, P. M.C., Swatman, P. A. and Fowler, D. C. (1994) *"A model of EDI integration and strategic business reengineering." Journal for Strategic Information Systems*, 3(1), 41-60.

Teng, J. T. C., Grover, V. and Fiedler, K. D. (1994) Business process reengineering: Charting a strategic path for the information age." *California Management Review*, 36(3), 9-31.

Venkatraman, N. (1991) "IT-induced business reconfiguration." Scott Morton, M. S. (Ed.): *The Corporation of the 1990s - Information Technology and Organizational Transformation*. New York; Oxford: Oxford University Press, 122-158.

Venkatraman, N. (1994) IT-enabled business transformation - From automation to business scope redefinition." *Sloan Management Review*, 35 (2), 73-87.

Wagenaar, R. W. and Heijden, H. G.M. van der (1994) EDI induced business redesign - A modeling approach towards improved intercompany coordination." Till, R. (Ed.): *Proceedings of the 5th World Congress of EDI Users* (Scientific Track). Brighton, June, 1-11.

Webster, J. (1995) "Networks of collaboration and conflict? Electronic data interchange and power in the supply chain," *Journal for Strategic Information Systems*, 4 (1), 31-42.

ENDNOTE

* An earlier version of this chapter has been published: Klein, Stefan and Schad, Heike. (1997). "The introduction of EDI systems in healthcare supply chains: A framework for business transformation." *International Journal of Electronic Commerce*, 2(1), 25-44 (reprinted by permission from M.E. Sharpe, Inc., Armonk, NY 10504).

Chapter VIII

Telecommunications as a Medicine for General Practitioners

Peter J.B. Lagendijk, Roel W. Schuring and Ton A.M. Spil
University of Twente, The Netherlands

The Internet is suffering from a continuous explosion of users, yet Internet communication in the healthcare chain is still on a low level. Most institutions that should be working together keep their information "for the patient's sake" in the house. This research studies the workflow that is concerned with the status of the patient in the healthcare chain. The functional integration of all healthcare chain components is an objective that might be utopia, but electronic prescription and electronic medical record combined with the strong communication facilities create many possibilities to put a step into the right direction. Communication is a strong weapon for the strategic use of information systems. Although at this moment most of the patient information is transmitted by paper or by phone, the near future will show the introduction of the e-life of the patient. Main results of the first phase of this study is that general practitioners should not be seduced with money and quality aspects to improve their information systems. What they need is a reduction of time pressure and means to communicate with the environment.

INTRODUCTION

The price of medicines used to inflate at a rate of 5% every year, but the last three years this percentage has gone up to 12% (Ankone, 2000). This means that this money (for the Netherlands alone more than half a billion dollars) cannot be spent on healthcare activities with a higher priority. Drug prescription is one of the most common tasks in the general practitioner's (GP's) office. Every year 610 million prescriptions (in Germany) are issued on paper, brought to pharmacy on paper and scanned at high expanse for the purpose of accounting, although 60% of the doctors are able to produce a prescription electronically (Wetter, 2000). In the USA it is estimated that there are potential savings of $36 billion annually from improving the methods by which medical providers and payers exchange data (Weinstein & Worman, 2000). The revenue from the electronic prescription system project should be $150 million a year (VWS, 1998) in the Netherlands from the year 2002.

Physicians no longer seem to have the attitude that computers will dehumanize care. They are positive about using information systems to access up-to-date knowledge, for continual medical education, for access to healthcare in remote and rural areas, for the quality of patient care and for the interactions within a healthcare team (Paré & Elam, 1999). Still many authors state that the behavior of physicians should change to make use of information systems effectively.

Information technology is pushing and transforming the way healthcare is delivered. Bergeron and Bailin (1999) give a good overview of technology-enabled evolutionary change but conclude that information technology is rarely the driving force for change. IT can serve as a change agent or enabler for those who are trying to improve upon existing processes. The quality of information systems in healthcare organizations seems troublesome. The systems, though technically correct and reliable, are not user friendly and are not integrated.

There is a lack of research on the use of formularies by Dutch general practitioners. There is an indication that information systems can support prescribing of medicines and laboratory requests (Althuis & Rikken, 2000). A study in the United Kingdom showed that the electronic prescription system "PRODIGY" is successful in altering prescribing behavior. The system needs to be further studied with a preferably large randomly selected group of practices (Sowerby Centre, 1998).

This chapter reflects research in progress that studies the workflow concerned with the patient. We studied how to enable positive change in healthcare with the use of information technology. First, an overview is given of the real life of a patient from the moment he or she starts having a complaint till the moment the patient is cured or deceased. The success of an information system is dependent on four variables (Saarinen & Saaksjarvi, 1992): success of the development process; success of the use process; quality of the IS product; impact of the IS on the organization. This chapter combines quality aspects of information systems and the innovation of technology literature to build a model of system success. This model is operationalized in the healthcare situation. The same model indicates that the resistance criteria in the healthcare organizations are of major importance to the success or failure of a new application. For the electronic prescription system, these criteria are elaborated.

RESEARCH METHOD

This research is in the process of analyzing the effectiveness of the electronic prescription system at the general practitioners' practice in the Netherlands. In a broader context as described in the section "the Real Life of the Patient," Twente University hopes to deliver a standardization description of all information transfers about the patient in the healthcare chain. These descriptions have to live up to standards that are already available in the healthcare organizations like diagnostic treatment combinations, HL7 (health level seven, a healthcare communication standard) and all quality standards applied.

The study describes the healthcare chain, first in a global way in the next section. We've chosen to deliver these standards on a regional level of three hospitals with their peripheral institutions.

To indicate the current problem we observe a practical case study in The Netherlands. The case we are observing is called the Electronic Prescription Support System (EPS). It is observed from the viewpoint of the patient as close to the primary process as possible. The overall aim of the system is to finally improve the quality of care, by supporting the decision of the general practitioner in prescribing (non-) medicamental treatment to the patient. The system will give support by giving opportunities for prescribing less and cheaper drugs with the needed quality, or no drugs at all. When we look at the model of the information-flows (see Figure 1) in the primary healthcare process, we conclude that the EPS system tries to support the input of external information (as a support or confirmation of the diagnosis) and tries to support the decision for the needed treatment.

REAL LIFE OF A PATIENT

It seems that the primary healthcare process will not work without the right information. The logical question you ask is, *What* information is needed to fulfil the process. Therefore we tried to get a clear view at the process and then combine the process with the needed information.

We have chosen to look at the information-flow through the eyes of a patient. To identify the several information-flows, it is necessary to describe the primary healthcare process. In this process every step has to do with an information-flow. In this process you can describe several dimensions. First there are three main parties within the process: the patient, the general practitioner and the healthcare specialist. The process starts at the moment a patient has a complaint and knocks at the door of his general practitioner. It ends with a treated patient. This does not necessarily mean that the patient will be healthy after the treatment. Aside from the healthcare specialist and the general practitioner, there is a person that will do the treatment (for instance a physiotherapist). The person will make his own (sub-) diagnosis and so will decide what concrete exercises will be done. Then there is the source of information needed to make or review the diagnosis. This can be the personal information from the physician, or the knowledge from other physicians. It is also possible to get information out of specific examination (for instance x-ray or blood tests) or decision support systems. Finally the diagnosis will result in a specific solution for the patient's complaint. This will be a mixture of the elements 'do nothing,' a medicine prescription, a specific treatment and a clinical treatment procedure. The steps that can be made are shown in Figure 1. Every arrow stands for a specific information-flow. The flows are randomly numbered.

After describing the primary process, it is now interesting to look at what information-flows are needed to establish the steps of the primary healthcare process. In total there are 14 specific information-flows shown in Figure 1. After shortly describing each flow below, we have picked the specific information-flows related with the EPS, to observe in more detail.

1. *Patient input.* At several points in the healthcare chain, the patient needs to give input. Aside from his personal information, he needs to specify his complaint.
2. *Describe the diagnosis.* At several steps in the healthcare process, physicians have to make a diagnosis. The diagnosis will be a source of information in the rest of the healthcare process.
3. *Referral-letter.* From general practitioner to specialist. When the general practitioner thinks (after making the diagnosis) that he can't handle the problem, he can decide to refer the patient to a specialist who *can* help the patient. To make this referral, he has to write a personal letter to the specific specialist.
4. *Examination request.* When an examination is needed, a request has to be sent. Most of the time a third party will do the examination (for instance making x-ray photographs or examining the blood).
5. *Examination result.* After the examination is accomplished, the results have

Figure 1: The Real Life

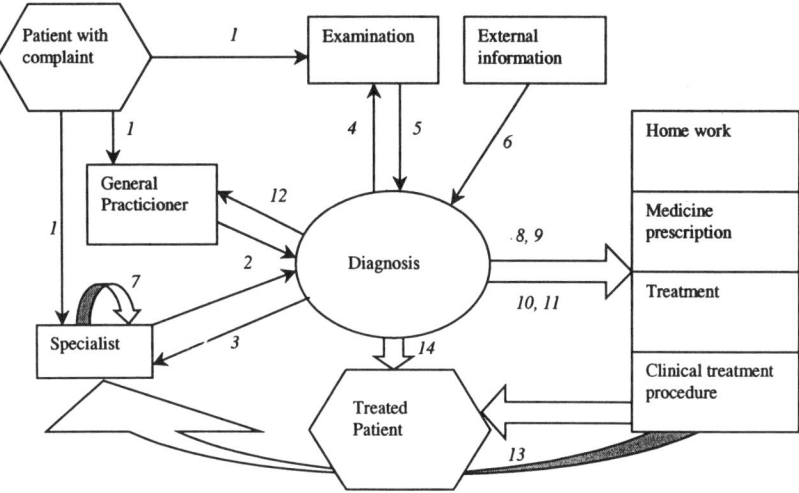

to be sent back to the person who requested it.
6. *Input from external information.* A method to take away all the doubt while making a diagnosis is the use of external information.
7. *Referral from specialist to specialist.* There are several diseases that aren't very simple to cure. In those cases most of the time there are more kinds of specialists needed (like for a bone-fracture that damaged one of the lungs).
8. *Non-medicamental homework for a patient.* When a physician has made his diagnosis, he can choose to prescribe a relatively simple solution that can be done at home (like doing exercises).
9. *Medicamental prescription.* When a physician decides to let the patient use a drug, he has to write out a drug prescription.
10. *Request for non-medicamental treatment.* One of the possible solutions to a patient's disease can be a specific treatment (for instance a plaster cast as a treatment for a bone-fracture). When the physician can't do the treatment himself, he has to request an institution or department to accomplish the specific treatment.
11. *Request for clinical treatment.* Like the request for a 'normal' treatment, there can also be a request for a clinical treatment. The difference is the receiver of the request and the content of the request. The patient has to be hospitalized.
12. *Feedback to general practitioner.* At several steps in the primary process, the general practitioner has to receive feedback about the status of his patient.
13. *Result from treatment.* It is possible that the result from a treatment procedure can be given to the patient himself. In another case the result will be presented to the specialist without informing the patient.
14. *Feedback to the patient.* Finally the patient will have feedback during the primary process. This can be information about the complaints, information about examinations or the treatment, but can also be the message that he is cured (or not). The information-flow will always come from the physician (the general practitioner or the specialist).

Information technology in the health care has done its successful work at business-related support systems in healthcare (like financial, logistic or administrative systems). At this moment the healthcare sector is trying to integrate the information and communication technology within the primary healthcare process. Many individual initiatives are already developed. It seems a problem to implement, apply and finally use the system at the operational level. This is because of a lack of standardization between information-flows. We first want to investigate the IT-possibilities in the individual information-flows with the aspect of standardization in mind.

DETERMINANTS OF IS SUCCESS

The three-level distinction, pragmatic, semantic and syntactic, is quite common in the information science literature (Iivari & Koskela, 1987), but in our opinion these three levels do not grasp the whole information concept. Iivari and Koskela (1987) give a good set of quality norms for each level. On the pragmatic level they state that quality should be a normal management judgement and that effectiveness is only a general term to be filled in specifically for the information system. However, the way they present this (economical, social, political, organizational, and technical) can span all quality-aspects. On the semantic level they give user satisfaction as quality criteria. On the syntactic level they give efficiency criteria to measure the quality of the information system.

The semiotic framework (Liu, 1993) is more precise. A social level is introduced because it is only when a social effect is obtained that information realizes any actual value and it must be remembered that the intentions of the information provider will not always lead (intentionally or not) to the desired effect. At the other side of the framework, the IT platform is more than simply a question of form. We should take into account communication channels, technical devices and people--these are the empirical level and the physical level.

When we regard the IT platform as a whole (physical/empirical and syntactical) then we can state that there are four determinants for the success of an information system (Spil, 1996), namely:
1. resistance on the social level;
2. relevance on the pragmatic level;
3. requirements on the semantic level;
4. resources on the syntactical, empiric and physical level.

On the social level, defining the resistance determinant can assess change.

Resistance is the negative attitude of all stakeholder groups towards the introduction of an information system. The main IS-quality aspect of resistance is the attitude and the willingness to change. Pare and Elam (1999) also choose for the attitude of the professional when they assess clinical information systems. Total quality management taught us that for this aspect, we have to deal with communication, information and deliberation. The end-users have an important role because their norms and values determine the effectiveness of the information system.

On the pragmatic level, the *relevance* determinant is defined to measure whether the provider-intention is the same as the user-interpretation (Sperber & Wilson, 1986). *Relevance is the comparison between the IS-specialists' intentions with the information system and the interpretations of end-user groups.* As main providers, we identify the suppliers and the national representative organizations of the GPs.

On the semantic level, the *requirements* determinant has to measure the meaning of the SISP system. *Requirements are the functional specifications that establish what the information system in a functional sense has to arrange.*

Resources are the people, the information technology, the money and the information needed and the interaction of these four elements for both developing and implementing the information system. The main focus of the quality determinant resources will be on the people and on the costs these people cause. Next to that the reliability of the information technology and the information systems are

Figure 2. The success factors of healthcare information systems

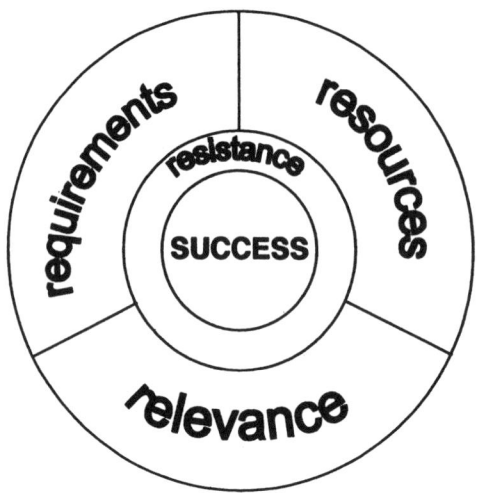

considered.

Due to the limitations of the research at this stage, we will not discuss the elements requirements and resources that can affect the attitude of end-users. We presume that it is technically possible to make a user-friendly system that will satisfy the demand, and that it is possible that the content has enough (clinical) quality so it won't be a bottleneck for the acceptance of the new formula of information-flow. For the research has left the environmental and the organization aspects that can influence the attitude, hence the acceptance of change. This chapter will concentrate on the relevance and the resistance determinants. To determine them in the EPS case, we need a more practical description of both determinants:

Relevance (Shepherd, 2000):
1. contain costs;
2. improve quality;
3. establish evidence-based medicine;
4. embrace consumerism.

Resistance (Spil, 1996):
1. fear of losing something worthwhile;
2. misunderstanding of the new situation;
3. belief that the new IS is worthless;
4. low tolerance of change.

E-LIFE

Currently, a technology push is trying to change the healthcare chain. Electronic medical dossiers have been made to collect and transmit all the necessary information about a patient's life. Information systems are developed for digitally archiving radiological files. Possibly for most of the information flows, there are some information systems available, but the application of the systems at the right place however will take years. The main question you can ask is what conditions are necessary to make specific elements of the technology push a success? After this question is answered, you can look at what elements of this technology push we can introduce in a paper-based healthcare organization.

In a case study we focus on just a small part of the e-life of the patient and that is from the moment a diagnosis is made by the general practitioner till the patient receives his or her (non-) medicamental prescription. In The Netherlands a national initiative of both the Dutch Association of General Practitioners (LHV) and the Dutch College of GPs (NHG) had to ensure that at the end of 2000 all general practitioners had to made effective use of an electronic prescription system. The University of Twente is asked to evaluate how the diffusion of this new system can be optimized.

The electronic prescription system (EPS) can be described as a decision support system for the general practitioners in making (non-) medical prescriptions, after the diagnosis is made. The aim of the system is to improve the quality of the prescriptions, to reduce the amount of steps to prescribe a drug and finally to lower the total annual drug-costs by reducing the number of drug-prescriptions and reducing the amount of drugs for one prescription.

In line with the described information-flows, the EPS will be an application that supports a part of the 'external knowledge' information-flow. The result from the EPS will subsequently influence the making of the drug-prescriptions.

To analyze this case we make (among other things) use of the diffusion theory of Rogers (1983). This is in combination with the elements, relevance and resistance.

User Characteristics

First we want to describe the environment wherein the EPS is applied. The two functions we are talking about are the use of external (static) knowledge for making the diagnosis and the final (drug-) prescription that is made. Without the EPS a general practitioner can use specific literature that can help him to analyze the patients' syndrome. All the knowledge of this literature is put into the EPS. This knowledge will not support the general practitioner in making the diagnosis, but it *can* support the general practitioner identifying contraindications. When the general practitioner enters a diagnosis, the system can propose a solution. Though the system can propose solutions that are non-drug-related, most of the time the solutions are drug-related. When a drug-prescription is made, the patient has to transport the prescription to the pharmacist so he can buy the needed drugs. Using this method neither the general practitioner nor the pharmacy can check whether the patient did buy and use the drug.

One of the most important characteristics is that the general practitioners do not mind in what proportions the drugs are prescribed. Their primary aim is to cure the patient. The result is that most of the time too much and too many drugs are prescribed. To decrease this problem, one of the goals of the EPS is that better proportions are prescribed.

Product Features

The electronic prescription system has its roots in standard (Dutch) literature for the general practitioner. It will give advice to the general practitioners in the Netherlands about:
- a non-medicine-based therapy,
- an indication for a medicine-based therapy,
- the set of considerations why to choose a specific medicine-based therapy.

Aside from the traditional method, the system can include several individual parameters (like age, gender or weight).

By prescribing drugs the following steps are taken:
1. the selection of the drug,
2. selection of the doses and frequency of use,
3. selection of the duration of the course.

The EPS launched a pilot in the end of the '90s. At 50 general practitioners, offices, the system was installed. It seemed that in 20% of the consultations, the system was used. In 80% of them times the general practitioners did follow the system's advice. It was shown that the use of the system leads to less and cheaper prescriptions because of the increased number of non-medicine-based prescriptions.

Communication Methods

The moment the EPS was introduced, the communication with the general practitioners was very important. The Dutch College of General Practitioners and the Dutch Association of General Practitioners have cooperated to tune the local information need from the general practitioners with the EPS. The general practitioners are using several information systems. It was possible to fit the EPS to the system already in use by making several versions. Furthermore, the Internet is used to communicate about the attitude of the general practitioners.

Relevance

Referring to Shepherd (2000), there has to be enough relevance to implement the proposed method of information-flow. One important element is the improvement of quality. In this case a system has to do more than create a specific information-flow. It has to improve the quality of the information-flow (or decrease the costs) *and* it has to improve the quality of care. The EPS tries to improve the quality of the information-flow by decreasing the amount of acts needed to prescribe a drug, and have information about complaints relatively quickly on the desk. It also tries to improve the quality of care by taking into account personal profiles in the prescribing process. Using actual, national authorized guidelines can also improve the quality of care.

Resistance

Though the EPS has profit on the quality of information-flow and quality of care, there will always be resistance of change from the end-user. In this case there are several reasons why the resistance can still be present:

- Every general practitioner has his private practice. When there are workflow methods introduced, there is the possibility that they want to work according to their own methods.
- The resistance can increase because a lot of general practitioners do not see the personal (short-term) benefit of the system. They rather see the profit of other shareholders like the assurance organizations and the ministry.
- The social attitude of people can have great impact in the resistance of change. Some of the general practitioners need a bigger push to accept the changes than other general practitioners. The costs saving can be not enough for some people to see the need of change.

At the moment all the general practitioners can freely implement the EPS system. Nevertheless the distribution and the use of EPS is disappointing. In practice it seems the EPS cannot give in to the needed personal benefits (gain of time and communication possibilities) of the general practitioner.

However all these issues can be the cause of misunderstanding and thus the inaccurate use of the new method of information-flow.

CONCLUSIONS

The relevance of an electronic prescription system to general practitioners can be lifted by reducing the time of consultation of the patient. This objective however is difficult to reach because the average consulting time is only about eight minutes. Only resources that are user friendly and quick can make a difference.

The resistance of general practitioners towards EPS stems mainly from a misunderstanding of the new system and a belief that the new system is worthless. In the first category the general practitioners are not yet ready for EPS because their level of automation is not yet high enough. In the second category general practitioners already have a satisfactory system or do not see their own benefit from the system. Improving the quality of the systems and supporting the general practitioners can get the automation level a step higher into the direction of EPS.

The objectives of the EPS implementation were to improve the quality of the general practitioners' practice and to lower the costs of medicine use in The Netherlands. These objectives have little or no relevance for the general practitioner because these subjects are not on his or her priority list. To improve the diffusion of EPS the objectives should change toward:

- reducing the time of a consult;
- improving the communication between general practitioners (especially desired when standing in for a colleague).

Telecommunication is high on the priority list of the general practitioner. The new electronic prescription system does not provide the practitioner with new communication possibilities. Our recommendation is that the diffusion of the new information system would improve if a telecommunication module will be offered and when the national organizations agree with a standard communication platform.

Conclusions from this work are that the technology push does not take the organizational needs into account. The assumption made in this chapter that we could ignore the requirement and resource success factors proves to be wrong. The next step therefore will be to investigate the quality of the information systems and the support given to general practitioners to use the resources given.

REFERENCES

Althuis, T. R. & Rikken, S. A. J. J. (2000) "Electronic support for general practitioners in prescribing drugs", *Health Information Developments in The Netherlands,* April, 62-66.

Ankone, A. (2000) "Tussen droom en daad, zin en onzin van FTTO en EVS"(in Dutch), *Medisch Contact*, March, 55(9), 308-311.

Bergeron, B. P. & Bailin, M. T. (1999) "Medical information technology: A vehicle for change," *International Journal of Healthcare Technology and Management*, 1(1), 29-45.

Hanseth, O. & Monteiro, E. (1998) "Changing irreversible networks: Institutionalisation and infrastructures," *Proceedings of the Sixth ECIS,* June, Aix en Provence, France.

Hanseth, O. & Lundberg, N. (1999) "Information Infrastructure in use", *Proceedings of the 22th IRIS Conference*, August, Keuruu, Finland, 1, 407-424.

Harmsen, J. (1997) "*Automatisering in de ziekenhuissector,* ",(in Dutch) NZI publication, ISBN 90-5376-314-7.

Iivari, J & Koskela, E (1987) "The PIOCO model for IS design", *MIS Quarterly,* September, pp400-417.

Lines, K. (1999) "MIS in local government health care organizations," *Proceedings of the 22th IRIS Conference*, August, Keuruu, Finland, 2, 337-348.

Liu, K. (1993) "Semiotics apllied to information systems development", PhD thesis, University of Twente, Enschede.

Pare, G. & Elam, J. J. (1999) "Physicians' acceptance of clinical information systems: an empirical look at attitudes expectations and skills," *International Journal of Healthcare Technology and Management*, 1(1), 46-61

Rogers, E. M. (1983) "*Diffusion of Innovations,*" The free press, New York.

Saarinen, T. & Saaksjarvi (1992) "Process and product success in information system development," *Journal of Strategic Information Systems,* **1**(5), 266-277.

Shepherd, S. G. (2000) " Integrated care pathways," *Electronic Proceedings of the E-health Europe Conference*, http://www.e-health-europe.com, Maastricht.

Sikkel, K, Spil, T. A. M., Weg, R. L. W. van de (1999) "A real world case in information technology for undergraduate students," *Journal of Systems and Software,* August, 1999.

Spil, T. A. M. (1996) *"The Effectiveness of Strategic Information Systems Planning in Professional Organizations,"* PhD Thesis, Enschede.

Spil, T. A. M. (1998) "From professional healthcare to where? A healthcare information management reference model," *Proceedings 1998 IRMA Conference,* Boston, USA, 285-294.

Sowerby Centre for Health Informatics (1998) "PRODIGY Phase two, prescribing performance (PACT analysis)," http://www.schin.ncl.ac.uk/, Newcastle.

Sperber, D. & Wilson, D. (1986) *"RELEVANCE, communication and cognition,"* Basil Blackwell, Oxford.

VWS. (1998) Meerjarenafspraak curatieve zorg (in Dutch), report Ministry of Public Health, The Netherlands.

Weinstein, D. R. & Worman, H. J. (2000) " Electronic prescription services offer potential savings and improvements in efficiencies," http://www.temple.edu/gisection/aganew19.html, Philadelphia.

Wetter, T. (2000) "Criteria for the introduction of electronic prescription of drugs," Project Plan, http://www.ukl.uni-heidelberg.de/mi/projects/presc/presc_ho.htm, Heidelberg.

Zviran, M. & Armoni, A. (1999) "Integrating hospital information systems," *International Journal of Healthcare Technology and Management.* 1(1), 168-179.

Chapter IX

Reengineering the Healthcare Supply Chain in Australia: The PeCC Initiative

Elizabeth More and G. Mike McGrath
Macquarie University, Australia

Reengineering is about fundamentally rethinking and dramatically redesigning business processes in order to lower costs and increase quality, service and speed. Such transformation is required in many industries today, perhaps none more so than the health sector. One enabling mechanism to allow for such large-scale change is found in information systems developments, most notably that of electronic commerce (e-commerce), offering a range of solutions for improving healthcare management.

This paper addresses the way in which the Australian health industry has grasped such opportunities for transforming itself through e-commerce strategies, allowing for improving cost-effective services to key stakeholders. A major achievement among a range of recent activities as outlined in the federal government's report, From Telehealth to E-Health: The Unstoppable Rise of E-Health (Mitchell, 1999), is that of Australia's first Internet trading community, The Project Electronic Commerce and Communication for Healthcare, otherwise known as PeCC, a key platform in transforming Australia's health sector.

---

* This study is supported by an ARC Collaborative Grant. The industry partner is IBM Australia.

Copyright © 2001, Idea Group Publishing.

INTRODUCTION

Recognizing the stark reality of economics can provide a strong imperative for reengineering an industry. This, coupled with the opportunities provided by evolving information and communication technologies in transforming healthcare delivery, provides a vital basis for radical change. Initiated in 1997, the *Project Electronic Commerce and Communication for Healthcare (PeCC)* emerged from just such a recognition by the federal government concerned over burgeoning costs in Australia's $37 billion health sector. This multi-stage project was developed and has received support from a number of federal government departments, but is a joint activity of both government and industry. PeCC was developed to introduce e-commerce practices into the health sector with almost 700 suppliers, automating pharmaceutical and other supplies to hospitals and retail pharmacies. While multiple projects occur within PeCC, the focus here is on the *Pharmaceutical Extranet Gateway (PEG)*, an Internet-based facility, developed to allow the automated passing of common order transactions between all parties and, in the process, to more tightly integrate their disparate systems. One of the most interesting features of the PEG project is that it has been developed and implemented by seven major pharmaceutical wholesalers, competitors operating in the same business but, nevertheless, collaborating in a critical and non-trivial endeavour.

During the PeCC study, interviewees at all points in the supply chain expressed concern at the fragmented nature of their IS, plus a good deal of frustration at the fact that accomplishing effective integration of their own IS suites had proved to be extremely difficult and, in most cases, impossible. Given, then, the difficulties encountered in IS integration initiatives *within* single organisations, one might expect that *inter-organisational* IS integration might be close to an intractable problem. Surprisingly, this is not what we found: certainly some fairly significant problems with inter-organisational collaboration were encountered but, in the main, the PEG architecture, combined with a heavy emphasis on standards, ensured that (within limitations) the project's data integration objectives were achieved.

The pharmaceutical industry is one of the first industry groups to have adopted a standardised approach to e-commerce. The project's impact, however, is significant within the broader healthcare industry. As one authority put it: *"The project heralds a global transformation of many aspects of health industry administration, putting barcode scanners into the hands of nurses and even replacing the doctor's hand-scribbled prescription. Every item used in hospitals, from cornflakes to soap, would eventually be covered"* (AH&HCJ, 1999, p.75).

Hart and Saunders (1997) have explored the way computer networks are increasingly being used to support the flow of information between and within organisations, and how such usage both influences and has consequences for inter-organisational relationships. Tapscott (1998) goes further and emphasises that the concept of community is vital for success in the new economy. An emphasis on relationships, both business-to-business and business-to-consumer, is central as organisations learn to coevolve into online business communities or, as he puts it, 'e-business communities.' Not many organizations, however, are far enough along the road of 'eTransformation' to realize the many benefits of such relationships online.

RESEARCH FOUNDATIONS, OBJECTIVES AND METHODOLOGY

Use the co-opetition mindset. Think about creating and capturing pie: competing and cooperating (Nalebutt and Brandenburger, 1997, p.35).

The goals of this study were to:
- explore innovations in Australia's healthcare management facilitated by information systems (especially e-commerce/Internet developments);
- understand how developments in IT enabled a change from interfirm rivalry alone to interfirm competition and collaboration; and
- extend work done elsewhere internationally in drawing on empirical research in Australia.

Our research was organized around the following general research objectives:
- test some current theories in the area of collaborative relationships;
- have an input into theory development;
- contribute to an improved understanding of the evolution of a particular industry; and
- focus on Australia as the locus of empirical testing.

The underlying theoretical perspective of this research was that of strategic alliances and competitive collaboration based on understanding that *"Alliances reshape not only the structure, but also the dynamics of competition* (Gomes-Cassseres, 1996, p.190)." While collaboration among competitors may at first glance seem rather strange, it appears that up to 70% of all interorganisational collaboration, at least in Europe and America--account for just such cooperation (Dussauge and Garrette, 1998). Others emphasise that what we are witnessing is the growth of 'collective competition,' that is competition between sets of allied organisations or 'constellations' of interlocking alliances (Gomes-Casseres, 1996). Nevertheless, the real nature of such collaboration is not always easy to comprehend.

There has been enormous diversity in approaches used to further understanding the rich area of interorganisational relations, cooperation and collaboration, cutting across a range of disciplines and perspectives, economics, politics, sociology, marketing, strategic and general management, and organisation studies, being among the major ones. In the past, there has been a heavy inclination towards the economics perspective. Now, however, there is growing agreement that one needs to move beyond a pure economics approach to understand the much wider variety of goals and purposes alliances may perform. Moreover, one needs to appreciate that certain approaches may not be valid, depending on the type of alliance under investigation. Indeed, diverse approaches offer the best solution to many of the difficult questions facing researchers and practitioners today. In this study we utilise the organisation studies and strategic management perspectives.

Our approach was that of a qualitative inductive case study with an emphasis on theory generation, propositions, rather than a sole focus on testing pre-existing theory (Eisenhardt, 1989; Yin, 1994). Case study methodology (Yin, 1994), while still not as widely accepted as other more traditional approaches, is increasingly recognised for its capacity to yield rich, dense data and to contribute to theory building.

The research also follows Glaser and Strauss' (1967) approach in developing 'grounded theory' that allows theory to emerge from the data. Furthermore, we adopted an interorganisational rather than dyadic perspective, stressing the alliance per se, instead of individual players and their particular relationships. This level was considered primary, although, much as Price (1996) has argued, the organizational and environmental levels were also encompassed.

Data collection was guided by theoretical preparation and literature reviews. Specific tools adopted to ensure triangulation (Yin, 1994) in our approach included the following:

- primary and secondary sources of information, minutes, contracts, policy documents, reports, publications, press, journals, academic and professional literature;
- minimally and semi-structured interviews with key stakeholders involved with PeCC and public sector agencies playing a key role (e.g., with senior executives, alliance managers, site managers, association representatives, etc.);
- participant observation such as attendance at meetings;
- linkage documentation and analysis using Netmap software (computerised recording and analysis of relationship links); and
- findings from previous related research (More and McGrath, 1996).

THE PECC PROJECT

PECC is the first project of its type in Australia where an entire industry supply chain is being revamped to take advantage of the Internet and Web-based technologies. It promises to create major savings to all the participants in the supply chain, particularly the publicly funded hospitals. (McRea, 1999, p.5)

A critical problem that needs to be overcome is the increasing cost of providing healthcare to an aging population, a problem common to most global healthcare models. Australia's current three-tier hospital system structure and its IT incompatibility problems have ensured that finding the real cost of the healthcare industry is an almost impossible task, as is the allied one of pinpointing wastage in the system. Improving supply chain management (SCM) by introducing IT dimensions of Global Numbering Standards (e.g., EAN), barcoding and e-commerce for tracking supplies from manufacture to point of consumption, was envisaged as providing a solution and ensuring *"the right item is in the right place, at the right time, in the most cost-effective manner" (PeCC and RCNA, 1998, p.3).*

PeCC is one of the leading-edge, innovative examples of Australian Internet commerce. This business-to-business e-commerce project has been driven by initiatives from both government agencies and industry partners. PeCC reform of the health sector supply chain commenced with the private sector (pharmaceutical companies and private hospitals) but is now spreading to public hospitals. It initially targeted pharmaceuticals but has extended to incorporate a wider range of products.

PeCC was designed to:
- accelerate the uptake of electronic commerce, Internet connectivity and the use of the EAN standard numbering system in the health sector manufacturing, professional community care and distribution environment; and
- demonstrate supply chain improvements that will become best practice for the management of product, inventory and allied services in the healthcare system (PeCC and RCNA, 1998, p.3).

PeCC follows closely the supermarket model of barcoding and scanning. In the pharmaceutical industry, distributors and manufacturers are encouraged to adopt common numbering and information exchange standards, as well as to use the Internet for e-commerce practices to distribute orders by wholesalers and to receive acknowledgments from manufacturers. Eventually the supply chain will be extended to include end-users (i.e., hospitals) which will allow pharmaceuticals to be optimally scanned by the bedside on consumption. Once PeCC is fully implemented and with industry products compatible, it is anticipated that those products not complying with the EAN barcoding system and e-commerce/Internet solutions will be excluded from purchasing panels and electronic catalogues.

PeCC itself consists of: a Council that provides policy direction for the project and meets three to four times a year; an Executive Steering Committee that decides on budget allocations, provides guidance to the project director and meets six times a year; a Project Director; Financial Stakeholders, including all PeCC Council members and all other organisations that have provided financial support to PeCC; Industry Sponsors, those organisations that have contributed financially but are not actively involved in any project; and Advisers. Of the $1 million PeCC budget, 60% has been provided by government agencies and the rest by industry sponsors and project participants.

On completion, PeCC will be Australia's first industry-wide Internet trading community. It will have achieved an open standards system allowing anyone to communicate with anyone else, instead of the traditional closed, proprietary networks dominated by IT-strong organisations. Moreover, uniformity across the pharmaceutical industry sector will be facilitated through PeCC. Additional benefits identified include more complete and readily available medical records for individual patients, better understanding of the costs of providing patient care inside hospitals and improvements in other hospital systems such as patient billing.

PeCC undertook a number of demonstration projects to show the viability of adopting common numbering and information exchange standards as well as using the Internet for electronic trading in the pharmaceutical industry. Figure 1 is a Netmap showing the complexity of linkages within the healthcare supply chain matrix and the positioning of the PEG within the supply chain.

PeCC's initial focus was to link five major competitive pharmaceutical wholesalers (Australian Pharmaceutical Industries, Faulding Healthcare, Hospital Supplies of Australia, Sigma Company and W.H. Soul Pattinson & Co), and the 700 manufacturers from whom they purchase. The CEOs of the five major wholesalers agreed on a handshake and then negotiated buy-in from their boards for collaboration on developing a common Internet-based EDI/EC platform, which would allow them to trade electronically with their suppliers at reduced costs (Head, 1998). The partnership that developed has culminated in the five wholesalers collaborating to use standard electronic order forms through PEG.

As illustrated in Figure 1, PEG provides a single common electronic ordering system that allows pharmaceutical wholesalers and suppliers to transact business through the Internet with the use of a common EAN-based bar coding or standardised numbering system. It enables wholesalers and suppliers to send purchase orders and to receive responses across the Internet rather than using the more expensive EDI option. EDI represents an alternative solution but, while satisfactory to large organisations able to invest in technology and skills required for the system, this is not a solution for smaller companies. The newer solution, as offered by PEG, is a single common electronic ordering system without much implementation time and minimum cost because of Internet utilisation. The wholesalers are subsidising the program by committing to the bulk of the development cost and paying for the operation of the central facility.

Sterling Commerce (which has worked extensively with U.S. and Australian pharmaceutical companies) won the tender for developing the e-commerce platform for the PeCC Trading Partners Program. Sterling is providing software (a suite of solutions for Internet trading called 'netCommerce') and services for PEG, and the service and technical expertise to connect wholesalers and suppliers to the PEG Bureau, PEG's central processing facility on the Internet. Sterling has chosen Telstra's Big Pond as the preferred Internet Service Provider (ISP), with Ozemail as second ISP and Hewlett-Packard providing the hardware. Datworks P/L serves as PEG marketing and integration specialist adviser. Alliance members all signed individual contracts with Sterling Commerce, with specific mention that no system changes could be made without the agreement of all PEG members.

Suppliers to the major wholesalers are generally small manufacturing companies with sales of up to $4 million annually and between 20-30 staff. Such organisations will be provided with the requisite Internet application software, connectivity and help-desk support for approximately $50-150 per month. Those already with these facilities installed will pay an annual fee for document transmission of between $600-2,200, depending on how many documents are processed (McIntosh, 1998).

Figure 1. Healthcare supply chain

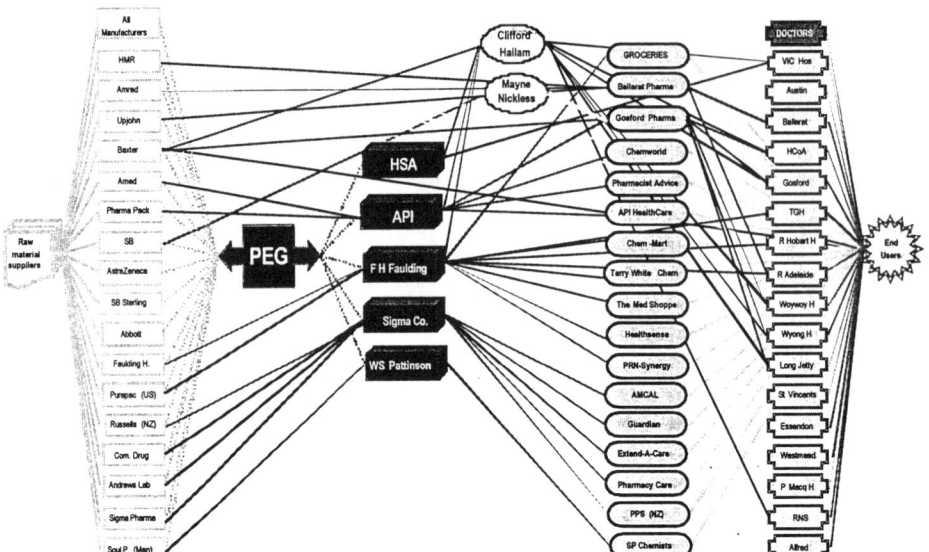

PEG is the most successful of the array of PeCC projects so far. It is aimed at overcoming problems of disparate databases and the current inefficiencies related to supply chain ordering via fax. These inefficiencies include re-keying orders, lack of confirmation of orders, multiple transmissions, delays and cost factors. PEG involves six EDI-forms, also in flat file and electronic Web browser format. Consequently, it offers accuracy in processing, advanced delivery notification, streamlined payments, and accurate and timely shared business information. It provides a network linking the major wholesalers to manufacturers and suppliers for purchase orders, acknowledgments and payments. Ensuring secure encryption, documents can be tracked through the system. Analysts estimate that the cost of placing an order through the normal manual process would be around $50 to $70, and with full implementation of PEG, this transaction cost will be reduced to a mere $2-5 per order.

PEG standards will be used to send orders by hospitals and pharmacies over the Internet; prescriptions may be sent; and PeCC standards will permit pharmacists and doctors to be paid by the government electronically. PEG allows for replacement of traditional fax transmission ordering. In reality: *"It is a single, common electronic ordering system for all wholesalers and suppliers. Small to medium enterprises can trade with their largest wholesale customers without the expensive EDI price tag or a lengthy implementation period" (Kilbane, 1999, p.2).*

PEG's formation and implementation, during 1998-2000, is leading-edge global practice, allowing a group of companies to use the Internet for exchanging messages, correspondence and product turnover ordering with approximately 700 potential trading partners. By the end of 2000, the project aims to have the majority of the 700 manufacturers' companies trading electronically. Furthermore, the project will enable e-trading between the PEG trading platform and transportation and logistics companies, an Australian first, pointing to the ability to track freight 'across docks.' The anticipated project completion date was the end of 2000, with wholesalers and suppliers connected and able to electronically trade the complete range of supply chain documents.

PEG: DATA AND SYSTEMS INTEGRATION

A view of the PEG architecture is presented in Figure 2. All parties (at whatever point in the supply chain) communicate with the central PEG databases using common, EDI-based transaction formats and, at the implementation level, through common, atomic-level (add, delete and modify) database access routines (DBARs). Furthermore, whatever supply systems or packages are employed at individual sites, all transaction details must conform to the PEG Catalog (which is based largely on EAN standards). Sterling Commerce (developers of PEG) assist each of the participants to develop interfaces for converting local data to standard PEG formats. Transactions with data in non-standard formats are rejected and are returned to initiators for investigation and correction.

While not obviously apparent, the PEG architecture presented in Figure 2 has much in common with data warehouses, federated heterogeneous databases and, indeed, the ISO 3-Schema Database Architecture. Essentially, all these approaches

Figure 2. PEG architecture

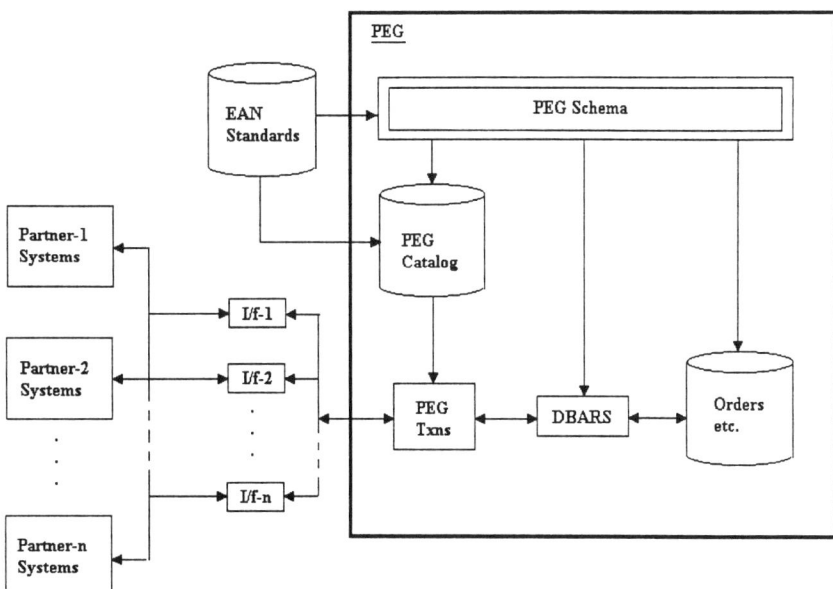

to data management are based on interfaces. With PEG, each partner in the venture may employ whatever internal systems they prefer and the interfaces, $I/f-1,—,I/f-n$, then convert their internal data to a form consistent with the PEG schema (which, in turn, is derived from EAN standards). The interfaces also handle conversion of data travelling in the opposite direction. The great advantage of the approach is that each partner has abundant flexibility in choosing software, hardware and applications to meet their particular needs. For example, if one company decides on a major upgrade of its IS and IT support platforms, neither PEG nor any of the other alliance partners will be impacted. Required changes will be restricted to that company's interface to the central PEG system.

Thus, in a sense, the necessity for inter-organisational coordination inherent in an e-commerce application dictates a system design (based on well-defined interfaces) that may result in a level of data integrity beyond that usually found in intra-organisational information architectures. As observed earlier, on the surface at least, this is a somewhat surprising result. It should be noted, however, that there are some significant limitations associated with this (PEG-type) approach specifically:

- Ideally, as transactions are rejected because of inconsistencies with the central schema and repositories, source systems and databases should be amended to bring them into line with the central system. Experience with data warehouses indicates that most organisations choose not to invest in (the admittedly expensive) data clean-up operations of this sort.
- Costs incurred in developing and maintaining interfaces can be prohibitive (even in an m:1 interfaces environment such as PEG). This is particularly the case for SMEs (such as many of the PEG manufacturers and suppliers).
- If data clean-up operations are not undertaken, inconsistencies between partner organisation and central (PEG) records can be a major source of errors and unnecessary work (e.g., reject investigation and other associated corrective activity).
- The approach does nothing to address data inconsistency and redundancy problems in partner organisations.

Figure 3. Data sharing, risk-taking and learning.

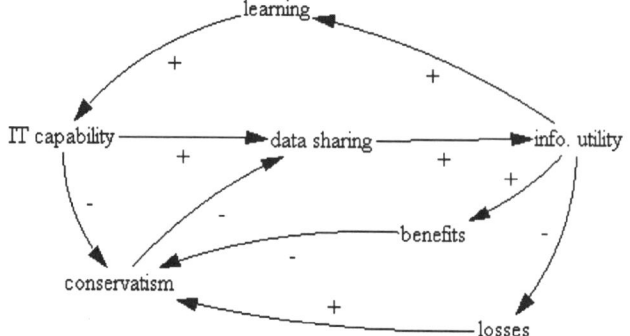

Finally, the central PEG databases constitute a potentially invaluable information resource that could be used to provide one or more partners with a significant competitive advantage. However, there are risks here as well as potential benefits and these are illustrated in the causal-loop diagram presented in Figure 3.

The question the partners must face is should they continue with the current system (albeit, in automated form), where they only have access to their own transaction data or should they allow each other to access the complete data set. If they opt for the latter course, they will be in an excellent position to use information for true strategic advantage: essentially, because each partner will now have access to information on the total business domain and not just their portion of it. Obviously, however, the risks here are high. So, effectively, those partners that favour data sharing will be backing their own organisation's IT capability against that of their collaborators/competitors. This, in our view, is one of the more fascinating issues still to be resolved among the PEG partners and goes way beyond basic, operational-level concerns with data privacy and security (important though these are).

OBSERVATIONS AND ANALYSES

Clearly if the central focus of PeCC, to reduce waste in the health industry by improving SCM, is achieved, this will be its major advantage. Savings of $340 million annually (Price Waterhouse, 1998) or more are predicted. Some specific benefits include:

- reduction in transition time from order placement to delivery and payment;
- reduction in costs of overall procurement (orders reduced from $50-70 to $2-5);
- comprehensive information on exact stock movements;
- establishing a foundation for a just-in-time ordering system;
- better matching of demand and supply by manufacturers and suppliers;
- greater accuracy and efficiency;
- error-free receipt of orders and integration with order entry systems by eliminating re-keying time and errors;
- rationalising of other trading documents, such as turnover orders and possibly electronic invoicing and payment instructions to financial institutions;
- improved service to customers (leading to faster payment for suppliers);
- improved inventory management and accountability within the hospital sector;
- increased efficiencies in hospitals and reduced shrinkage allowing funds to be better focussed on actual patient care;
- less reliance on proprietary IT systems;
- a major move towards standardisation opening the way for much greater interoperability;

- the ability to realise electronic commerce benefits without a massive investment in it; and
- the capability to more effectively utilise customer usage and ordering patterns information.

From our research it is clear that in its relative short history, PeCC has:
- set the agenda for improving supply chain management in the health sector;
- persuaded the major pharmaceutical wholesalers to use EAN numbering and barcoding in their supply network and to use an Internet-based 'any to any' common e-commerce platform;
- produced guidelines for barcoding in the healthcare sector;
- provided an array of publications for wide dissemination, to influential parties and existing and potential PeCC stakeholders;
- developed pilot/demonstration projects (Doz and Hamel, 1998);
- assisted with the re-engineering of hospital supply chains to e-business solutions;
- obtained agreement amongst most key stakeholders to common standards;
- established a common Internet-based gateway;
- worked towards establishing EAN as a standard for products;
- set agendas and raised awareness of critical ways of improving the healthcare sector; and
- obtained industry buy-in through in-kind and financial contributions.

Yet, from its inception, PeCC has had to contend with difficulties relating to the broad issue of change management in a fairly traditional and conservative industry. For example, resistance from those averse to technological development; concern from the manufacturing sector about waste and theft being reduced and leading to sales of fewer products; suppliers not wishing to alter culture and practice; some wholesalers also developing their own online systems connecting directly to customers; and difficulties within and across different levels of government relationships. Furthermore, there is concern over the pace and depth of change, especially given *"the entrenched, regimented views of some"* (Interviews, 1999). Many see it as too fast and radical, while those passionately committed perceive it as far too slow!

Finally, however, there is one overarching difficulty and challenge for the future that emerges from the data. This is that much of PeCC's work and projects are perceived in terms of IT rather than from a business strategy viewpoint. Consequently, from a broader perspective the real challenge in terms of PeCC projects is the complex one of ensuring appropriate change management in the industry. This incorporates the real need for attitudinal and behavioural change in the sector, including e-commerce being regarded as a critical first-tier strategic issue by senior executives and boards. As one executive we interviewed commented: *"Technically, the [PEG] system is complete and implemented ... What is needed now is awareness creation [of its strategic potential] in the organisations themselves"* (Interviews, 1999).

RESEARCH FINDINGS

Our industry is breaking new ground in the drive for greater efficiency because it is the first time competitive companies in one area have put themselves together. (David Murphy, CEO Faulding Healthcare).

The current research study provides a useful complement to work done for the Australian government by commercial consultants. These previous studies focused on analysis of e-commerce in managing the clinical supply chain in acute care and on mapping and evaluating the supply chain to hospitals. Our work demonstrates the role of competitive collaboration in required transformations, not only within industry but also across industry and government, and within government itself. All studies emphasize the need for reengineering health supply chains and developing integrated trading communities.

In particular, our study shows that *"PeCC is trailblazing and pace-setting ... Majors collaborate with different agendas and egos"* (Interviews, 1999). And that *"Collaboration exists because it makes sense for competitive reasons"* (Interviews, 1999).

In terms of competitive collaboration, PeCC's facilitation of agreement amongst the initial seven major pharmaceutical wholesalers in the PEG project stands out. It is a competitive alliance producing a new process, a new way of doing business, that can be learnt and distributed as both a private and common good among the alliance participants who are simultaneously PEG collaborators and competitors in the pharmaceutical markets. Interestingly the emphasis is to a large extent about learning with each other, not just learning from each other as is the case, for example, in many joint venture partnerships (Larsson et al., 1998).

Competition, however, is alive and well among the seven in the cut-throat pharmaceutical wholesaling market. Moreover, some (Interviews, 1999) suggest:

PEG is running far short on competitive collaboration. Trying to tackle the problem of getting lots of suppliers and reducing costs is as far as they are prepared to cooperate. But a lot are keeping strategies to themselves and have cordoned off that area of cooperation ... A lot of intelligence is not being shared ... use PEG to help individuals and then compete in their own area. (Interviews, 1999).

Furthermore, while there is competition in the retail pharmaceuticals market, there is growing competition for the hospital market. Others emphasized that *"The issue of competition is so strong between the States and Feds plus problems in Health with its own set of dynamics – they don't understand the nature of competitive collaboration"* (Interviews, 1999).

Certainly there are many barriers to smoothly implementing the major transformation envisaged at Australia's national healthcare industry level, at agency level, at supplier/distributor level. The diversity of players and interests creates problems, especially of commitment, trust, risk, the requisite critical mass, agreed standards, priorities, funding, policy, knowledge, technology infrastructure, and ways of managing and organizing.

The key research outcomes from our study are:
- confirmation of many current theories in change management leadership, communication, government support, strategic alliances and networks;
- falsifying the theory that dominant leading firms are not keen to cooperate with like firms within an industry (Doz and Hamel, 1998; Gomes-Casseres, 1996);
- reemphasizing the need to explore organization learning theory in terms of learning with rather than learning from, in collaborative e-communities; and
- finding a diminished role for trust as an alliance critical success factor (where a constrained alliance scope at the outset specifies the range of allowable collaborative activities).

The research has also attempted to bridge the divide so often evident between theory and practice and has tried to answer the call (e.g., Khanna, 1998) for case studies that move beyond outlining the decision to enter into partnership and into describing alliance development. It has done so by exploring an evolving alliance in the dynamic, new high technology area of e-commerce that challenges traditional ways of organizing and managing, individually and in relationships, competitively and collaboratively.

Major lessons from the particular case study described in the paper for the health sector broadly are as follows:
- ensuring that collaboration and the e-commerce community enable an equitable reaping of rewards by stakeholders;
- effectively managing the complex task of appropriate change management in the sector, including ways of overcoming resistance, the need for attitudinal and behavioural change, having senior management regard e-commerce as a critical first-tier issue, and keeping the momentum for radical transformation rather than an evolutionary pace of change;
- understanding the political dimensions involved in moving forward, both the 'big P' ones relating to governments, and those 'smaller p' ones relating to managing through the conflict and competition existing between governments, within and between government departments, between the public and private sectors, and within business communities and organizations themselves;
- appropriately handling cultural differences at the macro level between government and private-sector approaches, in terms of management styles, concerns and processes; and, at the micro level, cultural differences often relating to professional cultures such as those of administrators, healthcare professionals and IT personnel;
- improving communication with all key stakeholders about e-commerce and changes to the health system, and ensuring appropriate communication practices;
- resolving human resources issues relating to the enormous organizational changes e-commerce can bring to the nature of work in the sector, including concerns over job design and possible job losses;

- dealing with cost concerns for diverse stakeholders in relation to potential job losses, maintenance and upgrading costs, re-equipping and reengineering existing IT tools, training and education, and software products;
- securing appropriate funding for e-commerce innovations;
- overcoming the perceptions that e-commerce is focused on IT rather than the broader business strategy perspective, and shifting the agenda away from the technical domain owned by CIOs and into the realm of strategy and ownership by business managers;
- creating and implementing the appropriate governance structure to carry e-commerce initiatives forward, including the effective management of evolving e-commerce alliance and network management (especially in ensuring competition and collaboration are balanced to best effect);
- facilitating a critical mindshift in the sector – seeing healthcare as an industry rather than as a cost;
- grasping the challenge of e-health as symbolized by PeCC and enabling the requisite industry reengineering, transformation and paradigm shifts.

While it is clear that in the PEG alliance major objectives were met, in terms of the depth of skill improvement and knowledge acquisition, longer term research would also permit better evaluation of collaboration and performance than is at present possible. This would provide a more reliable basis for developing propositions and theory from the case. For example, the following tentative propositions certainly seem to merit further investigation:

- Constraining alliance scope, through the precise specification of the range of allowable activities, may well diminish the importance of *trust* as an alliance critical success factor (e.g., PEG within PeCC).
- A well-defined alliance scope may encourage partnerships where participants are more inclined to learn with (rather than from) each other.
- Benefits from alliance participation may be: commensurate with inputs, and a function of motivation for entering the alliance in the first place. With PEG, our observations were that those best placed to take maximum advantage of the collaborative arrangement are the participants most active at the operational level. Interestingly, a number of participants seemed to be motivated more by defensive considerations than by any real belief in the project and its objectives.

CONCLUSION

Today the health industry worldwide is being urged along a path of reinventing itself and reengineering its very nature, structure and way of functioning. Such transformation and renewal is continuous and necessarily results in changing ways of managing, organizing and fundamentally challenges traditional modes of thinking and management paradigms.

In the PeCC case study, we are witnessing an alliance and e-commerce revolution that will not only change industry players but the very way in which that industry itself is organised (Gomes-Casseres, 1996). We have been fortunate in being able to explore under the PeCC umbrella a number of bold initiatives and collaborative projects, particularly that of PEG, that will provide models for reinventing the Australian healthcare industry. Without the fundamental change such projects provide, the requisite reengineering and transformation of the health sector will not be achieved in Australia or elsewhere on the international stage.

REFERENCES

AH&HCJ (1999). *Australian Hospital & Health Care Journal.*

Child, J. and Faulkner, D.(1998). *Strategies of Co-operation,* Oxford, England: OUP.

Department of Communications, Information Technology and the Arts (DOCITA) (1999). Prepared by John Mitchell of John Mitchell & Associates, *From Telehealth to E-Health: The Unstoppable Rise of E-Health,* Canberra: DOCITA.

Doz, Y. and Hamel, G. (1998). *Alliance Advantage,* Boston: HBS.

Dussauge, P. and Garrette, B. (1998). "Anticipating the evolutions and outcomes of strategic alliances between rival firms," *Int. Studies of Mgt & Org.,* 27(4), 104-126.

Eisenhardt, K. (1989). "Building theories from case study research," *Academy of Management Review,* vol. 14, 532-550.

Glaser, B. and Strauss, A. (1967). *The discovery of grounded theory strategies for qualitative research,* Chicago, Ill: Aldine Publishing Company.

Gomes-Casseres, B. (1996). *The Alliance Revolution. The New Shape of Business Rivalry,* Cambridge, Mass.: Harvard University Press.

Harari, O. (1994). "Colluding with competitors is a dead end," *Management Review,* October, 53-55.

Hart, P. and Saunders, C. (1997). "Power and trust: Critical factors in the adoption and use of electronic data interchange," *Organization Science,* 8(1), 23-42.

Head, B. (1998). "A net cure for hospital waste," *Australian Financial Review,* 5 June, 45.

Khanna, T. (1998). "The Scope of Alliances," *Organization Science,* 9(3), 340-355.

Kilbane, D. (1999). "Australia pilots pharmaceutical EDI systems to save $340 million," *Automatic I.D. News,* Cleveland, January, 1-2.

Koza, M. and Lewin, A. (1998). "The Co-evolution of Strategic Alliances," *Organization Science,* 9(3), 255-264.

Larsson, R. Bengtsson, L. Henriksson, K. and Sparks, J. (1998). "The Interorganizational Learning Dilemma: Collective Knowledge Development in Strategic Alliances," *Organization Science,* 9(3), 285-305.

McIntosh, T. (1998). "Bringing the health industry online," *The Age and Sunday Age,* October 9, 13.

McRea, P. (1999). "Reducing the cost of supply chains," Unpublished paper, 1-5.

More, E. and McGrath, M. (1996). *Cooperative Corporate Strategies In Australia's Telecommunications Sector – The Nature of Strategic Alliances,* Canberra: DIST.

Murphy, D. (1999). *Sterling Commerce PR Sheet.*

Nalebutt, B. and Brandenburger, A. (1997). "Co-opetition: Competitive and cooperative business strategies for the digital economy," *Strategy & Leadership*, 25(6), 29-35.

PeCC and RCNA (1998). *Getting Business Online,* Canberra: NOIE.

Price, C.(1996). "The Evolution of Inter-Organizational Relationships: Exploration of the Implementation Phase," Unpublished dissertation, Boston University, Graduate School of Management.

Price Waterhouse (1998). *PECC – The Way Forward,* Canberra: DIST.

Tapscott, D. Lowy, A. and Ticoll, D. (1998). *Blueprint to the Digital Economy,* New York: McGraw Hill.

Yin, R. (1994). *Case study Research: Design and Methods*. 2nd ed. California: Sage Publications Inc.

Section 4

Network Organizations in Healthcare

Health Networks
Yolande Chan
Dave Ramsden

Networked Organizations
Ronald Spanjers
Willi Hasselbring
Ryan Peterson
Martin Smits

Chapter X

Understanding Health Information Networks in Canada

Yolande E. Chan and David J. Ramsden
Queen's University, Canada

ABSTRACT[1]

Findings from a preliminary survey of health information networks (HINs) established in various parts of Canada lead us to suggest that buy-in and participation in development of the alliance by physicians and other providers is critical. Also, most healthcare providers are not aware of the difficulties involved in establishing connectivity in the networks we examined. Nor should they be, perhaps. We found that networks that pursued a comprehensive set of applications closely linked to providing better care for patients were more likely to be considered successful by partner organizations and providers.

Alliance partners who had a history of interaction prior to the formal establishment of the health information network in question seemed to get to application development quicker than when the alliance was created only because a network was needed. Many alliances reported the positive effect that external players had in terms of helping alliance partners overcome differences, sustain momentum, and provide funds and expertise as needed.

INTRODUCTION

In 1997, the National Forum on Health in Canada recommended establishment of a culture of evidence-based decision making in which decision makers at all levels (providers, administrators, policy makers, patients and the public) would use high quality evidence to make informed choices about health and healthcare. Across Canada, health professionals, healthcare institutions and provincial Ministries of Health have begun to look for alternative ways to relay and utilize health information (Roos et al., 1998)[2]. Information has become an increasingly vital commodity in an effort to measure process, efficiency and patient health outcomes in an era where provincial governments grapple with rising costs in their healthcare systems, falling revenues from the federal government and uncertain provincial economies.

The Canadian healthcare system is largely publicly funded, publicly administered and intended to provide a uniform level of access to medically necessary care to all Canadians wherever they live or travel in Canada. Lacking the market discipline that is offered in a privately funded or managed system, the Canadian system has lagged in efforts to ensure and measure effectiveness. The constitutional authority to deliver healthcare rests with the provinces in Canada, although the federal government enforces national standards through the Canada Health Act, and contributes what many have described as a shrinking share of the overall costs of running the healthcare system.

Reforms within the Canadian system are typically initiated on a provincial basis, creating a patchwork quilt of approaches when viewed at the national level. Our examination of the emergence of health information networks across Canada

Figure 1. Map of Canada

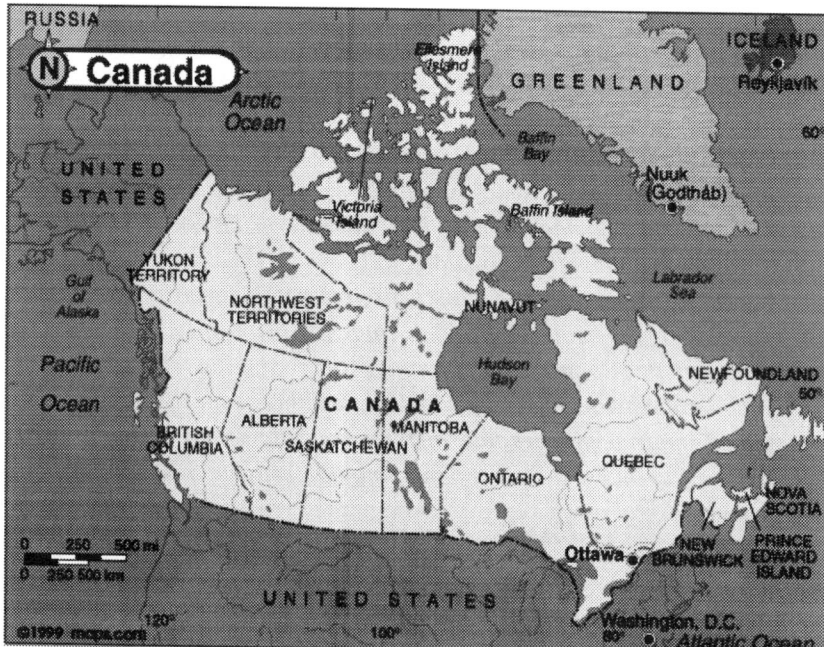

reveals a variety of approaches, and in fact, that the patchwork quilt exists within provinces as well as between provinces.

In this chapter, we outline the linkages between the structure of the healthcare system in Canada, its reform pressures and evolution of health information networks. We also comment on the issues within the Canadian healthcare sector that create difficulties in establishing and sustaining these interorganizational alliances.

Healthcare Technology Interface Challenges

It is important to acknowledge the extensive investment that hospitals and other healthcare institutions and organizations have made in diagnostic and information-related technology. The issue of prime focus is the dilemma of fragmentation. Systems within single institutions that have been developed to meet narrow purposes are often not well suited to share information with other similarly developed systems. Institutions have undergone structural change such that many have become allied or have merged with other institutions. Provision of specialized services has been rationalized such that single patients must traverse a variety of departments within single multi-site institutions. Without integration of patient information across these complex organizations, patients often end up being 'reprocessed' at each major service provision locale.

Provinces have invested significantly in database structures to track patient interactions and a broad range of disease conditions. Interconnection of these databases is only now being accomplished. Linkages between these pools of data and the service provision side of the healthcare system generally are poor. National datasets of service provision and health outcomes are similarly disconnected.

REVIEW OF THE LITERATURE AND DESCRIPTION OF THE RESEARCH MODEL

Definition of HINs

We have defined a network as a collection of interrelated organizations, typically supported by a technical infrastructure or network technology. The applications shared by the member organizations or participants within the network are called interorganizational systems (IOSs). Specifically, health information networks (HINs) are networks whose membership consists primarily or exclusively of organizations active in the management and delivery of healthcare services.

Guided by this definition, we included a variety of Canadian networks that encompass large regional health authorities as partners, networks that interconnect healthcare institutions and universities within a specific region, and networks populated by a mix of private and public organizations. We excluded networks such as the Edmonton Women's Health Network or British Columbia's Medilink since they operate as hubs providing service or information to a vast array of individuals who are otherwise not interconnected.

Nonetheless, the networks we included in our examination are different in many ways. We have compared and contrasted them in terms of their founding motivation, the path they developed along and the approach they have taken to governing themselves.

Framework for Analysis of HINs

We developed a framework to organize our findings related to this broad range of HINs, borrowing from literature on the establishment of interorganizational alliances and literature on the balanced score card (see Figure 2.) An examination of the motivation spurring partners to form an alliance is known to be an important factor, as is the process by which the alliance forms. In general, partners to the alliance must be convinced initially, and remain convinced, that they are able to accomplish outcomes as a member of a collective that are unavailable to them as separate entities. The success of the entity formed under the alliance is in part determined by the ability to set and accomplish a balanced set of goals addressing: 1) the needs of the human resources engaged in the work of the alliance, 2) fiscal constraints facing the alliance, 3) demands to support or improve business processes, and 4) the need to nurture learning within the alliance.

HIN Motivation

A common assumption made in the literature on interorganizational alliances (IOAs) is that a single organization will precipitate the alliance development process, in pursuit of strategic advantage, or to attain a higher level of operating efficiency. However, this is an oversimplification in the case of HINs.

Driving forces/context

Strategic advantage may seem at first glance to be a misnomer with respect to the healthcare field, but in an era of competition among institutions for scarce healthcare dollars, there may be reasonable application to this field, even in countries like Canada where healthcare is largely government funded. Certainly, the same

Figure 2. Precursors of HIN Success

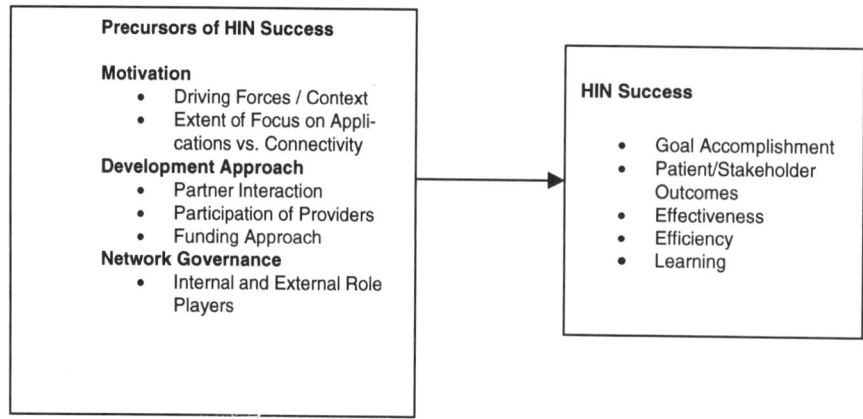

issue of scarce funding has caused many a hospital board or CEO to examine ways of improving efficiencies. A more appropriate characterization of the strategic motivation driving the formation of IOAs might be collaboration among public sector agencies. Given the nature of the evolving healthcare system in Canada, particularly in the larger urban areas, a broad array of agencies and institutions are responsible for providing different services to the same clients, suggesting the need for collaboration. Ferratt et al.(1996) argue that such collaboration can lead to greater efficiency and effectiveness of outcomes experienced by the shared client.

Strategic motivation, both in terms of intent and extent to which the initiating vision is held broadly by alliance partners, is a useful means of understanding the development and evolution of HINs.

Resulting focus on applications vs. connectivity

The nature of the interdependencies that draw organizations to the HIN may predict the focus on application or IOS development. While it is unlikely that each application will be uniformly valued by all partners, a sufficient subscription for each must be accomplished in order to cover the relatively high fixed costs of operating and expanding the technical infrastructure and supporting human resources (Ferratt et al., 1996). The source of application development initiation is likely to be important, as is the relative penetration that each application accomplishes across eligible partners.

Professional caregivers will be more likely to initiate and participate in the development of applications that appear to address patient care more directly, and less likely to participate or support projects that appear to address the needs of the governance or administrative structures of member organizations. A concern expressed most vehemently by professionals but shared by all, we believe, is the need to achieve a high degree of perceived and actual privacy and security of individual information.

Security and privacy of personal health information must be considered in a variety of terms, from inadvertent release of information to inappropriate persons, loss or theft of personal information, to release of information without individual consent. Contribution of information gathered as a result of professional interactions with patients will proceed slowly or not at all without robust confidentiality and security measures being in place for any exchange of information interorganizationally, electronic or otherwise.

The 'business' of providing healthcare services to people is similar in many ways across the country despite the fact that there are few national standards and minimal national health policy binding the actions of provinces. Canada's Constitution assigns responsibility for healthcare to provinces, with the federal government retaining responsibility for healthcare needs of aboriginal people on reserves, and the military. So, there are few structural constraints in the provinces that suggest that regional HINs will develop along similar lines, despite the similarity of healthcare services, needs and shared goals. The approach to development of the various HINs then is a likely source of variance.

Development Approach

We placed a particular focus on three elements typifying the development approach pursued by each alliance. In our research, we first examined the nature of the partners to the alliance, including their past history of interaction and interaction during formative stages of the HIN. Second, we examined the approach each network took in addressing and engaging the professional providers who carried out the work of each partner organization. The funding approach was our final attribute, of special interest because of the high capital costs that are often involved in IOS development.

Partner roles/interaction

An alliance may be borne of past experiences between two or more partners, or may stem from a search for a partner by a single organization. A related concept is the extent and nature of interaction amongst alliance partners, prior to and during the development of the HIN. Kumar and van Dissell (1996) propose a typology to differentiate classes of interorganizational systems (IOS) relied upon within an interorganizational alliance or network. Recalling that IOSs are the applications shared by participants within a network, Kumar and van Dissell (1996) distinguish various types of interdependence that exist between the partner organizations: reciprocal, pooled information resource and value or supply chain interdependence (supporting sequential interdependency).

Volkoff et al. (1999) suggest that the social and professional networks that underlay the development work influence the pace and process of development. The networks themselves evolve over time. The extent to which social and professional networks span the organizational boundaries of network partners prior to formalization of the network structure is expected to be positively related to the support of each organization's and the network's development and implementation plans.

The interactive nature of alliance development and collaborative application implementation suggests that a distinction be made between the extent of interaction a priori the alliance development compared to the extent of interaction that occurs during network formation. Social interaction that is borne solely out of network development or application implementation is more likely to cease once the flurry of project communication has ended.

Participation of providers

There is an extensive literature that argues for early and significant involvement of professionals in any organizational change, particularly where administrative or organizational and professional objectives appear at first blush to be in conflict (e.g., Etzioni, 1969; Guy, 1985; Wilensky, 1964)). An efficiency thrust, expected to reduce costs or increase patient 'throughput,' is potentially in conflict with a professional's concerns for quality of care, successful treatment of disease and retention of professional autonomy of practice.

In the paradigm of the healthcare provider, medical care is the primary means of improving health. With a clinical lens applied to measures of effectiveness, HINs are judged effective to the extent that they improve the interactions among providers and between providers and patients. Key evidence of success in this area includes the establishment of continuity of care, smooth transfer of patient information, the elimination of duplication, and the collection and use of clinical outcomes data (Satinsky, 1998). Providers can either participate openly in the change processes related to establishment and operation of these networks, or resist stubbornly the loss of professional autonomy (Blount, 1998).

We suggest then that the extent to which the affected provider community are involved in the overall development process is a helpful guide to understanding the way in which various HINs grow over time, and understanding the degree of success and acceptance they enjoy.

Funding approach

Funding is an issue at the core of network operations. A potential motivation for network formation is cost reduction, of particular concern in Canada where there is government fiscal shrinkage. Partners whose prime objective in joining an alliance is cost savings may seek early returns, and may not be willing or able to contribute to the working capital that is needed to fund network operations.

This concern is exacerbated in the high cost technology environment of communications-centered networks, which are intensely reliant on infrastructure. A lack of infrastructure can represent at least two threats. First, infrastructure construction is expensive and time consuming in its own right. Secondly, a need for infrastructure construction can delay the earning of returns from such capital investment. This may occur either because of the diversion of capital from applications projects to infrastructure projects, or simply because infrastructure delays defer the implementation of applications.

Network Governance

Alliances that represent a pooled or sequential interdependency may exhibit a strong, singular and constant leadership. Conversely, where the interdependency is collaborative or reciprocal, one might expect to find a shifting locus of leadership, or perhaps a more democratized governance structure. Volkoff et al. (1999) noted that during the development and implementation of a regional HIN, several distinct stages of development were noted during which both the focus and the source of leadership changed. Some of the management tasks seemed to require a sponsor that was external to all the partners, while other management tasks seemed to require the active involvement of an executive sponsor from within each partner organization. Such external facilitation or leadership is most likely required in the absence of a dominant or lead organization, to assist partners to find sufficiently common ground or to harmonize plans to proceed in pursuit of their vested interests.

For an external sponsor to be effective, they must be seen to be apart from the vested interests of all parties, and must be seen in sufficiently authoritative or at least credible terms by all partners, particularly when a power or expertise imbalance exists within the group of executive sponsors. External influence could also be derived from intervention from an overarching authority, such as government (Konsynski, 1993).

So, it seems that HINs that have at least one dominant partner will develop in ways that differ from more democratically or purely horizontally allied partners. However, the effectiveness of such 'relational' networks is likely tied to the availability of a credible outsider or neutral internal executive sponsor willing to intervene when necessary to help the partnership remain intact.

DATA COLLECTION AND FINDINGS

In this study, we undertook an extensive search of the Internet to gather information on Canadian HINs. We searched Web sites linked to the Federal Department of Health, and the Web pages of every provincial and territorial Department or Ministry of Health. We also relied on information contained in Web pages of Industry Canada, since that federal department has been responsible for much of the federal government's contributions to national network infrastructure. We relied on personal discussions and interviews with people connected to healthcare organizations involved in regional HINs, particularly in Ontario where a pan-provincial HIN has yet to be initiated. Table 1 provides URLs for each of the networks we examined.

Table 1. HIN URLs

Health Information Network	Scope	Province	URL
PharmaNet	Provincial	British Columbia	www.gov.bc.ca/hlth
We//net	Provincial	Alberta	www.albertawellnet.org
SHIN	Provincial	Saskatchewan	www.shin.sk.ca
MHINet	Provincial	Manitoba	www.gov.mb.ca/health
WED*net	Regional	Southwest Ontario	www.wednet.on.ca
LARG*net	Regional	Southwest Ontario	www.largnet.on.ca
HappIN	Regional	Southwest Ontario	www.happin.org
InfoLink	Regional	Southeast Ontario	www.seoinfolink.com
Healthlink	Regional	Southern Ontario	www.healthlink.com
OCHIP	Regional	Eastern Ontario	www.olsc.ca/ochip

Findings: Provincial Health Information Networks

In this section, we consider a broad range of HINs that exist on a provincial basis. That is, we include those health alliances that span entire provinces. In the section immediately following, we discuss HINs serving a specific regional or sub-provincial service area.

PharmaNet in British Columbia is a unique structure, given that it developed outside the direct healthcare delivery sphere in the province. This network was established to assist the province in monitoring overconsumption of drugs, to guard against adverse drug interactions, to enforce the provincial drug formulary and to streamline claims payments for pharmacies and individual claimants. All pharmacies and hospital emergency rooms are now connected to the network.

Alberta's Wellnet (or We//net) is a government agency jointly managed by the Ministry of Health and other major healthcare stakeholders. It was developed initially as a public private partnership comprised of government, the provincial telecommunications company and a large computing hardware / software firm. Membership in We//net spans the 19 regional health authorities in the province, professional practitioner associations, faculties of health science and the provincial research council. The HIN has supported development of a comprehensive data definition dictionary, security and privacy standards, and a broad range of healthcare applications ranging from an electronic patient record to a seniors drug information bank to telehealth services. The Saskatchewan government established the Saskatchewan Health Information Network (SHIN) in 1997. Its membership is similar to We//net's.

The Manitoba Health Information Network (MHINet) is a relatively new venture of the provincial association of registered nurses and universities. It was initially envisioned as an outreach service for nurses practicing in rural and remote areas of the province. However, work has commenced recently to link providers to patient records, link laboratories and hospital admitting offices, and community health centers.

We found little evidence of provincial-level HINs operating in Ontario, Quebec, Nova Scotia or Prince Edward Island. In a subsequent section, we will outline the regional HINs developing in Ontario in response to the approach to healthcare reform in that province. Nova Scotia recently revised its regional structure, creating a series of nine districts linked to community health boards. We note some degree of collaboration centered on the health science centre in the capital of Nova Scotia, primarily to facilitate the referral patterns for patients into that centre.

New Brunswick's healthcare system is managed on a regional basis, but governance still remains with the provincial government. The senior officer in each region is placed within the hierarchy, linked directly to the Ministry of Health. Institutions within the province can share patient data via Healthnet, but there is little evidence that significant collaboration occurs between those institutions.

Despite the relatively long experience of regional health authorities (RHAs) in Newfoundland, there is only recent activity related to technologically supported alliances. The government's 2000 business plan calls for work to be started on a "comprehensive, integrated, person-centered network," with an initial focus on the development of a Unique Personal Identifier registry. A fledgling HIN has emerged as a multi-province alliance in the west and north of Canada. Initially dubbed the Western Health Information Network, and recently renamed the WHI Collaborative, this alliance is aimed at inter-provincial initiatives such as the shared use or interconnection of provincial infrastructures. Partners to the Collaborative include the four western provinces and three territories whose residents obtain much of their secondary and tertiary care in institutions of the western provinces. The Collaborative was established in late 1999, and has set a modest initial agenda for itself. Initial projects are currently being identified. Initial support for this alliance appears to be stemming from Alberta We//net personnel.

Provincial HIN findings summary

Given the provincial nature of the healthcare system in Canada, it was perhaps not surprising to find provinces working ostensibly alone in development of province-wide HINs. We also noted at least one instance of interprovincial collaboration, albeit at an early stage. And then, finally, we noted the absence of a provincial-level HIN in Ontario, Canada's most populous province. In its absence, we noted the presence of several networks involving a broad range of healthcare-related institutions, covering various regions of Ontario.

Findings: Regional Health Information Networks

The regional health information networks we examined distinguish themselves from provincial HINs primarily in terms of reach, but also in the sense that the partners are typically drawn from a specific sub-provincial geographic area.

The majority of regional HINs (RHINs) that have formed in Ontario are built around large teaching hospitals affiliated with large universities or health science centers. These networks have typically created a strategic alliance or not-for-profit corporation to govern their activities, and to allow some corporate separation from the individual network members. We examined networks like these in Ottawa, Kingston, Toronto, Hamilton, Windsor and London.

The Ottawa Carleton Health Information Partnership (OCHIP) was formed in early 1998 as a not-for-profit corporation linking community, senior-level health professionals, educators and researchers. The initial proposal to form OCHIP came from a collaboration of universities, research institutions, major health institutions and the federal government, in response to demands from Ontario's Health Services Restructuring Commission (HSRC) for development of an integrated clinical information system. HSRC made similar demands of each of the major teaching hospital centers in the province, in 1996 and early 1997.

Kari+net, the Kingston Area Regional Information Network, was established in 1996 by four area hospitals, and the health sciences faculty of the local university. A more recent development has been the formation of InfoLink, representing an alliance of all healthcare provider institutions and agencies in southeastern Ontario. We grouped and examined these alliances together because they were interconnected.

HappIN, the Hamilton Area Public and Private Information Network, was established as a federally incorporated not-for-profit organization, which aspired to create a virtual healthcare community. By their own description, they were established as a doctor/patient-centered system. They drew on a large community, spanning teaching hospitals and health sciences faculty, public health, physicians, pharmacies, community care and the Ministry of Health in Ontario.

The London Area and Regional Global Network (LARG*net) is a not-for-profit organization encompassing stakeholders in a region to the west of that covered by HappIN. The network had been extensively supported by a local university from its inception in 1993 until recently, but also includes a broad range of partners drawn from mainly the public sector.

The Windsor and Essex Development Network (WED*net), formed in late 1994, is a consortium of health, education, municipal and industry stakeholders from the southwestern portion of the province of Ontario. Their key initial participants were the University of Windsor (including the health sciences faculty), the local college and school boards. They have incorporated with three levels of membership. Stakeholder members are the university, hospitals and the Cancer Center.

Healthlink was established in 1993 as a joint initiative of seven Toronto-area hospitals, along with three private-sector partners. They formed a private share corporation in 1996, and instituted a business plan in 1998 that saw them independent of government support. By 1999, they had grown to include 43 healthcare institutions.

Regional HIN findings summary

With the exception of the last example, these networks represent alliances between partners located in close proximity to each other. There appears to be no overlap in membership. Healthlink has developed a membership that reaches to institutions throughout the province, involving several who are represented in one of the other RHINs noted here.

In the next section we elaborate on various aspects of provincial and regional HINs, using the analytical framework discussed previously. We point out key motivating forces and the context from which they arose, the approach taken to develop HIN alliances and various approaches to network governance.

Motivation

The nature of th0e governance structure in the healthcare system in each province is likely to be most predictive of the nature and number of participant organizations potentially motivated to join or develop an HIN. Prior to the 1990s, the healthcare system was largely governed at the institution level, with each hospital, long-term care facility or health center governed by its own board and managed by separate administrations. Since that time, most provinces have initiated a regionalized structure of healthcare governance, representing a greater degree of centralization of authority than previously existed. Illustrative of this point is the progress experienced by Kari+net participants. In 1992, prior to formation of the alliance, the four institutions had independent patient information systems, despite the extensive movement of patients between the institutions. The institutions were isolated from each other, and for the most part, departments within a single institution could not share data electronically. By 1998, there was hospital-wide and multi-site integration for patient care information, including admissions and laboratory services.

Saskatchewan instituted a district structure in 1992, culminating in the formation of 32 districts by 1996. Alberta's regionalization occurred more swiftly, with the formation of 17 regional health authorities (RHAs) in 1994. These sub-provincial organizations have responsibility for all acute, primary and long-term care activity within their geographic regions.

Physician remuneration plans have been kept outside the regional governance structures in all areas where RHAs exist. Funding for the 'fee-for-service' plan for physicians typically remains with each provincial or territorial Ministry.

The 'bringing together' and eventual integration of agencies and institutions under regional umbrellas was key to eliminating many of the barriers to collaboration that existed previously. Similarly, with a vastly reduced number of stakeholder organizations, the government was able to leverage its view of how an integrated system would cooperate, communicate and allocate resources.

In other provinces, reform has occurred at a slower pace. Newfoundland implemented a regional governance system in 1994. Manitoba initiated 12 RHAs to govern healthcare delivery in that province as recently as 1997.

British Columbia began reform in their healthcare delivery system perhaps earlier than most jurisdictions, but has changed course along the way, possibly delaying the onset of alliances within their cadre of governing organizations. The reform resulted in a provincial structure of 11 RHAs in 1996.

Ontario initiated its health services restructuring in 1995, intending to make significant reductions in the number of hospitals and hospital administrations. It instituted district health councils across the province but they appear to have been given a largely advisory role to date. At the outset, there were 212 hospitals in Ontario, all separately governed. Currently, there are slightly more than 200 hospitals remaining, so closure has not been as significant as intended. However, there are approximately 160 hospital corporations remaining, indicating that what has happened is a series of mergers or amalgamations between previously independent institutions. The challenges of managing these multi-site organizations have in part motivated the regional alliances that we examined in Ontario.

Quebec and Nova Scotia have each decided to keep hospitals and other major institutions apart from their district or regional structure. The concentration of resources in major institutions is likely a factor increasing the 'power' differential between organizations and diminishing the likelihood of province-wide health alliances.

Given the change pressures evident throughout the country, it appears that provincial networks are more likely to reflect the interactions of individual organizations brought together by government edict. Regional HINs at this point are more difficult to describe, in the sense that most alliances exhibit some degree of proactive movement. Nevertheless, these alliances are struggling to cope with new merger partners, rising costs and an uncertain future.

Resulting focus: Applications versus connectivity

Basic connectivity has been an issue for all the networks, to some degree. Saskatchewan built an extensive fibre-optic network in the province some time before SHIN's formation, to support initiatives of the education system. OCHIP was able to take advantage of existing regional networks in their early stages of formation, although like all other networks, they soon experienced bandwidth restriction difficulties with subsequent applications.

Beyond the building of hardware infrastructure, most networks initiated development of standards pertaining to network use and network connectivity. Alberta issued an Information and Data Standards manual in late 1999. Alberta also

Table 2. Motivation: Driving forces/context /HIN focus

Motivation	Health Information Network
Driving Forces / Context	
Regionalization of healthcare system	Wellnet, SHIN
Merger of institutions	various RHINs in Ontario
Rising costs of healthcare	PharmaNet
Directives from government	all, except Healthlink
Information sharing	all
Connectivity	focus Larg*net, HappIN, WED*net
Focus: Applications vs. Connectivity	
Connectivity	WED*net, LARG*net,
Security, privacy	generally all
Electronic patient record	Wellnet, SHIN
Laboratory services reform	InfoLink
Tele-health	OCHIP, SHIN, LARG*net

requires that proponents of any application for use on We//net submit a Privacy Impact Assessment and have this assessment either accepted or rejected by the Office of the Information and Privacy Commissioner. To meet the security standards set for medical information transmission, SHIN has begun implementing security software, to encrypt email transmissions and ensure security of access to medical information databases.

HappIN set out early goals regarding connectivity and security. Early wins were described in terms of access to e-mail and discussion forums, access to the Web and development of electronic equivalents for routine inter-organizational forms. Considerable work went into resolving practitioner and public concerns regarding confidentiality, access to and sharing of patient information between institutions.

Early projects in We//net included development of a patient registration system and procurement standards intended to ease the purchase of desktop systems and accomplish desktop standardization amongst all network partners. One of SHIN's earliest and most clearly articulated goals was to broker and implement a shareable electronic health record for each individual in the province, across all RHAs. They initiated this project in 1998, one year after the formal inception of their network.

In mid-1999, We//net embraced projects related to telehealth, the establishment of a pharmacy network and a foundational application that was in essence a central birth registry. This registry was a key piece of one of the subsequent projects, the establishment of a metabolic screening program to track screening of all newborns in the province.

In the fall of 1998, SHIN supported a pilot project amongst three smaller communities within a single RHA, to automate the interactions between physicians, district office and health centers. By the end of 1999, 21 of 32 districts were in some way connected to SHIN. The balance of districts can be connected when they express interest. In the majority of cases, SHIN has taken a pilot project approach to implement their patient care IOSs. For example, two regional centres and the teaching hospital in Saskatoon are involved in a project to exchange CT scans between sites, thus avoiding expensive retesting and associated delays in care provision.

A pharmaceutical monitoring system has been developed by SHIN to assist in detecting duplicate prescription issuance, and to guard against adverse drug interactions. By early 2000, over 200 pharmacists were linked to and using this system. This system closely matches British Columbia's PharmaNet arrangements, as does We//net's system, although the latter services the senior population only.

By 1999, WED*net had begun to move into patient care IOSs, related to such advancements as image diagnostics, health record access and sharing, and intercampus connectivity between professional caregivers. LARG*net intended to 'design a large umbrella' and 'push down' small projects, but ironically did not seek to provide or develop specific applications for its members. In fact, in many of the RHINs we examined, there seemed to be a reticence to tread on the 'turf' of member organizations. For instance, in an early document from HappIN, they note a "non-turf" approach, where "we don't meddle in the internal business of others."

HappIN anticipated turning their focus to development of a community patient index, "Web-friendly clinical management system," and support for developing primary care networks of practitioners.[3]

Kari+net accomplished projects related to the sharing of patient information between member institutions. Another project, at an early stage of development, connects home care nurse providers to clinical information about the patients in their care, and allows these providers to query instructions or provide condition updates to institutional-based practitioners.

In its early stages, LARG*net initiated several projects, with the most high profile being a medical imaging initiative. This project was actively supported by 3M Canada and SUN Microsystems, whose presence was noted as a success factor early on, and a detriment to progress over time as the project moved through to maturity.

We noted several references in LARG*net documents to extensive communications between the various participants involved in establishing their metropolitan area network. Most participants attributed this level of communication to the project of connectivity, suggesting to us that it would prove to be unsustainable over time.

Healthlink first implemented projects pertaining to the movement of patient records and subsequently clinical test and laboratory information between institutions. In 1995, they implemented an application to move radiological image files between the seven initial partners. The system has since expanded to all departments.

Prior to the formation of OCHIP, the main participants had engaged in a series of pilot programs, primarily related to connectivity. Telehealth applications, including remote consultations with specialists, were also piloted. Key applications that received early attention after OCHIP's formation included electronic tracking and sharing of data related to pharmacy, laboratory and radiology departments, and the creation of electronic consultation reports and discharge summaries.

Beyond basic connectivity issues, most networks we examined moved quickly to the development of applications aimed at improving support to providers and improving the quality of care offered to patients. Of note though were the concerns evident in the documents from both LARG*net and HappIN expressing doubt that applications ought to be developed within the network entity itself. This might suggest disagreement among key partners regarding the purpose, objectives and priorities of the network.

Approach to Development

As noted earlier, our examination of the approach to development taken by each alliance looks at the nature of the partners to the alliance and their history of interaction prior to formation of the HIN, each alliance's efforts to involve providers as the HIN evolved and matters related to funding that potentially altered the path of development.

Partner roles/interaction

In most cases prior to the initiation of the HIN, there was little evidence of collaboration across institutional or professional boundaries. We noted that in the initial We//net pilot, there was considerable dialogue between providers on matters of security of access and emergent uses of new technology, where previously few of the participants had cause to collaborate.

The extensive planning effort that preceded many of the HINs speaks most clearly to the effort to engage participants from most if not all facets of the healthcare system. Alberta and Saskatchewan both completed extensive planning and consultation efforts, lasting in excess of a year. These planning efforts involved RHAs, medical associations, health science faculties and the public. InfoLink's sponsoring organizations conducted a similar effort, involving extensive surveying of member needs and expectations.

Members in the InfoLink alliance can point to an extensive dialogue between the member organizations for over two years prior to initiation of the HIN project. This dialogue was mainly centered on managing the restructuring that was taking place in the province, leading to the closure or merger of many institutions.

In many cases, given the high costs of connectivity within sparsely populated regions, it appeared that much of the initial motivation for alliance building was in pursuit of an 'order of magnitude' efficiency in provision of communication services, from a cost perspective. This may have been the case in WED*net's development, as there appeared to be little inter-organizational dialogue prior to the build-up of the customer base. The inevitable result was a partnership with few common interests.

Kari+net took a different tack when they initiated feasibility discussions with their partners regarding an information system to support their multiple site, multiple organization laboratory services reform. Lacking the necessary customer base to make the connectivity portion of their project affordable, they turned back to these same partners to examine a broader range of applications to use over the connectivity infrastructure. This 'marketing' effort was among established partners, and did not result in having to admit well-funded but dissimilar partners to the alliance.

Regional HINs have begun to enlist physician practitioners that practice outside institution boundaries, but have yet to link effectively with professional associations. As noted earlier, the RHINs have tended to form around or in close proximity to large teaching hospitals, and so have accomplished their linkage in that fashion.

British Columbia's PharmaNet is managed by the government, but maintains a close partnership with the College of Pharmacists and practicing pharmacists. The regional health authority (RHA) structure has no role to play in this alliance with the exception that access to PharmaNet was recently made available to hospital emergency departments.

Participation of providers

Connectivity is vital to the success of We//net, given the initial decision to maintain a distributed dataset architecture. Maintaining the data where it was collected was a vital step in securing practitioner 'buy in.' Another key element of attaining practitioner buy-in is the assurance of privacy and security of information. Kari+net's approach was to grant individual practitioners unique identifiers, allowing them to make inquiries regarding patients assigned to their care. Periodic audits to assess patterns of access have been conducted, to assure patients and practitioners alike, and to guide ongoing improvements to security measures.

SHIN has initiated a pilot program, which will allow physicians to receive lab results, access pharmaceutical information and perform automated verification of individuals' health insurance registration. This type of access is typical of similar projects in many of the other networks examined.

PharmaNet maintains a User Group Committee to assist in identifying problems, and to develop new policies, guidelines and legislation. Given the strong administrative and financial motivations that drove the province to institute this network, it is fair to say that the network still has its share of detractors, particularly in the prescribing physician community. This group of professionals has experienced significant constraints on their prescribing practices through enforcement of the drug formulary, so it stands to reason that the interactions that both governed the development and subsequent evolution of the network have not been all positive.

Table 3. Development Approach

Development Approach	Health Information Network
Participation of Providers	
Member	SHIN, We//net
Consultation	planning stages by all, ongoing by PharmaNet
Project initiation	LARG*net at start-up
We//net, SHIN	
Funding Approach	
Government agency	We//net, SHIN
Government funding	Healthlink
Private partners	LARG*net, We//net
Fee for service	Healthlink
Partner Relationship	
Predated HIN formation	InfoLink, OCHIP
Commenced at HIN formation	We//net, SHIN, LARG*net
Commenced after HIN formation	WED*net, HappIN

Healthlink was established as a clinically focused organization, with the goal to 1) provide electronic methods of locating and storing patient records, 2) distribute clinical information in a timely fashion and 3) provide access to online reference materials. Their work from the outset has been described as high involvement, engaging practitioners from all partner institutions in dialogue about clinical practice patterns and information needs.

Funding approach

SHIN and We//net are extensively government supported, although both have engaged private sector partners. Common to both is a partnership with the provincial telephone company, linked to infrastructure elements of the network. Both also engaged large computing and software firms as partners and project managers.

PharmaNet is also government supported, and was motivated from inception as a cost-saving innovation. The cost of pharmaceuticals is quickly becoming the single greatest component in provincial healthcare spending, and thus initial and ongoing investments in the network have been made with an expectation of short-term paybacks.

Healthlink was established in 1993 as a joint initiative of seven Toronto-area hospitals, along with three private-sector partners. They formed a private share corporation in 1996, and received over six million dollars in start-up funding from the provincial government. They now operate purely on the basis of revenues earned from partner organizations.

WED*net, early on in their project, was successful in attracting funding from both the federal and provincial governments. WED*net's primary partners spent nearly a year in implementation of their initial plans before seeking a dialogue with other regional players.

Other networks, such as OCHIP and InfoLink, have made extensive efforts to attract outside funding, primarily from a variety of government-funded initiatives. However, to date these fund raising attempts have been unsuccessful. These networks rely essentially on members' 'seed' funding to operate.

Network governance

The status of We//net and SHIN as quasi-government agencies, albeit with extensive non-government membership, suggests that governance options were

Table 4. Network Governance

External Partners Involved in Network Governance	Health Information Network
External Role Player	
Provincial Ministry of Health	PharmaNet, SHIN, We//net
Major institution	LARG*net, HappIN, InfoLink, OCHIP
Academic researchers	OCHIP, InfoLink
Private sector partner	LARG*net, SHIN, We//net

probably somewhat limited. British Columbia's PharmaNet is managed by the government, but maintains a close partnership with the College of Pharmacists and practicing pharmacists. The regional health authority (RHA) structure plays no role in this alliance.

From its inception in 1993 until the end of 1996, LARG*net operated in a relatively informal manner, pursuing growth and development. They pursued extensive community participation. It was after this initial period that the network adopted a formal governance and policymaking structure for themselves. A key change at that time was the decision to move all further application development out to consortium members.

InfoLink's governance board comprises senior representatives from each of the partner organizations. They determine the priorities of the alliance, and approve its operating budget funded through member contributions.

As we examine health networks across Canada, we see a range of successful approaches to network governance.

CONCLUSIONS

Health networks are a relatively new initiative. The services they provide to their member organizations will no doubt expand in the future. This will come through ongoing improvements in network infrastructure, through enhanced understanding of the value of information exchange and through measurement of enhanced outcomes for the patients they ultimately serve.

The technological base that underpins these alliances is constantly changing. Computers are becoming increasingly more capable of handling and compensating for human tasks (Lee, 1997). They can store information routinely gathered in healthcare service events, and assist in their retrieval through the click of a mouse. Health information networks aim to take advantage of this technology and, in doing so, accept the fact that they must continually improve their technological capabilities. Unfortunately these improvements will be costly in the short-run, and the potential long-run benefits, such as improved community health and lower hospital expenditures, remain at times uncertain.

At the foot of the path leading to each of these HINs lays a history of institutional mergers, fiscal cutbacks by government, government-imposed governance structures, and a growing and aging population. Funding agencies (primarily government in Canada) are becoming increasingly concerned that the systems they support provide effective care, and that the care offered reach those in the population most in need of care. At the same time, there is a growing recognition that a more seamless reliable approach to care, one that bridges institutions and levels of care, is needed. The extent to which these HINs aid and abet the clinical integration of services, as measured by enhanced health outcomes for patients, is the extent to which they will be able to continue to attract resources and support.

The framework we have proposed, and utilized, in this chapter addresses the elements we believe are important precursors to HIN success. The motivation underlying and guiding the work of the alliance has an important influence on the type of projects and the pace at which those projects are 'rolled out.' The alliance needs to engage partners in such a way that the entire continuum of care can be addressed within the alliance. Furthermore, we suggest that from its outset, the alliance needs to engage and involve and be persuaded by the input of the providers linked to patient care and support. Particularly in formative years, before partners can experience tangible positive results, funding availability will also be key. The pursuit of funding may lead to the inclusion of partners that create a more diffused approach to the alliance's operations; this should be handled with great care.

We also note that there is some skepticism pertaining to the faster flow of, and easier access to, patient information. Establishment and then maintenance of patient and provider trust will be key elements of the work of each alliance.

We examined the network governance approach taken and found a variety of forms and different experiences. Alliances that are centered on quasi-government agencies have not focused on governance issues at the alliance level. On a positive note, this appears to have spurred the attention of partners to patient-centred applications sooner than other networks. Only time will tell if these arrangements continue to spur development or serve to dampen the creative and collaborative engagement of practitioners.

Most alliances have commenced work on informal terms, and then slowly evolved or matured into more formal arrangements. We note one 'for-profit' alliance, and a variety of not-for-profit incorporated entities. At this stage in our work, we suggest that a form of governance that engages all partners continuously, remains focused on client (patient) needs and can sustain operations and a project pattern deemed valuable by members is apt to succeed.

REFERENCES

Blount, A. (Ed.) (1998). *Integrated Primary Care: The Future of Medical and Mental Health Collaboration,* W. W. Norton & Co., New York.

Etzioni, A. (Ed.) (1969).*The Semi-Professions and Their Organization: Teachers, Nurses, Social Workers,* MacMillan, New York.

Ferratt, T.W., Lederer, S.R. Hall, S. R. and Krella, J. M. (1996). "Swords and Plowshares: Information Technology for Collaborative Advantage," *Information and Management,* 30(3), 131-142.

Guy, M.E.(1985). *Professionals in Organizations: Debunking a Myth,* New York: Praeger, New York.

Konsynski, B.R. (1993). "Strategic Control in the Extended Enterprise," *IBM Systems Journal.* 32(1), 111-142.

Kumar, K. and Dissel, H. G. van (1996). "Sustainable Collaboration: Managing Conflict and Cooperation in Interorganizational Systems," *MIS Quarterly,* 20(3), 279-300.

Lee. F. (1997). "Evolution of Computer-Based Information Systems and Networks to Support Integrated Health Care Delivery Systems," *Top Health Information Management,* 17 (4)2.

Provan, K.G. and Sebastian, J. G. (1998). "Networks Within Networks: Service Link Overlap, Organizational Cliques, and Network Effectiveness," *Academy of Management Journal,* 41(4), 453-463.

Roos, N., Brownell, M., Shapiro, E. and Roos L. (1998). "Good News About Difficult Decisions: The Canadian Approach to Hospital Cost Control," *Health Affairs,* September / October.

Satinsky, M.A. (1998). *The Foundations of Integrated Care: Facing the Challenges of Change,* American Hospital Publishing Inc., Chicago, IL.

Volkoff, O., Chan, Y. E. and Newson, E.F.P. (1999). "Leading the Development and Implementation of Collaborative Interorganizational Systems," *Information and Management,* 35 (2), 63-75.

Wilensky, H.L. (1964). "The Professionalization of Everyone," *American Journal of Sociology,* 70, 137-158.

ENDNOTES

1 The authors wish to thank Patrick Legresley for his excellent work as a research assistant in this project. We appreciate the many hours he spent investigating Web pages of numerous health networks. The authors are also grateful to the Social Sciences and Humanities Research Council of Canada, and Queen's School of Business, for their generous financial support of this project.

2 In Canada, three levels of government exist: federal (across the country), provincial (across each province; 10 exist within the country) and municipal (across each city). Please see Figure 1.

3 In June of 2000, we noted the dissolution of the HappIN entity.

Chapter XI

Exploring ICT-Enabled Networking in Hospital Organizations

Ronald Spanjers, Ryan Peterson and Martin Smits
Tilburg University, The Netherlands

Willi Hasselbring
University of Oldenburg, Germany

This chapter describes an exploratory study of new organisational forms in hospitals. The study focuses on ICT-enabled networking in hospital organisations. Two Dutch hospitals (one general and one categorical) and a German hospital (university) are analysed. Hospitals develop through different levels of networking and phases of organisational focus. Strategic drivers and incentives are improvement of efficiency and effectiveness of the primary care process. Enabling conditions are a clear hospital strategy and an open and flexible hospital information system that supports network transactions and processes. The design and functioning of the network is conditioned by (a) the not-for-profit market, (b) the organisational focus and (c) the involvement of internal and external stakeholders. The measurability of performance increases as the organisational focus evolves. More research is called for to understand the complexity and dynamics of hospital network organisations.

INTRODUCTION

The healthcare sector is experiencing fundamental change, especially in and between hospitals (Tanriverdi and Venkatraman, 1999; Spil et al, 1999). While the role of information and communication technology (ICT) is certainly not new, the increasing dynamics of organisational and socio-economic developments, and the rapid technological advancements do emphasise the complexities and dynamics of a changing healthcare environment (Peterson et al., 1999).

Hospitals are subject to constant impulses from the national government and insurance companies to improve efficiency and effectiveness. For example, budget restrictions by the central and local government make it necessary to improve efficiency and to reduce costs; the general need to improve patient care makes it necessary to improve effectiveness. Hospitals are now becoming aware of the potential value of integrated services and the collaborative advantage of networking (Smits and Van der Pijl, 1999).

In this chapter, we focus on new ICT-enabled network organisational forms in hospitals. This study was conducted as part of a large-scale research programme on network organisations in healthcare and other industries. The ultimate aim of the research is to understand and improve the effectiveness of ICT-enabled networking in hospital organisations.

More specifically, the research questions are:
i) What are the strategic, organisational and performance features of hospital network organisations?
ii) What are the relationships and roles of the various stakeholder groups?
iii) What is the role of ICT in hospital network organisations, and how is ICT organised and managed?

The next section provides a theoretical background on network organisations in general and describes the research model underlying this exploratory study. The different organisational foci in hospitals, and the roles of stakeholders and ICT are outlined. The case studies in three ICT-enabled network hospital organisations are described and analysed. More specifically, the changing stakeholder coalitions and the strategic role of ICT are discussed. This chapter concludes with the main lessons learned and directions for future research.

THEORETICAL BACKGROUND

In the growing literature on network organisations, different definitions and typologies can be found for describing a network organisation. In general, three characteristics of network organisations are identified (Snow et al., 1992; Smits and Ribbers, 1999):
i) the network consists of at least three nodes;
ii) each node can decide independently regarding long-term relationships with other nodes;
iii) the relationship between the nodes must exist for some time and for more than one transaction.

In addition to this definition, two comments must be made. First, a network organisation can exist both inside a company (as a network of departments or

Figure 1. NEFETI research model

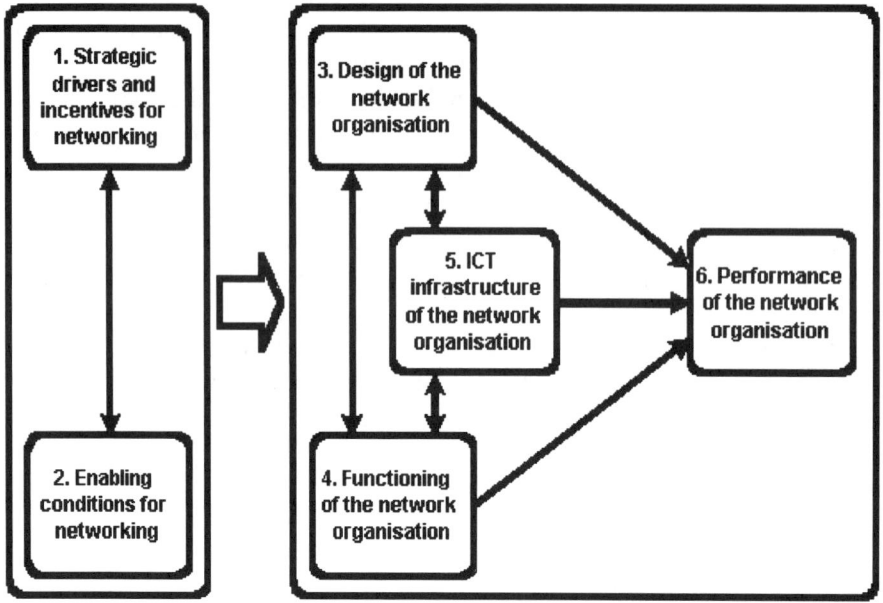

business units) and between companies. Second, a network organisation can exist as all kinds of cross sections in a value network, such as a network of suppliers, a network chain of suppliers and clients-organisations.

To analyse network organisations in practice, six interrelated aspects can be distinguished (Figure 1):

1. The strategic drivers and incentives of the stakeholders and organisations involved in the network (drivers can be commercial goals, improving internal quality, efficiency, etc.) (Grandori and Soda, 1995; Johnston and Lawrence, 1988; Normann and Ramirez, 1994).
2. The enabling conditions that stimulated the emergence and growth of the network (for instance the presence of a champion, previous experience with relevant technologies, the absence or presence of network standards) (Johnston and Lawrence, 1988; Norman and Ramirez, 1994; Moshewitz 1997a and b).
3. The design or structure of the network organisation, e.g., a chain, a star, a dyad, (Grandori and Soda, 1995); which parties or nodes are involved.
4. The way the network organisation functions, how the nodes in the network cooperate around inter- and intra-organisational processes (Johnston and Lawrence, 1988 [6]; Norman and Ramirez, 1994 [10]; Van Alsteyne, 1997 [19]).
5. The ICT infrastructure of the network organisation, e.g., the reach and range of infrastructure technologies and services (Weill and Broadbent, 1998). The role of ICT can vary from relatively simple closed systems (low reach, low range) to open flexible systems, capable of complex transactions between different inter-organisational units.

6. The performance of the network organisation, e.g., measured in terms of ICT and (inter-)organisational achievements and improvement (Grandori and Soda, 1995; Moshowitz, 1997a; 1997b).

These six aspects are regarded as generic for all lines of industry (Appendix A). The aspects can be evaluated at various moments during the development of network organisations. The research model is based on the theory of contextualism. Contextualism builds forth on theories concerned with the organisational, economic, technical and political aspects of strategic change in terms of conditions, arrangements, processes and outcomes in their context (Pettigrew, 1988). This study is specifically concerned with the conditions, arrangements, processes and outcomes of network organizations in healthcare (Walsham, 1993).

Network Organisations in Healthcare

Network organisations in hospitals can be distinguished at different levels:
- *Intra-departmental*: For example, within an organisational unit of the hospital the patient's needs are met, crossing the boundaries of the organisational units is not without hindering. Exchange of patients and information between departments is sub-optimal.
- *Inter-departmental*: For example, within a hospital that is patient oriented across organisational units. In multi-disciplinary sessions (gynaecology and oncology), the patient's needs are met without the hinder of formal internal boundaries.
- *Inter-organizational*: For example, in transmural care projects the physical boundaries of the hospital are crossed. Patient and information exchange from hospital to hospital or alms home without hindering.

In the past decade, hospitals tended to develop through three types of organisational focus (Figure 2) (Lorenzi and Riley, 1995):
1. functional-oriented organisational focus;
2. specialism-oriented organisational focus;
3. patient-oriented organisational focus.

In the functional-oriented hospital, processes are grouped by function. Ambulant and clinical wards, and services are separate organisational entities. Services and administrative functions are also centralised. Specialisms are weakly involved in the hospital top-management.

In the specialism-oriented hospital, processes are grouped in strategic business units. Specialisms become more involved in the hospital top-management. Services have the tendency to be centralised, although sometimes they are decentralised for reasons of efficiency and effectiveness. Enabled by ICT, the administrative functions become more decentralised and background process.

In the patient-oriented hospital, processes are grouped by flows of patients. Multi-disciplinary teams emerge. Administrative functions and services are outsourced when possible. The management of the hospital becomes more network based. The physical boundaries of the hospital disappear as processes become more transmural.

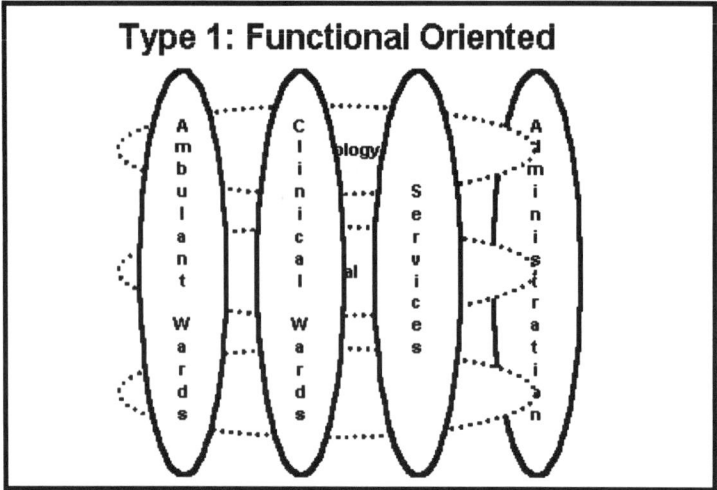
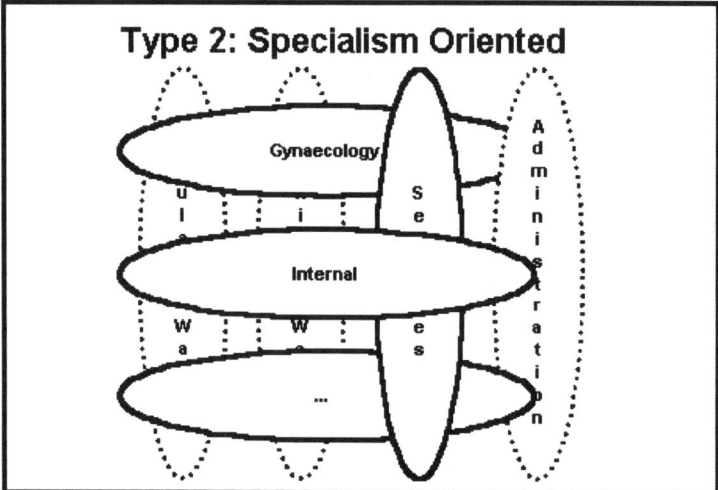
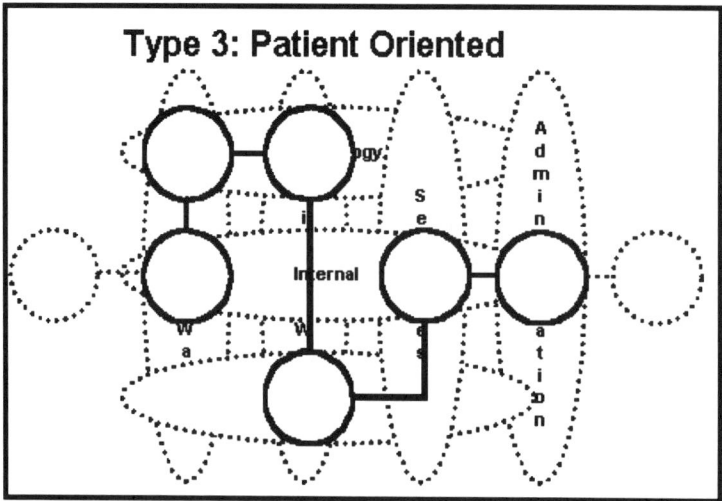

Stakeholders of Information and Communication Technology

With regard to the organisation, management and use of ICT, the following internal and external stakeholders can be identified in healthcare (Figure 3) (Glaser and Hsu, 1999; Hasselbring et al., 2000). These stakeholders play different roles with varying degrees of involvement.

Internal Stakeholders

The *top management* is interested in seamless and cost-effective operation of the hospital. The *administrative departments* expect quantitative information for billing and reports. The *physicians* expect an electronic medical record holding information on medical care and cure, such as prescription and diagnosis, with the possibility to conduct medical research. The *nurses* expect an electronic nursing record and a system for planning the resources such as operating theatres and beds. The ICT department in its role as enabler is mostly technically oriented and interested in clearly defined requirements for their work.

External Stakeholders

Increasingly, *healthcare organisation*s, such as general practitioners, hospitals and almshouses, have the need to exchange information with each other in order to achieve shared care for their patients. In theory, laboratory results, admissions and release notification can all be easily exchanged using electronic messages. *Funding institutions,* such as the government and health insurance companies, aim at an effective and efficient use of healthcare resources through deployment of new technologies. The *insurance companies* monitor the use of healthcare resources on behalf of the government. To accomplish this, hospitals have to manage statistical data on different levels of detail, which are not relevant to the primary hospital processes. In a complex ICT environment, such as a hospital, the make-or-buy decision often is in favour of buying. Given the commonly high degree of concentration in the hospital information system market, buying existing ICT solutions and hiring knowledge through *ICT vendors and consultants* implicates restrictions in terms of the ideal 'planned state.' Moreover, *patients* are getting involved in their treatment. For instance, the growing number of requested second opinions for diagnoses and the use of the legal right for patients to obtain information considering their own treatment, privacy and data security increase the demands placed on the use of ICT in hospitals.

CASE STUDIES

Three case studies were conducted to analyse network organisations in hospitals. The case studies cover the spectrum from intra-departmental to inter-departmental to inter-organisational network organisations.

Figure 3. Stakeholders involved in the organisation and management and use of ICT in hospitals

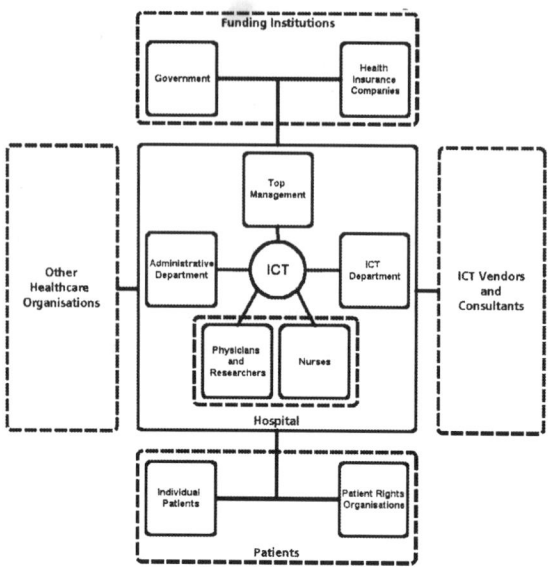

The studies comprised of semi-structured interviews with directors, department managers, project managers, technical staff and end-users of organisations participating in the network. Project plans and notes were gathered and analysed for further information. Document analysis is used to enrich and verify interview data. The validity and reliability of the study are enhanced through the use of multiple sources of information, the review of draft case reports by the interviewees and the use of a standardised case study protocol.

The analysis of the case studies is based on the research model, and focuses on the content and interrelationships among the different elements. Case analysis was conducted to identify patterns of similarities and differences within and across cases (Yin, 1994).

The three cases are described in the following subsections. An interpretation of the key findings is provided in Table 1.

University Hospital Leipzig (Germany)

The Universitätsklinikum Leipzig (former East Germany) is an academic hospital with a capacity of 1,500 clinical beds, 4,650 employees and 15 locations. Most specialisms have their own buildings, clinical wards, ambulant wards and service facilities (laboratory and radio-diagnostic). After the re-unification of Germany, the Universitätsklinikum Leipzig experienced dramatic reorganisations and updating of ICT. The Universitätsklinikum Leipzig plans to eventually reduce the 15 hospital locations to three main locations, and SAP R/3 software has been implemented.

In 1996 a 'Rahmenkonzept für die Weiterentwicklung des Klinikum-Informationsystems' was made, a general plan for the further development of the hospital information system. Main goals were identified as:
i) a central patient database,
ii) an integrated administrative resource planning system;
iii) a communication server,
iv) a medical knowledge server,
v) a clinical workplace system, and
vi) a data communication net.

The demand and supply of ICT is controlled centrally by a common project group of IMISE (Institut für Medizinische Informatik, Statistik und Epidemiologie) and ZMAI (Zentrum für Medizinische und Administrative Informationssysteme). In an annual budgeting cycle, plans concerning ICT priorities are set by a committee.

The main concern in setting priorities is to fit the plans to the budget. A large amount of the budget goes to the current implementation of SAP/R3 modules, particularly for the underlying hardware. Clinics are not free within the hospital policy to substitute a part of their budget to financing plans concerning ICT.

The Universitätsklinikum Leipzig network is perceived as successful when higher efficiency and effectiveness in control are reached, resulting in reduced costs without loss of quality in hospital healthcare. Financial and business outcomes contribute to the whole of the Universitätsklinikum Leipzig. Flexibility in organisation and ICT remain key factors in enabling the network organisation. Universitätsklinikum Leipzig has regional and national collaborations with other general and university hospitals. One would expect, considering the strong curative position of general practitioners in Germany, that from an efficiency and effectiveness perspective, networking would be more common.

Stated reasons for (future) networking are:
- marketing (attracting the 'right' patients),
- efficient and effective use of capacity and competence resulting in,
- cost reduction.

The current level of network organisation is best described as intra-departmental with progress towards the inter-departmental area. The University Hospital Leipzig is evolving from a functional-oriented hospital to specialism-oriented.

Bosch Medicentrum (General Hospital, Netherlands)

In January 1990, the Willem-Alexander Ziekenhuis and the Groot Ziekengasthuis merged into the Bosch Medicentrum. The Bosch Medicentrum is a general hospital, geographically divided in two locations in the Den Bosch area (approximately 25 km^2). It has a capacity of 780 clinical beds, 1,900 ftes (full-time equivalents), 2,600 employees and 140 physicians (divided in 30 specialties).

The annual budget is 118 million Euro (1998, the honoraria budget of physicians included), of which 65% is used for personnel, 20% for materials and 15% for the total hospital infrastructure. The Bosch Medicentrum is a traditional user of

HISCOM hospital information systems, provided by Hiscom in The Netherlands. The Bosch Medicentrum has regional and national collaborations with other general hospitals, leading to a merger in the near future.

In seeking improved efficiency and effectiveness, the Bosch Medicentrum started a reorganisation to evolve from an intra-departmental to a inter-departmental organisation structure in 1996. Units (nine Care Units, eight Supporting Care Units and two Service Units) were introduced to give the middle management the flexibility needed. In the Dutch healthcare this process is called 'tilting.'

The maximum size of the Bosch Medicentre network is 2,600 employees and 140 physicians. The network organisation takes place within the hospital. Its units are the nodes in the network. The nodes involve hospital-personnel and physicians, working together, attending to the patients' needs. Most physicians form a group within their specialty that has a separate legal entity. They form small companies within the hospital.

Incentives and enabling conditions for networking are influenced to a great extent by national and governmental rules and legislation. Dutch hospital healthcare has several barriers that prevent efficient and effective control of hospital organisations. Hospitals are not-for-profit organisations. The market does not freely determine barriers for entry and exit to this network. Hospital healthcare is considered to be a merit-good. One of the main barriers is that the current system of budgeting can work contra-productive on a micro-economic level (Raad voor de Volksgezondheid, 1999). Efficient and effective control of hospital organisations depends on the ability to determine the relation between input and output (Hofstede, 1981). Production parameters like admissions, short stays, nursing days and out-patients are still the backbone of the Dutch system budgeting hospitals. In an effort to stabilise the costs of Dutch healthcare, lump sum financing is now widely introduced. Obviously, these legislative ways of relating input and output influence the information systems of hospitals (Zuurbier, 1993). A more specific system of product-definition is needed. These changes demand a higher flexibility of ICT. This is an interesting challenge, because most hospital information systems were originally designed for hospitals with a functional management structure.

The Bosch Medicentrum uses the majority of the HISCOM hospital information systems (68 of the 109 modules available). In the area of specific hospital processes, information systems of other providers are used (Harmsen, 1999). Mainly hospital middle management, the functional operators and physicians are involved in the organisation and management of ICT. For each part of the hospital information system, at least one functional operator is assigned (totally 30). The functional operator is stationed at the unit and responsible for the quality and continuity of their part of the hospital information system. Functional operators exchange knowledge with colleagues grouped by care, supporting care and services. Technical support, implementation and central computing facilities are outsourced. The total outsourced costs of hospital information systems in 1998 were estimated at 4.3 million guilders (including 0,8 million guilders depreciation on computer equipment). The top 15 (20%) of the information systems induced 70% of the costs and 80 percent of the total computing capacity.

The demand and supply of ICT is controlled centrally by an automation co-ordinator. In an annual budgeting cycle, plans concerning ICT priorities are set by a committee. On an informative level plans are discussed in the groups of functional operators. The main concern in setting priorities is to fit the plans to the budget. A large amount of the budget goes to outsourcing, leaving only a small budget for innovation from within the organisation. However, units are free within the hospital policy to substitute a part of their budget to finance plans concerning ICT. In the near future the centrally controlled budget will be decentralised to the units.

The Bosch Medicentre network is perceived as successful when higher efficiency and effectiveness in control are reached, resulting in reduced costs without loss of quality in hospital healthcare. Financial and business outcomes contribute to the mission statement of the Bosch Medicentrum, i.e. providing a complete and coherent package of medical care that is recognisable and attractive for the patients from the region, in an integrated medical care organisation where employees can work under good conditions. Integrated medical care reaches beyond the organisational boundaries of the Bosch Medicentrum. The first transmural care projects have started. The performance of ICT is determined by how extensively and adequately it supports the network organisation. Flexibility in organisation and ICT remains a key factor in enabling the network organisation.

The current level of network organisation is best described as inter-departmental. The Bosch Medicentrum is a specialism-oriented hospital.

Roessingh Rheuma (Categorical Hospital, Netherlands)

Roessingh Research and Development is a research unit of the Roessingh Concern and employs approximately 40 people. The Roessingh Concern has approximately 140 beds and approximately 40,000 rehabilitation treatments per year. It is one of the largest rehabilitation centres in the Netherlands.

The Rheuma network was formed when a proposal was submitted to the Commission for Chronically Ill Patients to formalise and institutionalise communication lines between Medical Spectrum Twente and local clinics, and Leiden University Medical Centre and local clinics. The Roessingh Research and Development joined the Rheuma network to provide the technological know-how and services in supporting and enabling telerheumatology services. Their main role can be described as an 'internal' ICT vendor/consultant. The grassroots of the Rheuma network and the role of RRD originate from 1995, when Roessingh developed from a functional to a specialism-oriented hospital, with a focus on inter-departmental networking, through the use of multimedia technology.

Rheumatology requires a multidisciplinary approach across different lines and fields of expertise in healthcare, for example, general practitioners, physiotherapists, rehabilitation physicians. The level of network organisation is best described as intra-organisational. The Roessingh Rheuma network is a patient-oriented hospital.

The strategic objectives of the Rheuma network are to improve the efficiency and effectiveness of rheumatology services in order to meet patients' needs and care, across time and distance. In pursuing this objective, motivations mentioned by the network participants are to develop and formalise effective lines of communication between MST, LUMC and the respective local clinics, to leverage and share rheumatology expertise across the network and to exploit Internet technology for forming the Rheuma network and enabling inter-institutional communication.

The key enabling factor in the Rheuma network was the collaborative advantage by leveraging knowledge across the network and sharing expertise. Barriers to networking were building stakeholder commitment, communication and trust; spanning the traditional boundaries between institutions; and financing the network technology and infrastructure (i.e., investments, costs and reimbursements). By commencing on a small experimental scale and funding by the Commission, these limiting factors and barriers were crossed.

Different stakeholders at different levels take part in the Rheuma network. From an institutional perspective, three constituencies form the network organisation:
- Medical Spectrum Twente (MST) and the local network of physiotherapists.
- Leiden University Medical Centre (LUMC) and the local network of physiotherapists.
- Roessingh Research and Development (RRD) and the Roessingh Rehabilitation Centre (RRC).

Within each institute different stakeholders are involved from levels of general management to the physiotherapists and rheumatologists (users) involved in the telerheumatology services. In total, approximately 180 professionals are involved in the Rheuma network, spread across the different levels and institutions.

Different processes are distinguishable in the functioning of the Rheuma network. Key management processes are network coordination and stakeholder management. Frequent face-to-face meetings take place to discuss experiences and future directions. The primary processes and transactions cover telerheumatology diagnosis processes: communication and decision-making, collaboration and knowledge sharing. Within these processes, the main network 'transactions' are the provision of telerheumatology services across the network, the leveraging of rheumatology expertise across the network and the development and supply of multimedia network technology. Technology development processes focused on application and infrastructure design.

Demand and supply of ICT is differentiated across the network. ICT infrastructure is concentrated at RRD, while local applications are managed at MST, LUMC and RRC. The latter organisations are also responsible for ICT demand. A multimedia database, 'the post office,' based on Internet technology is used to facilitate the communication and diagnosis of rheumatology cases. Critical requirements are to support the current Rheuma network and to enable a synchronous multimedia communication, in order to provide efficient, effective, flexible and reliable

Table 1. Interpretation of key findings in the three cases, structured according to the model in Figure 1

Case	University Hospital Leipzig	Bosch Medicentrum	Roessingh
Level of network organisation	*intra-departmental towards inter-departmental*	*inter-departmental*	*inter-organisational*
Organisational focus	functional-oriented towards specialism-oriented	Specialism-oriented	patient-oriented
1. Strategic drivers and incentives for networking	Externally, marketing the hospital and attracting the 'right' patients.	Externally, to reduce costs.	Externally improve efficiency and effectiveness of rheumatology services, meet patients' demands, through the exploitation of ICT.
	Internally, efficient and effective use of capacity and competence resulting in cost-reduction.	Internally, to improve efficiency and effectiveness in control resulting in reduced costs without loss of quality in hospital healthcare.	Internally, to formalise effective lines of communication and develop expertise.
2. Enabling conditions for networking	A clear hospital strategy is needed to align the strategic information management with.	Efficient and effective control of hospital organisations depends on ability to determine the relation between input and output. These changes demand a higher flexibility of ICT.	The demand and supply mechanisms regarding rheumatology knowledge and ICT knowledge across the network. Sharing of costs (i.e., technical infrastructure) and risks (i.e., privacy).
3. Design of the network organisation	There is only one clear transmural example in which ICT plays a dominant role. However it is based on bilateral agreements (two nodes) and uni-directional data flow that is not integrated with the other information systems (low reach and range).	In seeking improved efficiency and effectiveness, a reorganisation took place to evolve from an intra-departmental to a inter-departmental organisation structure. Units (9 Care Units, 8 Supporting Care Units and 2 Service Units) were introduced to give the middle management the flexibility needed (moderate range & reach).	Separate responsibilities for rheumatology services and ICT services. Different functional roles and levels: 'sponsor,' 'network coordinator,' 'participants/users.' Enabling role of multimedia network technology (high reach and range).
4. Functioning of the network organisation	Mainly the ICT department and the administrative department are involved in the organisation and management of ICT. Technical support, implementation and central computing facilities are mostly insourced. The budget for innovation has been big.	Hospital middle management, functional operators and physicians and automation coordinator are involved in the organisation and management of ICT. Technical support, implementation and central computing facilities are outsourced. The budget for innovation is small.	Network and stakeholder management. Provision of telerheumatology services across the network. Leveraging of rheumatology expertise across the network. Centralised (concentrated) ICT infrastructure and dispersed ICT applications. Differentiated demand and supply of multimedia network technology.
5. ICT infrastructure of the network organisation	The implementation of a new hospital information (SAP R3) system, based on new technology, makes future networking possible.	To support the specific hospital processes, mainly HISCOM (market leader) information systems are used.	A multimedia database, 'the post office, based on Internet technology is used to facilitate communication and diagnosis of rheumatology cases. Critical requirements are a-synchronous multimedia communication.
6. Performance of the network organisation	The lack of a clear hospital strategy provides no triggers to reach beyond organisational boundaries in transmural care projects. There is no clear measure for performance.	Reduced costs without loss of quality in hospital healthcare. In this way a contribution is made to the mission statement. The networking is starting to reach beyond organisational boundaries in transmural care projects.	Improvement of inter-institutional collaboration and communication. Efficiency and effectiveness improvement of rheumatology services. Stakeholder satisfaction. Redefinition of stakeholder roles and (strategic) positioning in the sector.

telerheumatology services. The experiences with the Rheuma network have been successful. Stakeholders have experienced the 'collaborative advantage' of working together, sharing knowledge and developing expertise.

NETWORK ORGANISATIONS IN HOSPITALS AND STAKEHOLDER ROLES

To summarise the findings in the three hospitals, the Leipzig hospital is regarded to be an example of an intra-departmental network organisation, the Bosch Medicentrum hospital an inter-departmental network organisation and the Roessingh hospital an inter-organisational network.

Strategic drivers and incentives for the emergence of network organisations in all three hospitals are:

i) improvement of efficiency and effectiveness of the primary care process, reduce costs and

ii) meeting patients' needs and patient-information-streams. Internal and external stakeholders have different 'rationalities' regarding improvement of efficiency and effectiveness.

Enabling conditions for network organisations in hospitals are:

i) a clear hospital strategy, aligned with a clear ICT strategy and

ii) an open and flexible hospital information system that can support the transactions of the network.

More specifically, with regard to the role of ICT in hospital network organisations, we see that as hospital networks transform from an internally functional-oriented organisation towards an externally patient-oriented organisation, ICT plays an increasing strategic role, thereby shifting from a 'utility,' towards a 'dependent' and finally an 'enabling' role. The shift in network design and ICT role has consequences for the different stakeholder roles and the dominant coalitions.

The association between the organisational focus of the three hospitals and the involvement of the internal and external stakeholders in the organisation and management of ICT is described in Table 2. The following observations can be made:

- In a functional-oriented hospital, classical stakeholders such as the ICT department and administration dominate the use of ICT together with ICT vendors and consultants.
- In a specialism-oriented hospital, the use of ICT can come to a standstill as a result of the 'over'-participation in the number of stakeholders.
- In a patient-oriented hospital, internal stakeholders such as physicians, researchers and nurses dominate the use of ICT together with external stakeholders such as the funding institutions and other healthcare institutions.

As hospital network organisations evolve in network focus and design, the dominant coalitions of stakeholders also evolve and stakeholders assume different roles.

Table 2. *Organisational focus and stakeholder involvement in the organisation and management of ICT*

	External Stakeholders				Internal Stakeholders				
	Funding institutions	ICT-Vendors and consultants	Patients	Other healthcare institutions	Top Management	ICT department	Physicians and Researchers	Nursing	Administrative
Leipzig (functional-specialism)	-	++	-	-	++	++	-	-	++
Bosch Medicentrum (specialism)	+	+	-	+	+	+	+	-	+
Roessingh (patient)	++	+	+	++	+	++	++	+	-

With respect to the performance of network organisations in hospitals, it appears that:

- In a functional-oriented structure, performance is not defined in advance or performance measures are described in general terms, repeating the mission statement.
- In a specialism-oriented structure, performance is likewise described in general terms, with a focus on stakeholder expectations and networking agreements. Stakeholder roles are redefined and the performance is assessed in terms of stakeholder satisfaction.
- In a patient-oriented structure, stakeholder roles have been institutionalised and the 'benefits' of networking become clear. These include: healthcare efficiency and effectiveness gains, professionalisation and expertise development and stakeholder satisfaction.

Performance in financial terms remains difficult because the relations between input and output in a hospital are hard to determine since 'traditional' cost-benefit analyses of network organisations in healthcare are sub-optimal due to the inadequacy to account for all the (inter-/intra-organisational) changes that occur as a result of networking.

What emerges from the foregoing is a complex and dynamic picture of network foci and designs, and the role of different stakeholders and ICT in hospital network organisations (Figure 4).

The case studies indicate that when hospital networks transform from internally functional-oriented organisations towards externally patient-oriented organisations, the complexity of both the social infrastructure and the technological infrastructure increase in reach and range. In the case of Roessingh organisation, network formation started in late 1995, and over the past five years, the hospital network has gradually developed from an internally functional network towards an external patient network. The case findings suggest that both social and technological 'webs' need to be considered and managed in order for the hospital network to transform successfully through each of the networkability stages. Critical success factors for sustaining networkability are stakeholder roles and relationships and the ICT reach and range.

Figure 4. Trends in hospital network organisations

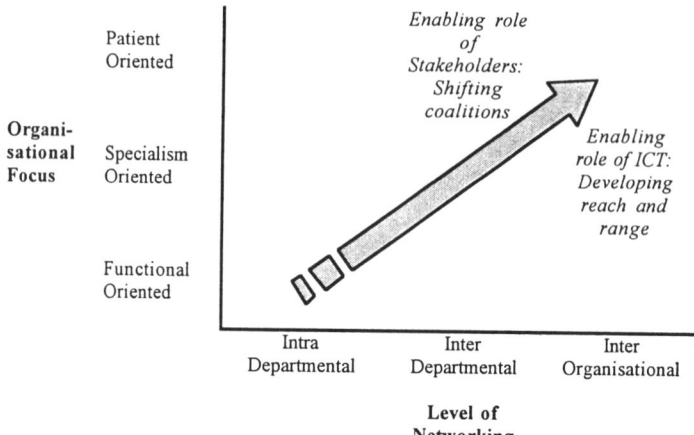

CONCLUSIONS

Two Dutch hospitals (one general and one categorical) and a German hospital (university) were analysed as examples of network organisations in healthcare. Three levels are distinguished: inter-departmental network, intra-organisational network and inter-organisational network. In the three cases in this study, the three levels corresponded with the organisational focus: respectively functional orientation, specialism-orientation and patient orientation. The case findings indicate that there is no such thing as 'one best' network organisation in hospitals.

Strategic drivers and incentives are improvement of efficiency and effectiveness of the primary care process. Enabling conditions are a clear hospital strategy and an open and flexible hospital information system that can support the transactions of the network.

The design and functioning is influenced by the not-for-profit market, the organisational focus and the involvement of internal and external stakeholders. The role of stakeholder groups with regard to the organisation and management of ICT varies between the different organisational foci. In the functional-oriented hospital, the impact of ICT vendors and consultants is very high; the role of patients, physicians, researchers and nurses low. In contrast, in the patient-oriented hospital, the impact of ICT vendors and consultants appears to be low, while physicians, researchers and nurses, funding institutions and other healthcare institutions are high. However, in the case of the Rheuma network, RRD fulfilled the role of an 'internal' ICT vendor and consultant. More research is necessary to investigate what roles (internal and external) ICT vendors and consultants play in ICT-enabled network hospital organisations.

With respect to the network structure in hospitals and the stakeholder model, the findings in the three cases suggest that hospital networks transform from an internally functional-oriented organisation towards an externally patient-oriented organisation. In this process, ICT plays an increasing strategic role, thereby shifting from a 'utility,' towards a 'dependent' and finally an 'enabling' role. The shift in network design and ICT role has consequences for the different stakeholder roles and the dominant coalitions. Eventually, the move to an external orientation will lead to a restructuring of the healthcare sector, as was the case the Rheuma network.

The measurability of performance seems to improve as the level of networking evolves from inter-departmental to intra-organisational. However, performance expressed as financial performance will remain difficult to measure, because the relation between input and output in a hospital is hard to determine, but also because network performance involves complex inter-organisational changes that cannot be expressed in financial terms only.

The findings and conclusions in this chapter are based on in depth analysis of three cases. More cases need to be investigated before generalisations can be made. Moreover, future research should specifically focus on the development of social and ICT networks that enable healthcare organisations to improve networkability and performance. Comparisons with network organisations in other sectors and lines of industry are likewise necessary and useful, in order to develop guidelines for the organisation, management and use of ICT; to enable effective, efficient and high quality organisational forms in healthcare.

REFERENCES

Glaser, J.P.& Hsu, L. (1999). *The Strategic Application of Information Technology in Healthcare Organizations,* The McGraw-Hill Companies.

Grandori, A. & Soda, G. (1995). *Inter-firm networks: Antecedents, Mechanisms and Forms,* Organization Science, 16(2), 183-214.

Harmsen, J., (1999) Automatisering in de ziekenhuissector, Stand van zaken 1998, Nzi publicatie, 198.1242.

Hasselbring, W., Peterson R., Smits M. and Spanjers R. Strategic information management for a dutch university hospital. In *Proceedings of the 16th Medical Informatics Europe Congress* (MIE2000), (Eds.), Hasman, A., Blobel, B., Dudeck, J., Engelbrecht, R. and Gell, G. H.-U. Prokosch, Hannover, Germany, IOS Press, 885-889

Hofstede, G. (1981). Management control of public and not-for-profit activities, *Accounting, Organisations and Society*, 6(3), 193-211.

Johnston, R. & Lawrence, P.R. (1988). Beyond vertical integration – The rise of the value-adding partnership, *Harvard Business Review,* 66(4), 94-101

Lorenzi, N.M. & Riley, R.T. (1995). Organisational Aspects of Health Informatics – Managing Technological Change, New York: Springer-Verlag.

Mowshowitz, A. (1997a), On the theory of virtual organization, Systems Research and Behavioural Science, 14(6), 373-384.

Mowshowitz, A. (1997b). Virtual organization, *Communications of the ACM*, 40(9), 30-37.

Normann, R. & Ramirez, R. (1994). *From Value Chain to Value Constellation: Designing Interactive Strategy*, 71(4), 65-77.

Peterson R.R., Smits M.T., and Spanjers R. (1999). Exploring IT enabled networked organisations in health care: emerging practices and phases of development, In *Proceedings of the 8th European Conference on Information Systems* (ECIS2000), Vienna, Austria, (Eds.), Hansen, H.R., Bichler, M. and Mahrer, H. 1253-1260.

Pettigrew, A.M. (Ed.) (1988). *The management of change*, Blackwell, Oxford.

Raad voor de Volksgezondheid & Zorg (1999), Prikkels tot doelmatigheid.

Smits M.T., Van der Pijl, G.J. (1999). Developments in Hospital Management and Information Systems. In R. Sprague (Ed.), *Proceedings of the 32nd Hawaii International Conference on System Sciences (HICSS '99).*

Smits, M.T., Ribbers, P.M.A. (1999). *Network Enterprises of the Future and Enabling Telematics Infrastructures,* NEFETI Report 99.01, Telematics Institute, Enschede

Snow, C.C., Miles, R.E. and Coleman, H.J. (1992). Managing 21st Century Network Organizations, *Organizational Dynamics,* 20(3), 5-20.

Spil, T.A.M., Meeberg, H.J. van de, Sikkel, K. (1999), The definition, selection, and implementation of a new hospital information system. In *Proceedings of the 32nd Hawaii International Conference on System Sciences.*

Tanriverdi, H., Venkatraman, N. (1999) Creation of professional networks, an emergent model using telemedicine as a case. In R. Sprague (Ed.), *Proceedings of the 32nd Hawaii International Conference on System Sciences (HICSS, '99).*

Van Alstyne, M. (1997). The state of network organization: A survey in three frameworks, http:/www.css.mit.edu/CCSWP192.htm.

Walsham, G. (1993). *Interpreting Information Systems in Organizations*, New York, John Wiley and Sons.

Weill, P. and Broadbent, M. (1998). Leveraging the new infrastructure, Havard Business Press

Yin, R.K. (1994). *Case Study Research, Design and Methods,* Sage Publication, London

Zuurbier, J. J. (1993). *Financial control in hospitals, the changing structure of internal financial control in Dutch hospitals,* Enschede.

Section 5

Knowledge Management Healthcare Information Systems

Distributed Knowledge Management
Michael Holm Larsen
Mogens Kühn Pedersen

Enabling Medical Group Practices
Nilimini Wickramasinghe
J. B. Silvers

Chapter XII

Distributed Knowledge Management in Healthcare Administration

Michael Holm Larsen and Mogens Kühn Pedersen
Copenhagen Business School, Denmark

The chapter addresses the electronic commerce application field of healthcare administration. Models for knowledge distribution are a rare commodity in healthcare Administration. Distributed knowledge management (DKM) is a concept that originated as an abstraction of a business model prepared for the mechanical and agricultural industry, but holds promises for a more general use. The contribution of this chapter is to suggest a new business model based on DKM and show the relevance and applicability of this concept in a totally new context of healthcare administration.

INTRODUCTION

As a comprehensive documentation of individual patient records is a prerequisite for efficiency improvements in a fragmented medical value chain, the healthcare industry needs effective means to manage data as well as information and knowledge. The purpose of introducing an abstract model for knowledge management is to ensure the problem is not only solved from a micro perspective with bilateral communications, but is brought into a macro perspective with structured multilateral business relations. Apart from the perspective of structuring business relations, an abstract model also may offer the opportunity to balance quality care with low cost efforts.

Copyright © 2001 IEEE. Reprinted, with permission, from
Proceedings of HICSS-34 (2001), digital text version.

These relations may be supported by information and communication technologies, which throughout the last decade have been more and more accepted in the healthcare industry and sector. Information and communication networks extend the reach and range of the firm's business opportunities (Keen, 1986). The information technologies of networks radically challenge management to consider the information separability of their major business processes (Sampler, 1998). Thus we are moving from business process redesign into a business network redesign era of strategic management (Hammer and Champy, 1993; Venkatraman, 1994; Hammer, 1995; Hax and Wilde, 1999).

The principles governing strategizing network reconfiguration cannot be found in the conception of knowledge management as purely an internal business affair. Moving beyond the boundaries of the firm into the extended enterprise (Konsynski, 1993) elevates the virtual organising of business into a knowledge-based strategy for a "dynamic portfolio of relationships to assemble and coordinate the required assets for delivering value to the customers" (Venkatraman and Henderson, 1998, 33). Business-to-business networks transcend the conventional image of value chains creating a complex exchange of specific information and in particular of specific knowledge (Choudhury and Sampler, 1997).

We argue that healthcare provision and administration represents an instance of applicability of a network distributed knowledge management (DKM) model. A case from the U.S. health sector proves this right.

The model to be presented caters for knowledge relations and the specific nature of network relations while stressing decision support (Sridhar, 1998). We argue that the exchange of asymmetric, specific knowledge in a network economy generates among all the participants a performance superior to that achieved without distributed knowledge networks.

KNOWLEDGE MANAGEMENT: CENTRALISED VERSUS DISTRIBUTED

This chapter emphasises the interorganisation perspective on knowledge management. Of particular interest is the capability of information technology to serve human purposes using symbols that are an integrated part of knowledgeable human behaviour. Information technology in this regard is a knowledge technology that processes meaningful, symbolic behaviour to manage extended economic organisations (Konsynski, 1993; Pedersen, Kühn, 1996). Knowledge management is therefore bound to rely upon information technologies including networks, the technologies of processing, transmission and storage, as these continuously experience diminishing costs compared to wages and capital equipment. Distributed knowledge management contemplates issues found in network theory exploring "co-specialised assets, joint control and collective purpose" (Alstyne, 1997, 86). These trends converge in the question: What does knowledge management need to provide for in economic organisations?

Knowledge management means the application of information technologies first represented in the acquisition of knowledge in a knowledge repository, and later represented in network models like intranet and extranet (Davenport and Prusak, 1998; Scott, 1998). The network perspective receives increasing interest in the management literature as "the future competition is not between companies, but between networks" (Kotler, 1994). Since the early dawn of knowledge management, several developments ensued.

The centralised knowledge creation model promotes the idea of making knowledge available to the whole organisation as the purpose of knowledge management (Nonaka, 1994; Nonaka, Byosiere, Borucki and Konno, 1994; Nonaka and Takeuchi, 1995; El Sawy and Bowles,, 1997; Favela, 1997; Davenport and Klahr, 1998). Thus knowledge management (KM) faces the challenge of how to ensure a dynamic updating of knowledge.

The alternative to a centralised knowledge management model, a distributed knowledge management model, generates knowledge among decision makers in interdependent businesses on a continuous basis while redistributing the outcome for a time-efficient knowledge use. The symmetries in knowledge and time specificity of the decision makers ensure that knowledge creation in an actor network is an incentive compatible exchange of knowledge (Pedersen, 1999).

The centralised KM model consists in a conversion from individual, knowledge specificity into organisational, collective knowledge made available to all individuals where each individual user on an ad hoc basis converts the global knowledge into local decision support. In contrast, the distributed KM model requires another conversion. The focus is on the exchange of specific knowledge to network actors in a mutual value-adding network. Each actor appropriates information and submits enhanced information that in return becomes enhanced by other network actors at other destinations, and thus returns to the originator more valuable than when originated. The latter process also makes for the difference between a centralised KM system that is passive in regard to decision making and an active distributed decision support system that takes advantage of the knowledge specificity related to different actors. And finally knowledge creation in terms of knowledge specificity encompasses both tacit and explicit knowledge since the same individuals or teams that create knowledge apply it (Polanyi, 1952; 1966; Spender, 1996). The emergent knowledge co-located with the actor results from acquired knowledge from the network merged with local, specific knowledge. Therefore, emergent knowledge resides with the actor and does not have to cross organisational boundaries. Only specific knowledge items are passed on in the network. This accounts for the use of both explicit and tacit knowledge in the DKM model.

The distributed KM widens the scope of knowledge management by including business partners in a broader network of knowledge exchange. In particular manufacturing and service suppliers in customer support knowledge may take advantage of the Internet by moving knowledge beyond organisational boundaries (El Sawy and Bowles, 1997; Hagel and Rayport, 1997; Venkatraman and Henderson,

1998). The supply chain attracted attention with its scope for increase of overall efficiency (Anderson, Day and Rangan, 1997). The linear model of a knowledge flow of the demands of customers to dealers and distributors though did not transform into value-added knowledge before considering the advantage from using the World Wide Web using rich information representations.

Today, the distinction between knowledge management in manufacturing and in professional services may seem to be overridden by the experience of knowledge management projects crossing previously relevant lines of demarcation Krogh and Roos, 1995; Krogh and Nonaka, 1997; Krogh, Roos and Kleine, 1998; Davenport, DeLong and Beers1998; Ruggles, 1998; Pedersen, 1999). The traditional dichotomy of acquiring information either in reactive mode (El Sawy and Pauchant, 1988) with a specific decision to make or in proactive mode to scan and monitor the environment to detect problems requires different decision management. Between the two we find a network of interdependent decision makers all acting on information specificity that derives from knowledge specificity and time specificity (Choudhury and Sampler, 1997).

The rise of knowledge management should be tempered by the concomitant rise of decision support systems, though in a new framework, viz. the distributed knowledge management. The model of supply chain management relates a significant share of all trade to opportunities of knowledge management for efficiency purposes thus representing a significant part of all business models. The supply chain network has been shown to benefit from information technology in the order fulfilment process (Strader, Fu-Ren and Shaw, 1998). Unlike previous, often hypothetical discussions of virtual organisations, the supply chain network decision support system provides an illustration of a robust knowledge-based structure where the knowledge exchange enhances the performance efficiency of all participating in the network.

The attributes of distributed knowledge management therefore carry implications for a broad range of business applications.

DISTRIBUTED KNOWLEDGE MANAGEMENT

The raison d'être of network distributed knowledge management resides in actor network role differentiation (Callon, 1991; Law and Hassard, 1999; Hull, Walsh, Green and McMeekin, 1999). Originating in innovation studies the actor network concept now permeates into the economics and sociology of organising entities ('intermediaries') and actors that are defined through their relationships. The nature of flows of knowledge (the 'intermediaries') between actors in computer-based networks takes on a dimension of symmetric incentives not otherwise found. In traditional economic analysis interdependencies across several market boundaries go unaccounted, an exception is Porter's clusters (Porter, 1990; 1998a; 1998b), and in sociology these are abstracted into institutional categories in neglect of actors. Actor network theory allows for both autonomy and interdependence of

Table 1. The Specificity of information (Choudhury & Sampler, 1997, p.29).

	Time Specificity	**Knowledge Specificity**
Specificity in Acquisition	Information that must be acquired immediately, or very shortly, after it first originates or becomes available	Information that can be acquired only by someone with the required specific knowledge
Specificity in Use	Information that decreases in value unless used immediately, or very shortly, after it becomes available	Information that can be effectively used only by someone with the required specific knowledge

actors in networks constructed by that which is exchanged, the intermediary, here specific knowledge taking account of each actor's specific role in the network.

In a business value chain, the division of labour allocates different tasks for each actor. These tasks require specific and global knowledge in varying combinations for their completion. The resource-based view of the firm argues that for each actor compared to others in the same market, the one succeeding the best in the value chain holds somewhat unique resources. The resource differential also explains the positioning in the value chain by reference to rents and quasi-rents from these resources (Wernerfelt, 1984; Milgrom and Roberts, 1992; Foss, 1997). The information associated with the resource-based view exhibits the characteristics of asset specificity from the point of view of transaction cost economics (Williamson, 1985; 1986; 1994). In this section this specificity is examined in more detail.

In this chapter the healthcare industry is regarded, but before presenting and discussing the appropriateness of the model, the main elements of DKM are presented (Larsen, Franck, Pedersen, 1999; Pedersen, 1999).

Information Specificity

Information specificity is defined as "the extent to which the value of information is restricted to its use and/or acquisition by specific individuals or during specific time periods" (Choudhury and Sampler, 1998, p. 29. Information specificity is in two forms, knowledge and time specificity. Knowledge specificity refers to either scientific or technical knowledge or "knowledge of context, or knowledge of particular circumstances of time and place" (Choudhury and Sampler, 1997, p. 30. If acquiring the information presupposes special training, insights, etc., the information is high in knowledge specificity in acquisition. Specificity in use often follows specificity in acquisition (Huber, 1982). Knowledge specificity may reside in different people or units in an organisation, called intra-organisational knowledge specificity. Inter-organisational knowledge specificity in a network economy refers to the existence of knowledge that is specific to each single organisation in the network reflecting that division of labour follows from a high degree of specialisation.

Time specificity can be found in the dictum that the right information at the right place at the right time prevails over all other information. Time specificity in use reflects a loss of value if the information is not used immediately, whereas time specificity in acquisition refers to an event like nature of information; an example is that the registration of the size of an earthquake must take place at the time of the quake. This example also conveys that specificity in use may not follow from specificity in acquisition.

The information time specificity argument can been extended to business in general due to the proliferation of time-based competition (Stalk and Hout, 1990; Wang and Barron, 1997). Competition leaves few without a sting from time pressures that are translated into information requirements equally time sensitive. In this sense much information acquires time specificity that if put aside devalues or makes the information irrelevant.

Timeliness no longer only resides with products like newspapers, flight tickets, tomatoes or sophisticated electronic products. Since timeliness is associated with business in general, the time specificity of information assets achieves a much wider relevance than that of a particular product or service characteristic. Further, shorter product lifecycles due to innovation speed up and due to customisations result in frequent change in product varieties, which makes necessary a careful product-customer tracking system demanding a management response like the timeliness claim.

Knowledge specificity traditionally plays a significant role in strategic technology collaboration for product development (Badaracco, 1991). As more technologies become systemic the knowledge interdependencies increase in use while relying upon knowledge specificity in acquisition (Teece, 1987; Chesbrough and Teece, 1996). In networks the knowledge specificity is a defining characteristic, whether explained by the transaction cost economics of relational contracting due to asset specificity or explained by beneficial (knowledge) cooperation (Johanson and Mattson, 1987). Knowledge specificity carries over into knowledge management issues of identification, storage and use.

The Actor Network Distributed Knowledge Management Model

The concept 'distributed' refers to an organisation in which activities are located to those locations or entities where it is best performed, determined for example by skills, costs or resources (Galbraith and Lawler, 1998). In our context, distributed normally also refers to independent organisations (companies) performing each of their value-added activities.

In an actor network distributed model of knowledge management, the acquisition of knowledge will not reside only within a single organisation. The inter-organisational knowledge specificity reflects the differences in specialisation and position in the network, for instance a supply chain. In any organisation external business partners are a source of important business information. Therefore it remains a target in the establishment of a repository to convert various partner-competitor systems into partnership systems sharing relevant and timely information about the significant environment of the company. Facing increasing competition in, e.g., customer response time, organisations are looking for tools to update the repository on a continuous basis, usually, when a certain threshold is reached that elicits signals calling for attention. The more the threshold information enters into daily routines, the more decision support is derived. The knowledge specificity of a partner may be merged with that of another that converts the information into new, specific knowledge. This knowledge fed back to the contributing partners' local applications generates new specific knowledge.

If we merge these aspects of information processing in an inclusive environment, we end up with a system holding distributed knowledge repositories at the same time as showing decision support qualities due to information timeliness and relevancy to the network actors. The network makes partners' time-specific knowledge available for processing along with the actor's own specific knowledge. This processing converts the actor's knowledge to a new, specific knowledge. The new specific knowledge or an item of it is passed on to another actor in the network. Also here specific knowledge received is merged with knowledge possessed forming a new, specific knowledge, items of which are passed on to another actor, eventually closing the circle as new specific knowledge arrives at the first mentioned actor. Of course, the actor that generates new knowledge items has to benefit from the received items in a non-intuitive way for the knowledge to be seen as vital to each actor's decision making.

The network distributed knowledge management process can be modelled in a data flow like the one of a public key system (Ghosh, 1998).

Figure 1 shows the decision process of each actor in the network and the distributed, specific knowledge passed on to the following actor. The figure represents a succession of nested knowledge creations in a distributed environment (Riempp and Nastansky, 1997). Each actor has independent, separate information management allowing for messageObjects for the exchange of specific knowledge items in the network.

In Table 2 the proposed model of a supply network decision support system, based upon well-defined knowledge repositories, is found. In the model we have stressed the requirements for viability, the knowledge repositories, the information exchanges required to convert localised, specific knowledge into properly converted specific knowledge entering decision making locally.

We have outlined a simplified business structure in which the company exchanges information with a representative dealer and an end-user (customer) of its product or service banking on its product state model (PSM). To analyse the nature of the relationships, we present the relationship in more detail. This is obtained if we consider a manufacturing company and the dealer as a service company whereas the end-user may be in any kind of trade. The determination of actors is meant as illustration of the model that is considered to be generally relevant in networks. For details see Larsen et al. (1999), where a manufacturing company produces agricultural machines (sprayers), dealers are trading in machines and spare parts and farmers are operating the sprayers vital in crop protection, reducing crop damage and yield losses.

In the matrix on the next page, only knowledge regarding product maintenance and replacement is entered whereas business information like prices, quotes, orders, payments, etc. all have been disregarded since there are standard information exchange in all businesses. In this example the business information interchange does not call upon a decision support model.

The knowledge management approach stresses source of knowledge and needs for sharing. In this model sharing is given by the nature of the relationships between

Table 2. The Knowledge Exchange Matrix (Source: Pedersen, 1999).

From: \ To:	Producer	Dealer	End-User
Producer	Internal knowledge handling	Product services knowledge Stock mix according to PSM	Self-service manuals Online advice End-user community
Dealer	State of stock mix Crisis management spare parts stock	Internal knowledge handling	Allocated (reserved) spare parts in stock Maintenance services
End-user	Hours of product use FAQs revealing usage problems Time-critical services	Maintenance support Replacement support Product support	Internal knowledge handling

Figure 1 The distributed knowledge network model (Source: Pedersen, 1999).

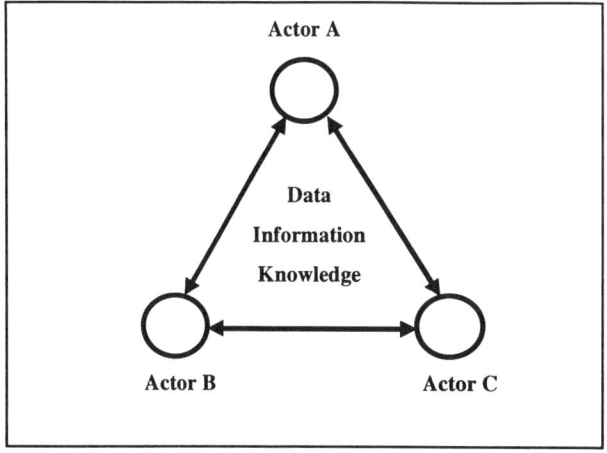

the three actors of the supply network. They are truly interdependent if all parties hold specific information. That is the case if the dealer's database on customers informs about the propensities of customers to repair rather than replace parts and components, and the propensity to cater for risk among their customers, all adding up to a knowledge of the immediate expected demand for services and spare parts. At the same time the dealers offer this knowledge, not in terms of a large amount of data but in terms of consolidated data, i.e., in the demand for allocated (reserved) stock and for a crisis managing stock to cope with unexpected demand.

The three actors of the supply network all hold privileged knowledge that, offered as continuous data to the other actors, make the aggregate information emerge as a new specific knowledge while being proper as decision support for each actor in his particular circumstances. The faster the information exchange cycle, the more the quality of relevance is supplemented with the one of timeliness, adding up to a new category, the distributed knowledge decision support.

Only by abandoning the dualistic model where the firm confronts an anonymous market does the nature of business-to-business and business-to-consumer relations emerge as complex, interdependent relationships, the ground for evolving strategic knowledge management options. The firm has to be perceived in a heterogeneous, structured rather than a homogenous, environment where identified complementors and customers represent opportunities but also challenges to the firm (Anderson, Day and Rangan, 1997). The co-existence of customer relations, business partners and relationships, and networks for distributed knowledge management coalesce into what Venkatraman and Henderson (1998) have named the "architecture for virtual organising," stressing that these are strategic characteristics applicable to every organisation.

THE CASE OF ARKANSAS DIVISION OF MEDICAL SERVICES

The case study is to a large extend based on the project presentation EDS presents on their Web site (see eds.com) in addition to Web site information from Arkansas Division of Medical Services (DMS).

Arkansas DMS administrates the Medicaid program that struggled to balance quality care with low program costs for low-income patients. The problem was that patients often went to emergency rooms and clinics for treatment. They seldom saw the same doctor more than once or twice. Therefore, doctors had to start over each time a new patient entered the clinic for treatment, which added unnecessary costs, wasted time and would furthermore potentially reduce the effectiveness of the healthcare.

Arkansas DMS officials recognised that doctors had the opportunities for serving patients best if they understood the medical history and treatments of each patient. As Arkansas DMS were faced with the fact that service to low-income patients under the Medicaid program increased, this called for the finding of a way to forge lasting relationships between patients and primary care physicians.

Those eligible for Medicaid fall into categories such as Supplemental Security Income receivers, i.e., people older than 64, blind or disabled adults and children, participants in aid to families with dependent children, or aged, blind or disabled persons in nursing homes who meet state eligibility requirements for long-term care, etc. (Medicaid, 1999). Persons who are not eligible for any of these programs may qualify for Medicaid through the medically needy program, depending on their incomes, resources and medical needs.

The Arkansas Medicaid Program covers 12 federally mandated services and several optional services.

With more than 415,000 potential Medicaid recipients in the state, program administrators faced three mandatory tasks for each case: confirm patient eligibility; find a primary care physician to stay with; and pay doctors, pharmacists and hospitals promptly. Failure to achieve any of these tasks could lead to untreated ailments, rising costs and reduction of the federal grants needed to fund the program.

The AEVCS System

Electronic Data Systems, EDS (1999), designed and built an electronic business system called Automated Eligibility Verification and Claims Submission (AEVCS). The key to accessing the system is a photo ID card with patient data on a magnetic strip.

The AEVCS system supports the processing of eligibility-verification and claims transactions through a network of point-of-sale devices or vendor systems. Each transaction is processed in real time, and a response is returned to the submitter immediately, noting whether the transaction has been accepted by Medicaid and informing the submitter of any errors.

The AEVCS system was developed jointly by the Arkansas Department of Human Services' Division of Medical Services and EDS, Arkansas Medicaid's fiscal agent. The AEVCS system, which was piloted in 1992 and implemented throughout Arkansas in June 1993, operates at more than 2,600 provider locations.

By using sophisticated VeriFone point-of-sale devices and a nation-wide packet-switching network, AEVCS lets providers determine, in real time and in one simple operation, a patient's eligibility for Medicaid. If the patient is eligible for Medicaid, AEVCS delivers an authorisation number to the provider, guaranteeing that any claim submitted for treatment on that date shall not be denied on the basis of ineligibility for benefits.

The system accepts most claim types used in the Arkansas Medicaid program, including HCFA-1500 medical; UB-92 hospital inpatient and outpatient; Early and Periodic Screening, Diagnosis and Treatment (EPSDT); pharmacy; vision; dental; and long-term care claims.

Knowledge, Information and Data Exchange

AEVCS can be accessed through point-of-sale devices, vendor systems, PCs

Table 3. The Knowledge Exchange Matrix for Arkansas Health Care

From: \ To:	Arkansas DMS	Doctors	Patients
Arkansas DMS	Internal knowledge handling	Confirmation of patient payment Display medical provider information	Assign primary care physicians
Doctors	Verify patient eligibility and benefit use	Internal knowledge handling	Care, treatment and advice
Patients	Request for payment status information	Patient medical history and treatment (patient card)	Internal knowledge handling

and both intranet and Internet Web sites. Office staff members of Arkansas DMS use the Web sites to display state-wide medical provider information and assign primary care physicians (PCPs) to patients. This set up allows eligible recipients to quickly choose their PCPs based on criteria important to them.

The patient's card is "swiped" through a terminal like those used with credit cards at the doctor's office. Hereby the system verifies patient eligibility and benefit use. AEVCS also confirms payment that will deposit electronically into the physician's bank account.

This flow of data, information and knowledge is collected in Table 3 in order to provide an overview of the communication of the business relations.

Compared to the knowledge exchange model in previous studies, the state model of this study is the patient medical history and treatment record. Hence, instead of speaking about a Product State Model, we might in this case speak about another kind of PSM, i.e., a People State Model. The actors holding resources relevant to the "people state model" are health service providers, i.e., primary care physicians, hospitals, dentists, pharmacies, etc., as well as the agency paying for these services. In this case Arkansas Division of Medical Services pays for the health services instead of an insurance company, as is the case for patients not eligible for Medicaid. In this case as well as in the case of the mechanical and the agricultural industry, the information exchange features specific information provided to an actor with capacity to exploit this information in actions guided by the actor's specific knowledge. The knowledge, information and data carried by the PSM is the core of the distributed knowledge management network.

Technical Specifications

The technical specifications suggested and implemented by EDS, EDI was a real-time SQL® with an online transaction processing database to support the AEVCS system, processing 17.1 million transactions per year. The AEVCS system resides on a Tandem® platform in Auburn Hills, Michigan. The Tandem platform is averaging a 20% capacity and uses approximately 7.4 gigabytes of disk storage. The Medicaid Management Information System (MMIS) processes paper claims and performs all "backend" claim functions. The MMIS resides on an IBM platform in the Plano, Texas, EDS Service Management Center. It processes 2.470 million instructions per second of processing power and 12.691 gigabytes of direct access storage. In addition to the Tandem and IBM platforms, EDS supports a decision support system in Little Rock, Arkansas, using the UNIX® operating system on a Sun™ platform.

Business Impact of the AEVCS System

By implementing the AEVCS system, paper bills, checks, envelopes or postage stamps were eliminated. All status information, e.g., payments, had to be accessed using the Web site.

In 1998, Arkansas Governor Mike Huckabee noted that the state "saved about $30 million in Medicaid costs as a result of the efficiency built into the system." That's a 17-month total drawn from achievements like the following. Governor Huckabee continues:

"Emergency room use by Medicaid patients dropped 60% — falling to 10% below the general population. Average claims processing time was reduced from 15 to 3.5 days. Collection expense, a fact of life for many care providers, is practically "zero" on Medicaid claims. The AEVCS system dropped costly claim denials from 12% to 1% of the Medicaid outpatient caseload of a large children's hospital. Before EDS initiated a decision support system, programmers developed 130 reports from the database in a one-year period. After system installation, staff members generated reports at an annual rate of 1,140. That's well over an eight-fold increase."

According to Ray Hanley, director, Medical Services for Arkansas Medicaid, another significant impact of the AEVCS system was that "With AEVCS, we went from an error-prone paper claim system that took weeks or months to process a claim to an average turnaround time today of 3.8 days with an extremely high degree of accuracy."

Also, denied claims have fallen from 33% to less than 4% because the new system instantly flags errors for providers. Providers all over the state are gladly accepting Medicaid patients, which has improved both the access and quality of healthcare across the state.

In savings of postage fees alone that went with the old paper eligibility card system, the state saved $60,000 per month.

DISCUSSION OF THE MEDICAL SERVICES CASE

To argue for the relevance and applicability of the DKM model to healthcare administration, we intend to trace the knowledge management aspects in the case, including knowledge creation and sharing.

In the case of the Arkansas Division of Medical Services, the product state model serves the purpose of containing pertinent data about patients, providers and claims. These data are translated in the Medicaid Management Information System into valuable information to save the State of Arkansas's money and provide adequate, cost-effective healthcare to Medicaid beneficiaries. The information acquired in a well-specified context is knowledge that becomes a platform for action.

The healthcare administration case was presented in terms of a business model that required a distributed knowledge management based on product state models. Our interpretation of the case bridges the two worlds: the Medicaid systems already developed and operating, and our theoretical model of distributed knowledge management. Our interpretation structures the data in accord with the multiple organisations approach of DKM and traces the impact upon product state models, i.e., the Arkansas DMS, the physicians and the patients.

Finally, a distributed decision support can also be tracked. Firstly, data acquisition and sharing (AEVCS) generate up-to-date patient eligibility and medical history. Secondly, the recurrently acquired physicians' and other health service providers' patient treatment data are made available as timely eligibility data accessed online by the very same health service providers when visited by patients. The eligibility is the knowledge exploitation outcome of the PSM of the Arkansas DMS. The treatment offered patients is the knowledge exploitation outcome of providers' access to tracking patient medical and treatment history across different providers. Patient healthcare satisfaction reflects the patients' use of a primary care physician and procedure information, helping to ease access to relevant health service provision.

CONCLUSION AND PERSPECTIVES

Knowledge management schemes based on symmetric incentives are rarely found in literature. The distributed knowledge model merges specific knowledge with knowledge from other actors into a decision support specific for each actor in the network in recognition of actor role differences.

Traditionally, knowledge management is conceived in a bilateral model where information acquisition is separated from information use in the sense that the acquisition is done without any conception of who will use the knowledge and when. In the distributed knowledge model, the acquisition takes place in a structure where the usage and user is known, as both the acquisition and the use of the specific information of each actor relies upon a network-based exchange with other actors. In this model symmetric incentives ensure sustainable knowledge acquisition and use emphasising the robustness of the model. The idea of a network of repositories each exchanging partial, specific knowledge giving and gaining value when distributed in the network is substituted for a common organisation-wide knowledge repository.

The strength of a network distributed knowledge management system is the push forward of relevant knowledge to decision makers on a recurrent scheme, making economising on critical resources a strategic option. One option necessary to consider also in the framework of healthcare administrative is cost drivers. Concurrent enhancement of the quality of health service at diminishing costs vouch for benefits shared by payers, patients and healthcare personnel.

REFERENCES

Alavi, M. and Leidner, D. E. (1999). Knowledge Management Systems: Issues, Challenges, and Benefits. Communications of the Association for Information Systems. Vol. 1, Paper 5, January.

Alstyne, M. van. (1997). The State of Network Organization: A Survey in Three Frameworks. Journal of Organizational Computing and Electronic Commerce. 7(2&3) 83-151.

Anderson, E., Day, G. and Rangan, V.K. (1997) Strategic Channel Design. Sloan Management Review, June. 59-69.

Badaracco, Jr. Joseph L., (1991) The Knowledge Link. Harvard Business School Press. Boston, Mass.

Chesbrough, H.W. and Teece, D. J. (1996) When is Virtual Virtuous? Organizing for Innovation. Harvard Business Review, 74, Jan-Feb. 65-73.

Choudhury, V. and Sampler, J. L., (1997) Information Specificity and Environmental Scanning: An Economic Perspective. MIS Quarterly, March 21(1) 25-53.

Davenport, T. and Prusak, L. (1986) Working Knowledge - How Organizations Manage What They Know. Harvard Business School Press, Boston, MA. 1998.Keen, P. G.W. Competing in Time. Ballinger Publishers.

Davenport, T.H. and Klahr, P. (1998) Managing Customer Support Knowledge, California Management Review 40(3) 195-208.

Davenport, T.H. and De Long, D.W. and Beers, M.C. (1998) Successful Knowledge Management Projects. Sloan Management Review. 39(2) Winter, 43-57.

EDS. http://www.eds.com/case_studies/arkansas/cs_ak_si.shtml. 1999 Callon, M., Techno-economic networks and irreversibility. In J. Law,ed. A Sociology of Monsters. Essays on Power, Technology and Domination. Sociological Review Monograph 38. London: Routledge. 1991.

El Sawy, O.A. and Bowles, G. (1997) Redesigning the Customer Support Process for the Electronic Economy: Insights from Storage Dimensions. MIS Quarterly December 457-483.

El Sawy, O.A. and Pauchant, T.C. (1988) Triggers, Templates and Twitches in the Tracking of Emerging Strategic Issues. Strategic Management Journal 9(5) 455-473.

Favela, J. (1997) Capture and Dissemination of Specialized Knowledge in Network Organizations. Journal of Organizational Computing and Electronic Commerce 7(2 & 3) 201-226.

Foss, N. J. (1997) (Ed.), The Resource-based Perspective on the Firm. London: Routledge Kegan Paul.

Galbraith, J.R. and Lawler III, E.E. (1993) Organising for the Future. The New Logic for Managing Complex Organizations. San Francisco: Jossey-Bass Publishers. 1993.

Ghosh, A. K., E-Commerce Security. Weak Links, Best Defenses. Wiley Computer Publ. N.Y.

Hagel, J. and Rayport, J. (1997) The Coming Battle for Customer Information. Harvard Business Review, January-February, 53-65.

Hammer, M. and Champy, J. (1993) Reengineering the Corporation – A Manifesto for Business Revolution. Harper Collins Publishers, New York.

Hammer, M., Beyond Reengineering. Harper Collins Publishers. N.Y. 1996.

Hax, A. and Wilde II, D.L. A Delta Model: Adaptive Management for a Changing World. Sloan Management Review 40 (2) 11-28. 1999.

Huber, G., Organizational Information Systems: Determinants of Their Performance and Behavior. Management Science 28 (2) February. 138-155. 1982.

Hull, R.,V. Walsh, Green, K., and McMeekin, A. The Techno-Economic: Perspectives for Analysis and Intervention. Journal of Technology Transfer, 24. 185-195. 1999.

Johanson, J. and Mattsson, L.-G. Interorganizational relations in industrial systems: a network approach compared with the transaction-cost approach. International Studies of Management and Organization. 17. 34-48. 1987.

Konsynski, B.R., Strategic Control in the Extended Enterprise. IBM Systems Journal, 32(1), 111-142. 1993.

Kotler, P., Marketing Management: Analysis, Planning, Implementation and Control. Prentice Hall. 1994.

Krogh, G. von and Roos, J. (1996) Managing Knowledge - Perspectives on Cooperation and Competition. Sage, London.

Krogh, G. von and Nonaka, I. and Ichijo, K. (1997) Development Knowledge Activists. European Management Journal, 15(5), 475-483.

Krogh, G. von, Roos, J. and Kleine, D. (1998) Knowing in firms - Understanding, Managing and Measuring Knowledge. Sage, London.

Larsen, M.H., Franck, L. R. and Pedersen, M. (1999) Kühn. Frontline CALS – Extranet Enabled Support of Customer Relations Based on Product State Information. Proceedings of the 7th European Conference on Information Systems. Copenhagen, June, 302-319.

Law, J. and Hassard, J. (1999) Actor Network Theory and After. Blackwell. 1999.

Medicaid. http://www.medicaid.state.ar.us/index.htm.

Milgrom, P. and Roberts, J. (1992) Economics, Organization and Management. Englewood Cliffs, N.J. Prentice-Hall International, Inc.

Nonaka, I. (1994) A Dynamic Theory of Organizational Knowledge Creation. Organization Science, 5, 14-37.

Nonaka, I. and Byosiere, P. & Borucki, C.C. & Konno, N. (1994) Organizational Knowledge Creation Theory: A First Comprehensive Test. International Business Review. Special Issue on Knowledge in Organizations, Knowledge Transfer, and Cooperative Strategies. 3/4, 337-351.

Nonaka, I. and Takeuchi, H. (1995) The Knowledge Creating Company – How Japanese Companies Create the Dynamics of Innovation. Oxford University Press.

Pedersen, M. Kühn (1996) A Theory of Informations. The Business Cycle Model. Copenhagen. Samfundslitteratur.

Pedersen, M. Kühn (1999) Professional business service innovation: A distributed knowledge approach. Proceedings, CISTEMA Conference, Mobilizing Knowledge in Technology Management. October 24-27. Copenhagen Business School, 2 vols. 478-501. 1999.

Polanyi, M. (1962) Personal Knowledge: Towards a Post-critical Philosophy. University of

Chicago Press, New York.
Polanyi, M. (1966) The Tacit Dimension. Anchor Day, New York.
Porter, M. E. (1990) The Competitive Advantage of Nations. Macmillan, N.Y.
Porter, M.E. (1998) Clusters and the New Economics of Competition. Harvard Business Review. November-December 76(6) 77-90.
Porter, M.E. (1998) The Adam Smith Adress: Location, Clusters, and the "New" Microeconomics of Competition. Business Economics. Washington, January 33(1) 7-13.
Riempp, G. and Nastansky, L. (1997) From Islands to Flexible Business Process Networks- Enabling the Interaction of Distributed Workflow Management Systems. Proceedings of the 5th European Conference on Information Systems. Vol. 1, 481-496.
Ruggles, R. (1998) The State of the Notion: Knowledge Management in Practice. California Management Review. 40(3), 80-89.
Sampler, J. L. (1998) Redefining Industry Structure for the Information Age. Strategic Management Journal 19. 343-355.
Scott, J. E. (1998) Organizational Knowledge and the Intranet. Decision Support Systems. 23, 3-17.
Sridhar, S. (1998) Decision Support using the Intranet. Decision Support Systems, 23, 19-28.
Spender, J.C. (1996) Organizational Knowledge, Learning and Memory: Three Concepts in Search of a Theory. Journal of Organizational Change Management, 9, 63-78.
Stalk, G. and Hout, T.M. (1990) Competing Against Time. N.Y. The Free Press.
Strader, T. J.; Fu-Ren Lin; Shaw, M.J. Information Infrastructure for electronic virtual organization management. Decision Support Systems 23, 75-94. 1998.
Teece, D. J. (1987) Profiting from technological innovations: Implications for integration, collaboration, licensing and public policy. in Teece, D.J. Ed., The Competitive Challenge. Cambridge. Mass.
Venkatraman, N. (1998) IT-Enabled Business Transformation: From Automation to Business Scope Redefinition. Sloan Management Review, 35, Winter 73-87. 1994.
Venkatraman, N. and Henderson, J.C. Real Strategies for Virtual Organizing. Sloan Management Review, 40(1) Fall, 33-48.
Wang, E. T.G. and Barron, T. (1997) Computing services supply management: Incentives, information, and communication. Decision Support Systems 19, 123-148.
Wernerfelt, B. (1984) A Resource-based view of the firm. Strategic Management Journal 5, 171-180.
Williamson, O. E. (1985) The Economic Institutions of Capitalism. New York: The Free Press.
Williamson, O. E. (1986) Economic Organization. Brighton: Wheatsheaf Books Ltd.
Williamson, O. E. (1994) Transaction cost economics and organization theory. In Smelser, N.J. and Swedberg, R. (eds) The Handbook of Economic Sociology. Princeton U P. 77-107.

Chapter XIII

IS/IT: Enabling Medical Group Practices in a Managed Care Environment

Nilimini Wickramasinghe
University of Melbourne, Australia

J. B. Silvers
Case Western Reserve University, USA

The U.S. spends significantly more money as a percentage of GDP on healthcare than any other OECD, country and this amount is expected to increase exponentially (Folland, Goodman and Stano, 1997). In this high cost environment, two important trends have occurred: 1) the movement to managed care and 2) large investments in IS/IT (information systems/information technology). Managed care has emerged as an attempt to provide good quality, cost-effective healthcare treatment. Yet its implications and impact, especially on medical group practices, are not well discussed in the literature. The repercussions of large investments in IS/IT on the healthcare sector in general and on medical group practices in particular are also largely ignored by the literature. By analyzing three different types of group practices, we investigate the impacts of these two central trends on healthcare in general as well as on the medical group practice in particular.

Copyright © 2001 IEEE. Reprinted, with permission, from
Proceedings of HICSS-34 (2001), digital text version.

INTRODUCTION

Several recent changes in the healthcare industry have resulted in increasing competition which has had a significant impact on hospital and medical group practice activities, including financial and strategic planning, as well as marketing. Managed care in the private sector is a key element behind such changes.

Unfortunately, in many cases, existing IS/IT (information systems/information technology) do not support the sophisticated data-collection and analysis requirements that are needed to enable strategic planning and the generation of meaningful data on costs and utilization demanded by a managed care environment (Knight, 1998). To cope with these environmental demands, new practice management/billing IS/IT are emerging. However, little research attempts to understand the impact of these systems on the medical group practice.

This study addresses this deficiency by focussing on the impact of the implementation of practice management/billing IS/IT by three different types of medical group practices in a managed care environment taking an agency theory perspective. Modelling the situation of the managed care organization (MCO) and primary care physician (PCP) in terms of agency theory in the context of the *knowledge worker* agent, we analyze these three medical group practices. We then discuss why the adoption of these IS/IT systems is both necessary and prudent given the demands of a managed care environment. We present findings from our empirical research to support this predication. Our data also show that the structural distinctions between types of medical group practices (i.e., the structural distinctions between the IPA, multi-specialty group practice and faculty practice) are blurring as a result of the implementation of IS/IT. We believe this to be a significant finding. Drawing on legitimacy theory to explain the significance of the change in structure, we conclude that this observed structural change is a key impact of managed care on the medical group practice, with IS/IT serving as the catalyst.

MOVE TO MANAGED CARE

In the U.S., the healthcare industry is in a state of flux (Chandra, Knickrehm & Miller, 1995; Applegate, Manson & Thorpe, 1986; Wolper, 1995; and Kongstvedt, 1993). This "turbulence and change" (Huber, 1990) is summarized by Kongstvedt (1997, p. xvii) in the following description: "The rate of the rise in healthcare costs has been variable. The shocking increases experienced in the early 1990s has slowed in the mid-and late 1990s, but there is no guarantee that they will continue to do so." The reasons for this include but are not limited to the following: rapidly developing technology, cost shifting by providers, shifting demographics, expectations for a longer life, legal environment, administrative costs as well as wide variations in inefficiencies, variation in provider income regardless of efficiency or quality and decreased public dollars (ibid). In other marketplaces buyers are sensitive to the price of the product and thus calculate a cost-benefit analysis. "In the medical marketplace, however, the buyers and users of medical services and technologies have been relatively insensitive to the cost of these services ..." 'The traditional financing and reimbursement policies of the healthcare industry are felt to be largely responsible for this price insensitivity, inhibiting the forces of competitive supply and demand economics (Applegate, Mason and Thorpe, 1986, p. 80). Therefore, it is necessary for providers of medical care to develop ways to control and manage costs as well as increase productivity without compromising quality.

As an attempt to stem the escalating costs of healthcare, managed care has emerged. It is aimed at creating value through competition in order to combat "...an extremely wasteful and inefficient system that has been bathed in cost-increasing incentives for over 50 years" (Enthoven, 1993, p.400). The intended result is to provide adequate quality healthcare and yet minimise, or at least reduce, costs.

The principal participants involved in any managed care arrangements include the following five categories of stakeholders: the managed care organization (MCO), the purchaser, the member, the healthcare professional and, if applicable, an administrative organisation (Knight, 1998). MCOs contract with individuals, employers and other purchasers to provide comprehensive healthcare services to people who enroll in their health plans. "MCOs are entities that offer an HMO (health maintenance organization), preferred provider organization (PPO) or POS (Point-of-Service) plans or any combination of these" (ibid, p. 22).[1]

ROLE OF THE PCP

The essential difference between MCOs and more traditional types of medical care is connected with the distribution of financial risk among the purchaser of healthcare, the provider of the care and the insurer (Hillman, 1987). MCOs typically reduce this financial risk for the purchaser of healthcare insurance by guaranteeing a comprehensive range of services at a fixed price to them. To do this of course, the MCO must keep the use of healthcare resources within a budget, thus making critical a focus on managing medical care.

"It is impossible to understand the problems of medical care without understanding the physician. And it is impossible to make significant changes in the medical field without changing physician behaviour" (Jensen and Meckling, 1973, p. 56). The primary care physician (PCP) plays a significant role in a managed care environment. A key issue in the effective management of these organizations is how MCOs relate to their PCPs.

In a managed care environment, the PCP usually acts as a gatekeeper since the PCP is typically the first physician with whom patients have contact. Thus, it is the PCP who makes the initial decisions about the type of disease or illness and then the corresponding course of treatment required. In such a gatekeeper model then, the PCP is directly or indirectly responsible for all costs associated with medical care.

"Information holds the key to improving productivity" (Enghoven, 1993, p. 94), since it enables physicians and administrators to engage in discussions concerning practice patterns, variations and costs. Managed care has put much emphasis on the need to collect, transmit, manipulate and store a variety of information which is central to the operation of these health plans. Meaningful data on costs and utilization support every aspect of a health plan's operations, including financial planning, pricing and underwriting, provider capitation and profiling, quality measurement and medical management. These requirements complicate the information collection and sharing process. By using IS/IT, plans can reduce administrative costs, improve planning efficiency, eliminate timing lags and enhance quality management [16]. In the following section we model the relationship between the MCO and PCP in terms of agency theory for the knowledge worker agent in order to identify the critical role for IS/IT.

AGENCY THEORY

Agency theory (Wilson, 1968; Alchian and Demsetz, 1972; Jensen and Meckling, 1973) is concerned with the misalignment of goals when an agent (employee/contractor) performs a task for a principal (employer/purchaser). Therefore, the principal needs to guard against sub-optimal behavior, and the divergence between the agent pursuing activities, which facilitate his/her own goals being achieved, in preference to the achievement of the principal's goals. In order to achieve goal-aligned behavior, two mechanisms available to the principal are contracts and ex-post monitoring. We focus on the latter because it is in connection with monitoring that opportunities exist for IS/IT to have a considerable impact.

In attempting to achieve goal alignment, the principal must incur some costs, which are made up of the following: a) monitoring costs,[2] b) residual loss and c) decision information costs (Jensen and Meckling, 1992; 1973). Monitoring costs (M) result from the principal having to perform activities to check that the agent is performing his/her task appropriately. Residual loss (RL) represents the cost to the principal of misaligned goals.

Decision Information (DI) costs represent the cost of transferring localized information (acquired by the agent throughout the course of doing his/her job) from agent to principal so that the principal can make better, more informed decisions. When hiring an agent to perform a specific activity, the principal also has the option of relinquishing the decision right to the agent, i.e., empowering the agent to make key decisions which collectively and over time have a significant impact on the organisation. Locating the decision rights with the agent, though, means a low level of goal alignment, since agency theory predicts that the agent will make decisions in his/her best interest not necessarily in the best interests of the principal. Thus, as Jensen and Meckling (1992) note, the principal, in order to maintain high levels of goal alignment, usually retains the decision right when hiring an agent.

In keeping the decision right, yet not carrying out the activity himself/herself,

Figure 1. Agency Costs I

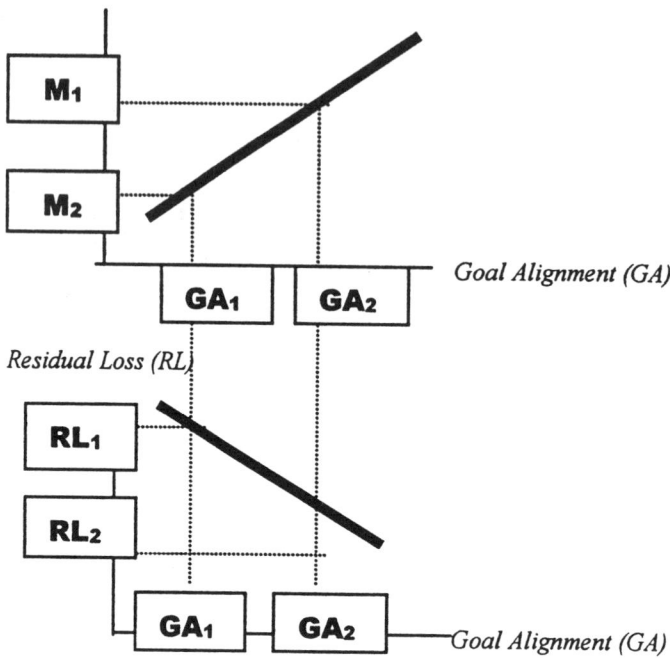

Figure 2. Agency Costs II

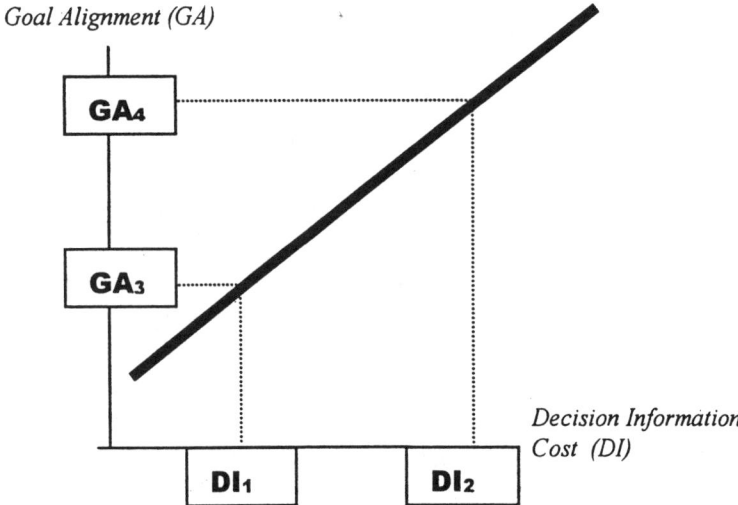

the principal does not have access to the localized information or idiosyncratic knowledge that is generated from carrying out the activity and is necessary to make superior decisions. In order to make optimal decisions, the principal requires the localized information or idiosyncratic knowledge that the agent has acquired and the transferring of this information from agent to principal so that the principal can make better decisions incurs a cost, namely, the decision information cost (Jensen and Meckling, 1992).

These three types of costs and their impact on goal alignment are depicted in Figures 1 and 2. Specifically, Figure 1 shows that as the monitoring cost (M) increases so does the level of goal alignment (GA), and hence the residual loss (RL) decreases. In other words, increasing monitoring (incurring a higher monitoring cost) is effective in achieving a higher amount of goal alignment. By achieving a higher level of goal alignment, the residual loss or loss due to a mismatch in goals is naturally reduced.

Figure 2 depicts the typical positive relationship between the decision information (DI) costs and the level of goal alignment. In this diagram, for higher levels of goal alignment, greater expenditure is required to transfer localized information from the agent to the principal. Underlying this graph is the assumption that the principal is utility maximizing; however, the principal doesn't carry out the specific tasks that generate key information defined as localized information or idiosyncratic knowledge (Jensen and Meckling, 1992). Furthermore, this localized information is necessary to make "better" decisions, i.e., more consistent with the specific goals. The ability for the principal to make decisions consistent with his/her goals then is dependent on receiving this localized information or idiosyncratic knowledge generated by the agent. Increasing DI cost by moving this information to the principal, as depicted in Figure 2, is associated with higher goal alignment.

Applying this construct to our problem, one would expect the goal alignment, as represented by the match between the MCO's budget and the practice's actual performance, to be positively related to the monitoring costs incurred by the MCO. However, our situation is more complicated because the PCP is a knowledge worker agent, not the "regular agent" of agency theory. Having a knowledge worker agent has an unique impact on the agency costs, especially the DI cost and hence, the level of goal alignment, as we elaborate in the following section.

Agency Theory with Knowledge Worker Agent

The actual interaction of these agency costs is situation specific. We classify our PCP as a knowledge worker agent. Hence, we must focus on the interaction of these costs in the case of the knowledge worker, a specific type of agent (Wickramasinghe, 1999). We justify our assertion of the PCP as a knowledge worker agent in the next section.

We define knowledge workers as a subset of employees who: 1) own their means of production, i.e., their knowledge; 2) possess specialized skills and training which they have acquired by investing significant resources (time and money) towards their education; and 3) are empowered to make decisions that have far-reaching consequences for the organizations for which they work (Kelly, 1990; Drucker, 1993; Nonaka and Takeuchi, 1995). Given the preceding definition of the knowledge worker, let us now turn to how this impacts agency costs.

The key here is that the knowledge worker is hired because of his/her possession of special skills and knowledge. Thus, it is rational for the principal to give the decision rights to the knowledge worker agents. In fact, this is consistent with our definition of knowledge workers being empowered to make key decisions which have significant consequences for the organisations for which they work. The principal, even if he/she had access to all the localized information, could not make these key decisions since he/she does not possess the special skills and knowledge of the knowledge worker. For instance, in our healthcare example, the MCO could not make the treatment decisions.

Now that the knowledge worker agent has the decision rights, the DI cost is *low* and ***constant***. It is *low* because little localized information or idiosyncratic knowledge is passed to the MCO pertaining to patient treatments so that the MCO can decide appropriate patient treatments. We note here that information such as referral information is passed to the MCO from the PCP, but this is not so that the MCO can make the treatment decisions. Thus, the cost of passing this information is not a DI cost, rather a monitoring cost. This distinction while subtle is significant.

DI costs are *constant* because the PCP is continuously making these decisions not the principal, i.e., the PCP is a knowledge worker agent hired specifically to make these types of decisions. We illustrate this in Figure 3a, where the DI cost is at DI_1 and this DI cost curve is horizontal. The horizontal DI cost curve with a low DI cost intercept indicates that the knowledge worker agent, the PCP, possesses the decision rights, and little localized information or idiosyncratic knowledge is being passed to the principal, the MCO. We can also see from this figure that the level of goal alignment is low at GA_1.

Since the principal has relinquished the decision rights, he/she now is faced with the problem of low goal alignment (refer to Figure 3a). It becomes critical for the principal to resolve this problem; the solution is found through monitoring. Thus, what the principal requires is a tool to perform effective, efficient monitoring; from this higher goal alignment will result.

Figure 3 depicts the interaction of agency costs with goal alignment in the context of the knowledge worker agent. Of key significance is the impact that IS/IT has in shifting or rotating the monitoring cost curve. It is the basis for the movement from line M to M' (in Figure 3b) where the same increment in monitoring costs buys a larger increase in goal alignment.

Figure 3a-c highlights this key role for IS/IT by comparing three separate scenarios each involving a knowledge worker agent. Thus all three scenarios begin with a level of goal alignment at GA_1 as per Figure 3a. The material difference is the level of IS/IT use for the monitoring activity. Scenario 1 (labelled with subscript index 1) involves no monitoring, i.e., the null case. Based on agency theory this means that the residual loss is significant and goal alignment will remain low at GA_1.

Scenario 2 depicts monitoring with low (essentially very little, if any) IS/IT use. This is consistent with the arguments provided by Jensen and Meckling (1973) (and consistent with Figure 1) that the monitoring activity will enable an increase in the level of goal alignment.

Finally, Scenario 3 depicts the situation with significant IS/IT use for the monitoring activity, i.e., the use of an enterprise-wide system to perform the monitoring activity. We show how this increased level of IS/IT use shifts or rotates the monitoring cost curve from M to M'. Furthermore, the level of goal alignment has also significantly increased; for example if we take point M1 (Figure 3b), we can see that the level of goal alignment has increased from GA_2 to GA_3. In addition, we can see that the residual loss has decreased significantly (Figure 3c) from RL_2 to RL_3, and our total costs--which include decision information costs, monitoring costs and residual costs--are much less. In short, the use of IS/IT has had a dramatic impact on agency costs.

PCPs as Knowledge Workers

Doctors are sophisticated knowledge workers with areas of knowledge covering medical and procedural facts, tacit knowledge or expertise of their specific discipline that has developed over time, access to other medical professionals as well as patient information (Wheeler, 1995). Further, PCPs have autonomy and are empowered to make treatment decisions. In addition, they influence the quantity, type and quality of service rendered to patients.

Therefore, the relationship between PCPs and the MCO can be modelled in terms of agency theory in the case of the knowledge worker agent. Goal alignment as represented by the match between the MCO's budget and the practice's actual performance is likely to be low (ceteris paribus) since the PCPs have the decision rights. Hence, we expect that the MCO will turn to IS/IT to perform monitoring activities and by doing so will ensure a high level of goal-aligned behavior ensues. From Figure 3 we can see conceptually that IS/IT enables the level of goal-aligned behavior to increase. Let us briefly discuss why IS/IT enables this rotating of the monitoring cost curve to occur, thereby enhancing the effectiveness of the monitoring expenditure.

Role for IS/IT

Underlying the need to achieve goal alignment in the principal/agent relationship is the need to alleviate the problem of asymmetry of information. That is, the agent may have important knowledge not readily available to the principal. This is clearly the case with physicians and health plans.

IS/IT can be used most effectively and efficiently as a tool connecting these two parties (principal and agent); in particular IS/IT can have a crucial impact in aiding communication and decision making (Huber, 1990). IS/IT is particularly useful

Figure 3. Agency Costs III

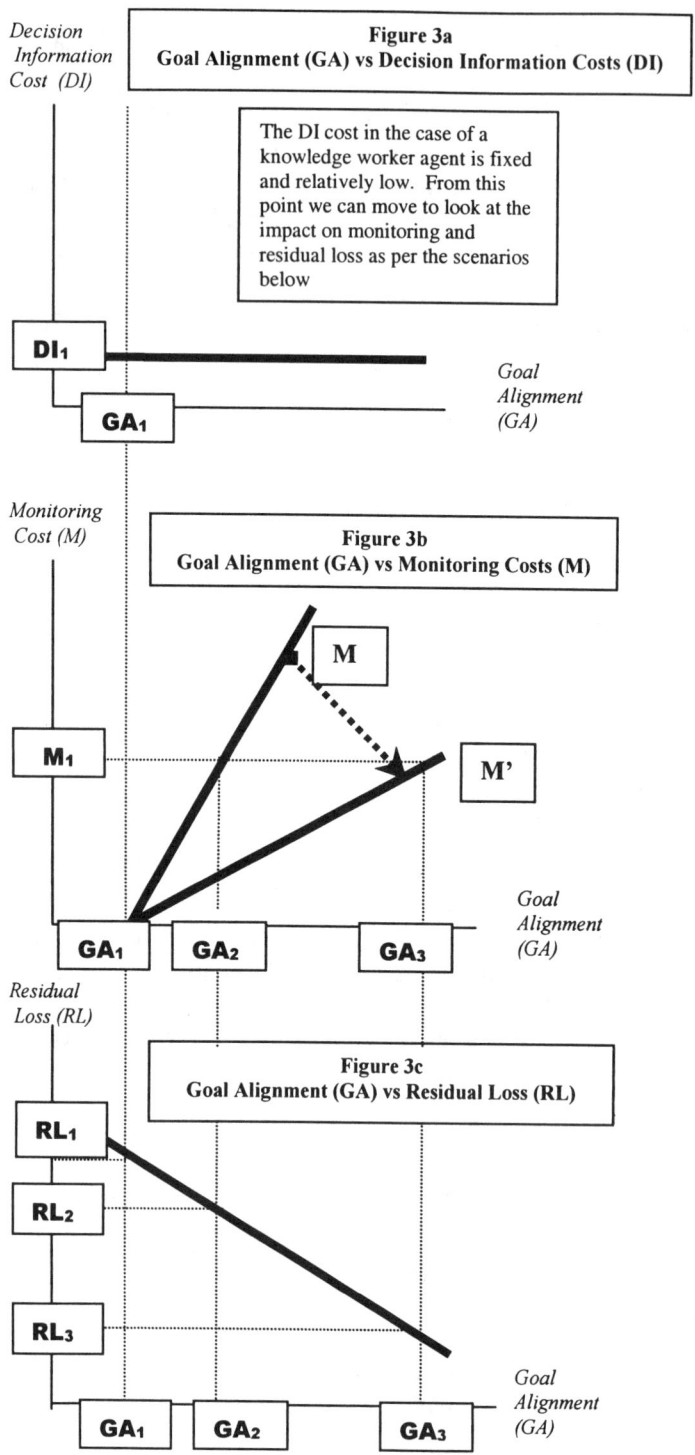

when codified information must be shared among highly diffused groups (Simons, 1995). The cost and utilization information demanded by a managed care environment precisely falls into this category. Further, MCOs require this type of information to be shared amongst highly diffused groups of PCPs. Thus, it would appear to be the perfect situation to implement IS/IT and benefit from its impact.

By investigating the impact of three different medical group practices operating in a managed care environment, we are able to test if IS/IT does in fact enable a higher level of goal-aligned behavior to result. However, as evidenced in the empirical findings, IS/IT goes beyond its impact on the level of goal alignment to also perform an enabling role. Specifically, we show that the IS/IT that was implemented in our medical group practices enabled them to move to a centralized structure.

CASE STUDIES

Exploratory multiple case study research was conducted to enable the generation of rich data in a non-restrictive manner (Wickramasinghe, 1999). The cases represent one MCO (MCO Z) and three medical group practices (Cases 1, 2 & 3) located in the Northeast Ohio area of the U.S. In the language of agency theory, the *principal* under consideration is the MCO and the knowledge worker *agent* is the PCP in the respective organizations.

Within the healthcare industry in the U.S., medical group practices vary with respect to their structure, the power of a particular MCO and the varied duties PCPs must perform (i.e., teaching, research and clinical focus) (Wolper, 1995; Kongstvedt, 1993). These factors combine to make up the micro environment for each case. The three cases were chosen as they represent major, distinct types of group practices in existence, which contract with multiple MCOs, i.e., differing with respect to the number of conflicting goals and power of the MCO.

Information was gathered from several sources including semi-structured interviews, the collecting of key documents and memos, numerous site visits and the direct observation of various steering committees and meetings, thus enabling the triangulation among different data sources (Eisenhardt, 1989). Rigorous coding and extensive thematic analysis was conducted to analyze the qualitative data gathered (Boyatzis, 1998; Kavale, 1996). What follows are brief descriptions of MCO Z and the three cases that serve to highlight the empirical evidence. Each of the points listed was confirmed by multiple interviews, written documentation and passive observation.[3]

MCO Z

This organisation was founded on the belief that doctors and other health plan professionals can and should maintain the quality and control the costs of medical services. MCO Z is one of the larger health plans in Northeast Ohio. As of 1997, the organization had more than 500 employer groups and more than 100,000 individuals enrolled. Succinctly stated, the goal of MCO Z is to provide cost-effective quality healthcare treatment to its enrollees.[4].

The provider contracts adopted by MCO Z do not vary significantly across the three cases under consideration. In fact, these contracts are essentially typical of standard provider contracts in their format [16] consisting of the following sections: A) Purpose, stating the purpose or intent of the parties to establish a contractual relationship as well as defining the parties in the contract. B) Definitions, defines the terms used throughout the agreement. C) Obligations of parties, which states the obligations of the MCO and provider, including responsibilities for administrative procedures, verifying member eligibility, obtaining pre-authorizations for hospital admissions and specialty care referrals, submitting reports and reimbursing providers. D) Term & termination, which outlines the effective date and duration of the contract as well as specifying its renewal and termination provisions. E) Miscellaneous, including provisions relating to amending the contract and disclosing information.

MCO Z's program does, however, adopt a distinctive organizing approach for its PCPs called medical care panels. These are contractual relationships among a small number of physicians (5-20) who know each other and may already have established professional ties, and hence represents the one unique feature of these otherwise relatively regular provider style of contract. Panels are the program's accountable care giving and economic teams, and they form the organisational heart of the program for MCO Z. The panel, therefore, fulfils a number of distinct and critical functions which include the following: 1) panels are the focal point for data collection, analysis of use patterns, patient care outcomes and they provide a decentralized peer review function, 2) the panel is the unit that is profiled, 3) they form the basis to pool enrollee cost experience and compare it to premiums collected for enrollees, 4) each panel constitutes its own limited risk pool with explicit stop-loss protection built in and 5) panels are the program's economic unit for bearing limited risk (via fee withholds and/or bonus incentives). From an agency theory perspective, the panel mechanism enables the idiosyncratic knowledge of the physician to be utilised and shared as well as enabling MCO Z to conduct monitoring activities on a statistically meaningful group of providers and enrollees.

The agency costs for Principal MCO Z are as follows: 1) *Monitoring Costs*, these are mainly driven by the provider profiling activities performed by MCO Z. Provider profiling involves "the collection and analysis of various information (including medical claims, utilization data, member satisfaction surveys, patients' medical records and hospital admissions records) to assess the practice patterns, quality, service and cost efficiency of participating providers" (Wilson, 1968, p.86). 2) *Residual Loss*, for MCO Z this represents the costs it must bear as a result of its PCPs not meeting or beating accepted utilization levels, and hence, the costs of medical care exceeding MCO Z's budget allowance. 3) *Decision Information Costs*, as discussed earlier these costs are essentially non-existent since the PCPs possess the decision rights and MCO Z does not itself make treatment decisions.

Case 1

The group practice in Case 1 represents a closed staff multi-specialty medical practice, historically engaged in clinical care delivery without parallel focus on teaching or research. This practice has been in operation since the mid-1940s. The practice itself has three ambulatory care sites and four single specialty offices. Its primary care specialties include ob/gyn, pediatrics and internal medicine. About 500 of its physicians are PCPs.

This practice contracts with many MCOs. The percent of income received by the group practice from the MCO can serve as a proxy for the relative power of MCO Z as compared to other MCOs. MCO Z accounts for 15% of the group practice's income and thus has less power than other MCOs connected with this group practice that account for 20%-30% of the income. Given the relatively low power of MCO Z, agency theory would predict a low level of goal-aligned behavior would exist with MCO Z, simply because of the lower attention it would command. However, over a period from 1992-1997, based on panel performance data, Case 1 has consistently achieved its budgeted targets and thus had high goal-aligned behavior. The achievement of high goal alignment at Case 1 is largely attributed by this practice to the IS/IT implemented.

The specific IS/IT implemented here was an IDX[5] billing system that was to enable a common physician practice management to result across the group practice. After the implementation of the system, the group practice formed among its physicians an administrative arm and a clinical arm. This structural change was deemed necessary in order to best use the IDX system and meet the demands of the managed care organizations it contracts with, such as MCO Z.

Case 2

The practice in Case 2 is a comprehensive ambulatory healthcare centre. It was founded in the early 1970s by a group of university-affiliated physicians. It represents an independent practice association, a group of physicians that have formed a medical group so that they appear as one legal entity, which is advantageous when contracting with various managed care organisations. In addition to its clinical focus, this group practice has some research and teaching focus. Hence, in contrast with Case 1, where interests were purely clinical, this practice has other conflicting goals.

The group practice has both fee-for-service and managed care contracts. The managed care contracts are with various MCOs. MCO Z accounts for about 10% of their revenue contracts. Goal-aligned behaviour is low between this group practice and MCO Z as evidenced from panel performance data from 1992-1997, where they frequently had total medical costs for their panels in excess of their actuarially determined budget.

Case 2 is currently channelling all their energies into the development and rollout of a new billing/scheduling system. This system coincides with the expansion of the group practice, and thus several issues need to be addressed. IS/IT is driving and enabling this structural change. In the long term, they envision a move to computerized medical records. The more immediate introduction of the new billing system will allow more meaningful utilization data to be collected. In addition, the group practice is adapting its structure to take best advantage of the benefits of the new billing/practice management system, as seen from the comments by the medical director for this group practice which indicate the central role of IS/IT in their plans.

"The environment is changing and cost focus is critical. We are currently in the process of getting a new system...In conjunction with this new system, we shall also be changing our structure...there will be a central location to schedule all docs' patients, also we will all have the same billing format and that too will be centralized. We will also have a practice manager whose job it will be to analyse data off the new system and see how the practice flow and utilization are, if docs are over-utilizing or under-utilizing." [Medical Director]

Case 3

Case 3 is a faculty practice within a university setting. By the mid-1980s, 23 different groups existed as independent practices. Overall, these faculty practices had a strong affiliation with a university school of medicine. The percentage of revenue from MCO Z was only 5%.

Case 3 is in the process of converting to the IDX[6] system, essentially the identical system implemented in Case 1 with a few minor differences with respect to inclusion of certain specific modules. This is a slow process being performed sequentially as each of the 23 specialties switch to the billing system one at a time. Many issues regarding the updating and consolidating of systems across this group practice are proving to be problematic.

The critical issue for this group practice is to ensure that the transition to its new administrative structure moves smoothly. Creating a single large contracting and management organization out of 23 independent practices has been a major political and practical task. Yet this new structure is critical in the coordination of operations across the practices, as well as the formation of a single IS platform throughout. Ultimately, the IS/IT is planned to help in developing improved practice patterns. The next step in this direction is for the group practice to implement the IDX system. This will not be an easy task given the difficulties experienced by the practice in creating a single organization structure.

Discussion of Case Findings

The preceding descriptions of the medical group practices serve to highlight several changes taking place in these organizations as a result of a managed care environment. These changes can be categorized as follows: the respective group practices 1) on assessing the demands of a managed care organisation reformulated their current strategy and operations in order to meet the requirements given the exogenous change, i.e., impact of managed care, 2) realized the role for IS/IT in this process and thus implemented (are in the process of implementing) appropriate billing/practice management systems that will enable/enhance better practice management and 3) realized the need for organizational transformation and thus moved to (are moving to) a centralized structure and standardized approach. In all three cases the implementation of the IS/IT is coupled with a restructuring towards a centralized structure and standardized approach to operations.

What appears most interesting in these three cases is that many of the traditional structural distinctions that had existed between the IPA, multi-specialty group practice and faculty practice are becoming blurred as they all move to a centralized structure and adopt a standardized approach to operations. In order to explain this unexpected yet significant finding, we turn to legitimacy theory.

"Legitimacy is a generalized perception or assumption that the actions of an entity are desirable, proper or appropriate within some socially constructed system ..." [33 pp. 878]. The changes in structures and the movement by all the medical group practices to a centralized structure can be rationalized in terms of enacting a managerial legitimation process.

Applying managerial legitimacy in this instance, we have the professionals in the medical unit, i.e., the PCPs, accepting the importance of management (MCO Z) and its tools (such as IS/IT) as desirable, proper and appropriate. The move to centralized structures within all the group practices is an attempt to construct a system to use the IS/IT and thus legitimize their activities or in terms of agency theory, legitimize their decision-making functions. From the findings of Ruef and Scott (1998), we know that a high degree of managerial legitimacy is needed when dealing with formalized relations. We can categorize the principal-knowledge Worker agent relationship between MCO Z and the respective PCPs as such a formal relationship. Further, Ruef and Scott (ibid) note that organizations are not passive recipients of the legitimation process but work to ensure they receive legitimation from their multiple audiences; one way of achieving this is through their organisational structure. The relationship between the medical group practices and MCO Z can be characterized as a formalized relationship and thus managerial legitimacy is required for the survival of these group practices.

By drawing on legitimacy theory, we are able to show that the unexpected (and at first appearance, trivial) finding of the move to a centralized structure and standardized approach to operations that was evidenced in all three cases is indeed significant. Not only does our evidence strongly suggest that this change to the traditional structures of the group practices is related to operating in a managed care environment but also that IS/IT was clearly the enabler.

CONCLUSIONS

In this chapter we set out to shed some light on the impact of managed care on the medical group practice. We did this by focussing on the implementation of new IS/IT by three different types of medical group practices in a managed care environment. On comparing pre- and post-structures of the respective group we show that the distinct structural differences that have existed between IPAs, multi-specialty group practices and faculty practices have become blurred. In addition, IS/IT serves as an impetus for internal responses within the three groups as seen in their new information systems and organizational structures. The occurrence of the adoption of billing/practice management systems and then restructuring of the respective group practice in all three cases adds external validity to our findings. Our results also suggest that the large investments in IS/IT currently being experienced in healthcare are prudent, and we urge for further research.

REFERENCES

Alchian, A. & Demsetz, H.(1972). Production, Information Costs and Economic Organisations, *American Economic Journal Review*, 62(5), 777-795.

Applegate, L., Mason, R. & Thorpe, D. (1986). Design of a Management Support System for Hospital Strategic Planning, *Journal of Medical Systems*, 10(1), 79- 94.

Boyatzis, R. (1998). *Transforming Qualitative Information Thematic Analysis And Code Development,* Sage Publications, Thousand Oaks.

Chandra, R., Knickrehm, M. & Miller, A. (1995). Health Care's IT Mistake, *The McKinsey Quarterly*, Number 5.

Drucker, P. (1993). *Post-Capitalist Society.* New York, Harper Collins.

Eisenhardt, K. (1989). Building Theories from Case Study Research. *Academy of Managmenet Review*, vol 14, 532-550.

Enthoven, A. (1993). The History and Principles of Managed Competition, *Health Affairs*, 25-48.

Folland, S., Goodman, A. & Stano, M. (1997). *The Economics of Health and Health Care* Prentice Hall, New Jersey.

Fuchs, V. (1974). *Who Shall Live?* Basic Books, New York.

Hillman, A. (1987) "Financial Incentives for Physicians in HMOs" *New England Journal of Medicine*, 317(27), 1743-1748.

Huber, G. (1990). A Theory of the Effects of Advanced Information Technologies on Organisational Design, Intelligence, and Decision Making, *Academy of Management Review*, 15(1), 47-71.

Jensen, M. & Meckling, W. (1992). Specific and General Knowledge, and Organizational Structure in L. Werin & H. Wijkander (Eds.), *Contract Economics*, Blackwell, 251-291.

Jensen, M. & Meckling, W. (1973). Theory of the Firm: Managerial Behaviour, Agency Costs and Ownership Structure, *Journal of Financial Economics*, vol. 3, 305-360.

Kavale, S. (1996). Interviews An Introduction to Qualitative Research Interviewing, Sage, Thousand Oaks.

Kelly, R. (1990). Managing the New Workforce, *Machine Design*, 62(9), 109-113.

Knight, W. (1998). *Managed Care: What It Is and How It Works*, AspenPublication, Maryland

Kongstvedt, P. (1997). *The Managed Health Care Handbook*. Aspen Publication, Maryland.
Kongstvedt, P. (1993). *The Managed Health Care Handbook*. Aspen Publication, Maryland
Nonaka, S. & N. Takeuchi. 1995. *The Knowledge Creating Company*. New York, Oxford University Press.
Ross, S. (1973). The Economic Theory of Agency: The Principal's Problem, *American Journal of Economic Review*, vol. 2, 134-139.
Ruef, M & Richard, S. W. (1998). A Multidimensional Model of Organizational Legitimacy: Hospital Survival in Changing Institutional Environments, *Administrative Science Quarterly* vol. 43, 877-904
Simons, R. (1995). *Levers of Control*. Harvard Business School Press, Boston.
Wheeler, M. (1995). Perfect Knowledge: The Physician's Role, *Health Management Technology*, 16(4), 26-30.
Wilson, R. (1968). The Theory of Syndicates, *Econometerica*, vol 36, 119-132.
Wickramasinghe, N. (2000) *IS/IT As A Tool To Achieve Goal Alignment In The Health Care Industry* Int. J Healthcare Technology and Management, Vol. 2.
Wickramasinghe, N. (1999). IS/IT As A Tool To Achieve Goal Alignment In The Context Of The Knowledge Worker In The Health Care Industry, PhD Dissertation, Case Western Reserve University.
Wolper, L. (1995). *Health Care Administration*, Aspen Publication, Maryland.

ENDNOTES

1 Since these issues are not significant to this study, we shall use the term MCO rather than differentiate among HMO, PPO or POS, which essentially differ in the degree and ease enrollees may move among various providers in the community.

2 Jensen and Meckling [13] also discuss a bonding cost which comes about due to the agent performing bonding activities to align themselves to outside investors. These activities are not relevant in the context of the PCP in the healthcare industry and are thus not discussed in this chapter.

3 An appendix detailing the methodology, coding and thematic analysis will be supplied upon e-mail request.

4 This goal was stated by all interviewed at MCO Z, written in key documents, and activities conducted by MCO Z were consistent with the achievement of this goal. Further, this goal enables the delivery of cost-effective quality treatment, the reason for the existence of these MCOs (Knight, 1998).

5 For a full description of the IDX system itself, please refer to the following Web site: http://www.idx.com/.

6 http://www.idx.com/.

About the Authors

Stuart Barnes is a faculty member in the School of Management, University of Bath, UK. After starting as an economist, Stuart later pursued a professional interest in information systems by completing a PhD at Manchester Business School. He joined Bath in 1996. His current research interests include IS implementation in healthcare, emerging ICTs in healthcare, evaluating e-commerce quality, knowledge management systems, and business applications of mobile technologies.

Marc Berg is Associate Professor at the Institute of Health Policy and Management, Erasmus University Rotterdam, the Netherlands. He has published widely in the field of information systems research, medical sociology and science and technology studies, focusing on the role of information systems and other formal tools (protocols, records, and so forth) and standardization in medical work. Core book publications are *Rationalizing Medical Work. Decision Support Techniques and Medical Practices* (Cambridge: MIT Press, 1997) and *Differences in Medicine. Unraveling Practices, Techniques and Bodies* (Durham: Duke University Press, 1998, with Annemarie Mol).

Yolande E. Chan is an Associate Professor of Management Information Systems at Queen's University. She holds a PhD from the University of Western Ontario, an MPhil in Management Studies from Oxford University, and SM and SB degrees in Electrical Engineering and Computer Science from the Massachusetts Institute of Technology. She is a Rhodes Scholar. Prior to joining Queen's, Dr. Chan worked with Andersen Consulting as an information systems consultant. Dr. Chan currently conducts research on health information networks, knowledge management, the alignment of information systems strategy and business strategy, and the business performance impacts of information technology investments. She has published her research in a number of refereed books and journals such as *Information Systems Research, Journal of Management Information Systems, Journal of Strategic Information Systems,* and the *Academy of Management Executive.*

Willi Hasselbring is associate professor and head of the Software engineering Group at the University of Oldenburg, Germany. His research interests include software engineering for heterogeneous information systems, information management, and medical informatics. From 1998 to 2000, he was assistant professor at the INFOLAB in the Department of Information Management at Tilburg University. Formerly, he was researcher in Software Engineering at the Universities of Essen and Dortmund. In between, he visited Trinity College, Dublin, and the University of Edinburgh. He received his Diploma in Computer Science from the Technical University of Braunschweig in 1989; PhD in Computer Science from the University of Dortmund in 1994.

Stefan Klein is professor for information systems at the University of Muenster, Germany. He has held teaching or research positions at the University of Koblenz-Landau, University St. Gallen, Switzerland, Harvard University, German National Research Center for Computer Science (GMD), and University of Cologne. His research and teaching areas are interorganizational systems, information management and communication systems. He is program committee member or track chair of several international IS conferences (Bled International Conference on Electronic Commerce, ECIS, ENTER) and member of the editorial board of *European Journal of Information Systems* (Associate Editor), *Electronic Journal of Organizational Virtualness*, *EM - Electronic Markets*, *e-Services Quarterly*, *Informatik/Informatique*, *International Journal of Electronic Commerce* and *Information Technology & Tourism*. About 100 publications, among them several books and numerous refereed articles, document his research.

Michael Holm Larsen received his MSc (Eng) in 1996 and is a PhD candidate from the Department of Manufacturing Engineering, Technical University of Denmark. Currently, he is a research fellow at the Center for Electronic Commerce, Copenhagen Business School. He has published in *International Journal of Intelligent Automation and Soft Computing* and in various international conference proceedings such as HICSS, ECIS, and in conferences on production research and intelligent manufacturing systems. His current research interests are in e-business, knowledge management, and CALS.

Nina Lundberg has a PhD in informatics from the Department of Informatics, Gothenburg University, Sweden. Presently she is CEO at eCare AB, a company developing software for healthcare. She is the author of several scientific articles within IT and healthcare. Her research work has focused on how we can improve the design and implementation of information systems within healthcare.

G. Michael McGrath gained his PhD from Macquarie University in 1993. He is currently Deputy Director of the CSIRO-Macquarie University Joint Research Centre for Advanced Systems Engineering (JRCASE), where he heads a research strand focusing on socio-technical aspects of systems and software engineering. He has more than 20 years experience in the IT industry - mostly at Telstra, Australia, where he worked in a variety of positions. These included Senior Project Manager, responsible for the development of Telstra's multi-million dollar supply systems applications, and an executive-level position, as Manager Information Architecture within the organisation's Corporate Strategy Directorate. His current research is focused mainly on the development of business and IS process models that incorporate the critical "softer" or "people" issues, on the investigation of strategic alliances within the communications and healthcare industries (plus other sectors), and on the enabling role played by e-commerce in these partnerships.

Elizabeth More is Professor of Management and Director of the Graduate School of Management at Macquarie University and Director of MGSM Pty Ltd. She has a BA (1st Class Hons.) and PhD from the University of N.S.W. and a Graduate Diploma in Management from the University of Central Queensland. She has presented numerous conference papers and published widely, both locally and internationally, in the field of organisation studies, particularly in the areas of organisational communication, culture, change, communications technology and policy. She is a past President of the Australian Communication Association and, before entering academe, had wide experience working in the theatre, television, and advertising. In addition to her academic work, Professor More has extensive experience in consulting to both private and public sector organisations (e.g., Royal Australian Navy, Royal North Shore Hospital, Anglican Retirement Villages, Commonwealth Bank, 3M, Australian Taxation Office, Hallas Trading Co., the Hilton Hotel, Zurich Insurance, and the Office of Public Management). She was also appointed by the Commonwealth Government in 1992 for a five-year term as a Member of the Government's Telecommunications Industry Development Authority (DIST) and was appointed to the Tax Concession Committee of the IR&D Board from 1996-98.

Mogens Kühn Pedersen is research professor at the Department of Informatics in the Copenhagen Business School. He holds a DrMerc From Copenhagen Business School (1996) and has done research for the Danish government and the European Commission, and has more than 100 scientific publications. He is chairman of the PhD School in Informatics at CBS. His current research interests are in business informatics including e-business, knowledge management and e-services.

Ryan R. Peterson is assistant professor in Information Management at the Tilburg University (the Netherlands). His interests span Governance and Management of Information Technology (PhD), IT Strategy Development and Decision Making, IT Assessment, IT Change Management, Electronic Business and Network Organizations. He has contributed articles in these fields at numerous local and international conferences, Prior to joining the Department of Information Management, he worked as a business consultant and research associate at the Telematics Institute. He is also a lecturer at the Department of International Business and the TIAS Business School.

David Ramsden is a PhD candidate in Management Information Systems at Queen's University at Kingston. His research interests are in investigating the role of information technology in support of multi-professional integrated healthcare teams and inter-professional knowledge exchange.

Heike Schad is a CapGemini Ernst & Young E-business consultant. She holds a doctorate from St. Gallen University where she worked at the Competence Center Electronic Markets and was a research fellow at the Haas School of Business, Berkeley, CA. Her research is focused on interorganizational business process redesign and Electronic Commerce.

Roel W. Schuring, PhD, is associate professor Management of Health Care Organizations at the University of Twente, the Netherlands. His particular research interest is the organizational design of healthcare processes. This offers the opportunity to use both his operations management and organizational studies background. His PhD is about the process modeling of organizations.

J. B. Silvers, PhD, is the Elizabeth M. and William C. Treuhaft Professor of Management at the Weatherhead School of Management and Director of Research at the Health Systems Management Center, Case Western Reserve University and holds a joint appointment in the School of Medicine. Dr. Silvers' research in the areas of finance and health has been published in the *Journal of Finance*, the *Journal of the American Medical Association*, *Health Services Research* and many others. He currently holds a Robert Wood Johnson Investigator Award in Health Policy Research to study the creation, distribution, and destruction of value in the changing health care market. From 1997 to 1999, while on leave from CWRU, he served as President and Chief Executive Officer of QualChoice - a 160,000 member, $200+ million health plan which is a subsidiary of University Hospitals Health System, Cleveland, Ohio. During this time, QualChoice grew by 30%, gained $10 million in bottom line results and was recognized by JD Powers as the best HMO in the area. Professor Silvers was a Commissioner on the Prospective Payment Assessment Commission (ProPAC, the predecessor of MedPAC) for over six years advising the U.S. Congress on Medicare payment and testifying twice before the Ways and Means Committee. He also has served on other state and national policy commissions. He received his PhD in Finance from Stanford University and served on the management faculties of Stanford, Harvard and Indiana University, and Case Western Reserve University.

Martin Smits is associate professor of Information Systems at Tilburg University (Netherlands). His research focuses on strategic information system planning, group decision making, interorganisational systems and new organisational forms. He started his research career in 1981 and was involved in the development of computer based teaching and management information systems in healthcare. He holds a DMD (1981) and a PhD in Medicine (1987) by the University of Groningen (Netherlands) and Master degrees in Information Management (1989) by Tilburg University and Washington University (USA).

Ronald W.L. Spanjers, beagn in 1992 as a Financial Consultant in the Bosch Medicentre (general hospital) for the Social and Financial Department. From 1998 he worked as a Manager in the University Medical Centre Utrecht (academic hospital) for the Division Obstetrics, Neonatology and Gynaecology. In the present time, he is working on his PhD research at Tilburg University where organisational and ICT development in hospitals are main topics.

Ton A.M. Spil is assistant professor at the department of Technology & Management at the University of Twente. He is teaching in the area of Business Information Systems, mainly in project based education. In 1988 he finished his master's in Computer Science and started his own company consulting big firms on strategic information systems planning. In 1996 he finished his PhD thesis on the effectiveness of these plans and after that he specialized in the application area healthcare and professional organizations. In 2000 he was project manager on a big e-health research project and chaired a track on HICSS 33.

Robert A. Stegwee is professor of Information Management and chair of the Business Information Systems department of the Faculty of Technology & Management at the University of Twente. He holds a master's in Computer Science from the University of Amsterdam and a doctorate in Organisation and Management from the University of Groningen. Within the Center for Telematics and Information Technology, one of the research institutes of the University of Twente, he is area leader for Electronic Process Interaction and Communication (EPIC). On several occasions he chaired an ICT in Healthcare Track at international conferences. With Cap Gemini Ernst & Young he gained practical experience through extensive consultancy work in ICT for the Healthcare Consultancy Group. He is member of the board of HL7 The Netherlands.

Pieter Toussaint studied Information Science and General Linguistics at the University of Leiden. After his graduation he was employed at the research department of a vendor of Hospital Information Systems in the Netherlands. He performed PhD research, and defended his thesis on integration of information systems in 1998. After that he was employed as an assistant professor at the technical university in Delft. Currently he works at the clinical informatics department of the Leiden University Medical Center. He is involved in a number of research projects on electronic patient record implementation, and the evaluation of ICT use in care processes.

Nilmini Wickramasinghe, PhD, MBA, GradDipMgtSt, BSc. Amus.A (piano) Amus.A(violin), currently is a senior lecture in Management Information Systems at The University of Melbourne, Australia, in the Faculty of Economics and Commerce, Department of Accounting. Here she teaches in the areas of Management Information Systems and Knowledge Management at the undergraduate and graduate levels. In addition, Nilmini is actively researching in many areas of Information Systems including the integration of ERP and e-commerce with knowledge management, e-medical records and the impact of IS/IT on the health care domain both in Australia and the US. After graduating with a Bachelor of Science in mathematics and computing and completing an MBA at The University of Melbourne, in Australia, Nilmini accepted a full scholarship to undertake PhD studies at Case Western Reserve University, in the U.S. During this time she was involved with many research projects focussing on health care issues and the impact of enterprise wide Information Systems/Information Technology (IS/IT) particularly on health care organisations.

Index

A

actor network distributed model 187
AEVCS 191
agency theory 201
application area 70
applications 147

B

business network redesign 91
business-to-business e-commerce project 130

C

capital requirements 3, 4
case mix 14
centralized knowledge creation model 184
client adapter 84
client application 83
communication 114
communication standard 68
computational viewpoint 81, 84
concern for quality 3
concerns of quality 4
connectivity 147
consultation tools 38
control level 3, 4
customer 34
customer support tools 38

D

decision support provision tools 39
dependencies 17
describe the diagnosis 117
DICOM 51
distributed knowledge management 184

E

e-life 121
EDI 91
education 33
electronic commerce 182
Electronic Patient Records 78
electronic prescription system 121
electronic standards 46
end-user 188
engineering viewpoint 81, 84
enterprise viewpoint 81
examination request 117
examination result 117
external pressures 13

F

feedback to general practitioner 118
feedback to patient 118
feeder adapter 84
feeder system 83
fragmented industry structure 33

H

handcrafting traditions 33
healthcare administration 182
health information networks 143
healthcare 67
hierarchical organization structures 33

I

information and communication technology 31
information specificity 186
information strategy 2
information structure 2
information viewpoint 81
input from external information 118
inter-organizational IS integration 127
inter-organizational process innovation 91
interaction 148
interaction support tools 38
Internet 54
interorganizational alliances 146
interorganizational systems 148
INTHES 92
IOS development 148

K

knowledge management 7, 183
knowledge worker 199, 205

L

level of acceptance 70

M

managed care environment 199
managed care organization 199
management model 184
management tools 40
medical diagnostics 92
medical group practices 198
medicamental prescription 118
money-related support tools 39

N

national differences in processes 33
network organizations 7
network organisations in hospitals 167
network technology 145
networks 35
new technology 36
non-medicamental homework for a patient 118

O

object request broker 85
object 71

P

PACS 49
patient input 117
Pharmaceutical Extranet Gateway (PEG) 127
preparation tools 40
price level 3, 4
primary care physician 199
private sector 12
process innovation 3
process support tools 39
product and market breadth 3, 4
product and process innovation 3
product state model 188
professional culture 33
Project Electronic Commerce and Communication 127
prototype strategy 61
providers 148

R

radiology 56
reengineering 127
referral from specialist to specialist 118
referral letter 117
regional health information networks 152
relevance 119
request for clinical treatment 118

request for non-medicamental treatment 118
requirements 119
resistance 119
resource management initiative 13
result from treatment 118

S

specification strategy 60
standardisation 5, 67
strategic IS 11
strategy 3
supply chain management 129
synapses 79, 80
synapses server 84

T

technology 3
technology requirements 4
technology viewpoint 81
telecommunication 124
transformation 5

U

UK health sector 11

W

weak customers 33

NEW!
Healthcare Information Systems: Challenges of the New Millennium

Adi Armoni
Tel Aviv College of Management, Israel

ISBN 1-878289-62-4
(soft cover) • $69.95
256 pages • © 2000

Healthcare information systems are crucial to the effective and efficient delivery of healthcare, to the performance of healthcare organizations and to patient care and welfare. Medical information systems drive and impact many aspects of the healthcare system, including structure, economics and performance. **Healthcare Information Systems: Challenges of the New Millennium** reports on the implementation of these systems, looking at both the success stories as well as the reasons for failure in the design, development and implementation of these systems. The book covers the major elements of healthcare information systems: core systems (ATD, logistics, finance), electronic patient record, the use of artificial intelligence in the medical domain (expert systems, robotics, etc.), clinical databases, and integrative medical information systems.

Relevant to all people working in the healthcare industry, **Healthcare Information Systems: Challenges of the New Millennium**, is an excellent reference tool and a must-read for all those concerned with staying up-to-date in the ever-changing arena of healthcare information systems. This timely new book makes an ideal reference tool for physicians, students and information systems administrators and academics alike.

An excellent addition to your library

For your convenience, the Idea Group Publishing Web site now features "easy-ordering" for this and other IGP publications at
http://www.idea-group.com

Idea Group Publishing

1331 E. Chocolate Avenue • Hershey, PA 17033 USA
Tel: (717)533-8845 • Fax: (717)533-8661 • cust@idea-group.com
http://www.idea-group.com

NEW!
Managing Healthcare Information Systems With Web-Enabled Technologies

Lauren Eder
Rider University, USA

ISBN 1-878289-65-9
(soft cover) • $69.96
288 pages • © 2000

Healthcare organizations are undergoing major reorganizations and adjustments to meet the increasing demands of improved healthcare access and quality, as well as lowered costs. As the use of information technology to process medical data increases, much of the critical information necessary to meet these challenges is being stored in digital format. Web-enabled information technologies can provide the means for greater access and more effective integration of healthcare information from disparate computer applications and other information resources.

Managing Healthcare Information Systems with Web-Enabled Technologies presents studies from leading researchers and practitioners focusing on the current challenges, directions, trends and opportunities associated with healthcare organizations and their strategic use of Web-enabled technologies.

An excellent addition to your library

For your convenience, the Idea Group Publishing Web site now features "easy-ordering" for this and other IGP publications at
http://www.idea-group.com

Idea Group Publishing

1331 E. Chocolate Avenue • Hershey, PA 17033 USA
Tel: (717)533-8845 • Fax: (717)533-8661 • cust@idea-group.com
http://www.idea-group.com

RA
971.23
.S74

2001